Interpersonal Skills

Interpersonal Skills

A Handbook for Management Trainees

Sue Smithson and Jan Whitehead

Croner Publications Ltd
Croner House
London Road
Kingston upon Thames
Surrey KT2 6SR
Tel: 081–547 3333

Published by
Croner Publications Ltd,
Croner House,
London Road,
Kingston upon Thames,
Surrey KT2 6SR
Telephone: 081–547 3333

British Library Cataloguing in Publication Data
Smithson, Sue
Interpersonal skills at work.
1. Organisations. Personnel. Interpersonal relationships
I. Title II. Whitehead, Jan
158.26

ISBN 1–85524–038–6

Contents

Preface

This book has been written to help all those who are entering management careers or who are in the early stages of their work lives. It aims to improve communication and interpersonal skills in relation to people within the work organisation and outside it.

Since business skills are an integral part of all BTEC courses at Higher Level, whether full-time or part-time, readers will find it useful as a text book to support such skills on business, catering, engineering, leisure and science HNDs and HNCs, as well as on BTEC Continuing Education Diplomas and Certificates.

Those studying for professional qualifications will find it a valuable companion to develop business skills alongside the more specialist subjects on their courses. Management trainees should find the book useful as a self-study text which provides a firm base for the practice of managerial skills and a boost to confidence.

This book is organised into three sections. The first concentrates on basic communication principles. These principles underpin all the skills mentioned in the rest of the book. The second section examines skills needed to relate effectively to other employees within the organisation, eg interview skills, team building and leadership, conduct of meetings, the giving of instruction. The third section deals with developing effective relationships with those outside the organisation, eg presenting a good image, handling face-to-face and telephone contacts, dealing with awkward customers, and negotiating.

The style of writing is simple, direct and addressed directly to the reader. The provision of self-evaluation activities at frequent intervals allows readers to consider their own attitudes and behaviour and those of others; collectively, they are a useful open learning mechanism.

Although there is no set order for reading this book — it is a constant reference book to assist in a skill needed at any particular time — we would suggest the first section should be read straight through first to provide a firm grasp of the basic principles of communication which form the foundations of more specific techniques. Readers will find some cross-referencing between chapters where a particular technique builds on information provided elsewhere.

We hope all those who use this book will find it helpful in gaining the qualifications they need and in enabling them to operate more effectively at work.

Sue Smithson
Jan Whitehead

SECTION 1: EFFECTIVE COMMUNICATION SKILLS — THE BASICS

INTRODUCTION: THE COMMUNICATION ASPECT OF A MANAGERIAL ROLE

If you are using this book, you have already made some decisions about your career. You are studying for, or already working, in engineering, science, hotel and catering, leisure management, marketing, personnel, finance, computing, etc. You are involved in developing the specialist knowledge required and probably expect to spend most of your work time making/implementing decisions related to that specialism.

In fact, you will find that a significant proportion of your working day will involve relating to other people. These may be individuals within your organisation at various levels — colleagues or superiors — or those outside it — customers, clients, suppliers, agents, Government officials or the general public. If you are a student, your first contacts of this kind may be in the context of part-time work or on a sandwich placement.

You may find that many people will claim that communication "comes naturally" and is one of the easiest parts of their job. Do you support this idea? If you scan the range of training courses that are provided for management at all levels, you will soon realise that this is far from the truth. The number of courses in written communication skills, making presentations, team building and leadership, personal selling, negotiation, assertiveness, etc, bear witness to the fact that communicating effectively at work can present a great many problems.

Ineffective communication costs money — in time, lost business, delays and wrong decisions; it also has a considerable social cost; the atmosphere at work can suffer and unhappy relations at work often mean unproductive activity, poor motivation, frustration and stress.

This first section of the book will help you to understand and put into practice the basic principles which underpin all effective communication with other people, ie a knowledge of the communication process and the ability to present yourself effectively orally, in writing and visually.

1 The Communication Process

Although communication is a process that one undertakes every day without much thought, it is important to understand fully what that process involves if one is to acquire the range of skills needed by supervisors and managers. A definition of the communication process is simple:

> A process by which a message is passed from one individual or group to another and achieves the required response.

When you begin to examine the process, however, you will find that it can be quite complex.

THE COMMUNICATION PROCESS

It may help to begin with a simple diagram which represents what we believe happens in the communication process and then build up a picture of the problems which can occur at each stage.

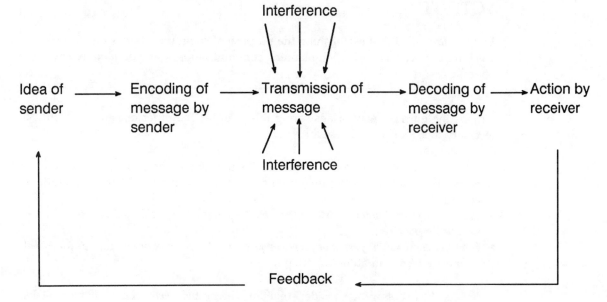

Diagram of the Communication Process

The diagram shows that effective communication should be a two way process which achieves understanding and the required results. It is interactive and requires response and feedback if it is to be successful. Let us consider each stage in the diagram more carefully.

Conceiving an Idea

This stage is concerned with formulating an idea of what to communicate. Too often we open our mouths to speak or commit words to paper before we have really thought through the idea. Effective communication at work needs careful planning; otherwise, mistakes will be made. There are a number of factors to consider before attempting to write or speak. These considerations can be expressed as a number of questions you should ask yourself at this preliminary stage.

Why do I need to communicate and what am I trying to achieve? In other words, you must establish the purpose.

There are numerous reasons for communicating at work. One may want to:

▶ inform
▶ explain
▶ persuade
▶ reprimand
▶ encourage
▶ thank

▶ appraise
▶ propose
▶ consult
▶ apologise
▶ praise.

ACTIVITY 1

We have identified that establishing the purpose of communication is one factor which must be considered when planning communication. Can you identify any other factors?

Perhaps the quickest way of answering this is to list the other questions which it is necessary to ask oneself. These are:

▶ *Who will receive the message?* What do I know about them in terms of level of authority, degree of familiarity with the matter I am communicating, their attitudes and age?
▶ *What method of communication will be most appropriate to achieve my purpose and be suitable for the receiver?*
▶ *How do I approach the person or people in question?* What tone, style and approach will be most effective in attaining my purpose?

It may also be necessary to consider sometimes *where* and *when* people will be available and most receptive to what one has to communicate.

Only when these questions have been answered are you ready to formulate your message.

ACTIVITY 2

Consider the following situation. You have to request time off from work from *your* immediate superior/tutor because you have won a holiday in a prize draw.

(a)   What attitude is your existing superior/tutor likely to have to your request?
(b)   What approach will you use as a consequence?
(c)   What method will you use to communicate your request?

Your answer to (a) will obviously condition your answers to the other two questions. If your superior/tutor is very approachable and normally sympathetic you will be more likely to discuss it with him or her fairly informally. If not, you may wish to request a formal interview by memo. This will give you some idea of the need to plan. In both cases, of course, you will need to decide how such a request can be made as acceptable as possible, eg by suggesting cover or altering your present holiday arrangements (if you are an employee), or suggesting arrangements for covering the work you may miss (if you are a student). Thinking about the *recipient* and his or her concerns is the main principle.

Encoding the Message

The above activity shows that the next step is to present the message in a form that people will understand; this is not always easy. It is necessary to choose the right medium of communication so that the message is:

(a)   understood and

(b)   acted upon in a favourable manner.

As a reminder, here are some of the media for communicating a message from which a selection may be made:

(a)   *Written*: letters, memos, reports, minutes of meetings, telex, telemessages, telegrams

(b)   *Oral:* conversations face-to-face, interviews, meetings, conferences, training, telephone, teleconferencing

(c)   *Visual:* diagrams, graphs, illustrations, slides, VDU, video, body language.

The table on the next page lists some of the main advantages and disadvantages of each form of communication.

Advantages and Disadvantages of the Three Types of Communications Media

	Advantages	Disadvantages
Written	Permanent record which can be kept for later reference	Production and delivery of message is slower than other methods
	Necessary for contracts and agreements	One-way method of communication, therefore feedback is delayed or non-existent. This can mean that misunderstandings cannot be sorted out immediately
	The recipient can take in the message at his or her own pace	
	More accurate for complex or technical information	May be used to avoid facing up to a person
Oral	A more personal contact between sender and recipient	Not very good for conveying complex or technical information
	Tone, phrasing and (in face-to-face situations) body language, can help to convey the message	There is no formal record
		The recipient can be more easily distracted by noise
	Possible to secure faster feedback	
Visual	Can be used where it is difficult for people to read or hear because of environmental difficulties or physical disabilities	No control over interpretation and feedback unless supported by spoken or written words
	Possible to convey information to mass audiences	Personal contact between sender and recipient not easy to establish
	Can overcome language difficulties	May require additional skills to understand diagrams and graphs

In some situations, it will be necessary to choose more than one medium to convey a message properly. The choice of media will depend on a number of factors, the most important of which are:

(a) effectiveness of medium in achieving the required purpose

(b) effectiveness of medium in persuading the receiver to act favourably

(c)   whether or not a permanent record is required

(d)   whether or not instant feedback is needed

(e)   the complexity of the content of the message

(f)   the time taken to convey the message

(g)   the cost involved in conveying the message.

Currently, one not only has to make decisions about which medium of communication to use to send a message but also the specific method and the technology used to transmit the message. The choice of such technology may have an impact on both understanding and favourable response. For example, if you want to query something with another member of your organisation, you may choose to go to see him or her, telephone, send a written memo, send a message by electronic mail, leave a telephone message with a secretary, bleep the person on a pager, or ask for him or her over the public address system.

If you want to process a report you may have the choice of having it typed, or produced by word processor or by means of desktop publishing (DTP) software. As new office technology develops the choice of media can become more complex.

ACTIVITY 3

Identify what media and methods of communication you would use in the following situations and why.

(a)   You are a senior researcher in charge of a laboratory. One of the technicians has been arriving late for work recently. You have already called the technician aside and had an informal word about his behaviour.
(b)   You want to remind staff who operate computers that they should not bring coffee into the room and drink near their terminals.
(c)   A client has rung your hotel to complain about an upset stomach after eating a meal in your restaurant. Your receptionist took the call and has passed the message on to you.

Check your answers with ours at the end of the chapter.

Selecting the wrong medium for your message can be costly. This may be in terms of time wasted, expenses incurred, or by creating unfavourable attitudes and responses.

Transmitting the Message

This stage involves its own problems. The first of these is trying to ensure that the recipient is ready to receive your message. You need to attract his or her attention.

Switching on the recipient   In any form of communication it is necessary to "switch on" the recipient to the fact that a communication is coming before beginning the crucial part of the message. After all, the message may be only one of many hundreds he or she will receive that day and his or her mind may be focused on other matters. Each individual is pre-occupied with his or her own life, problems, priorities, etc. Also, all work environments, whether factory, research laboratory, kitchen, office, shop, leisure centre, farm or estate, have their own activities which can distract people from being receptive to a particular message.

One of the advantages of face-to-face communication is that the communicator can observe whether someone is concentrating or not. Even so, it may be necessary to switch the person on to the subject, so that he or she is already thinking about the topic before a specific message is delivered. There are some special techniques which can be used to do this.

(a) *Make a statement of purpose:* "I would like to talk to you about the Wilson contract".

(b) *Ask a question about the matter in hand:* "Did you receive the memo I sent you yesterday about your appraisal interview?".

In each case, the mention of the subject is valuable in focusing the attention of the person on the matter to be discussed.

ACTIVITY 4

Here are two questions relating to methods of catching the attention of a recipient. See if you can answer them and then check your answers with ours at the end of the chapter.

(a) What method does user-friendly computer software employ to catch the attention of the operator?
(b) How can you switch on your reader to the subject in a letter or a memo?

The way the message is delivered needs careful thought.

Designing a message to suit the recipient   In many specialisms we develop our own jargon and certainly become familiar with many technical terms, abbreviations and initials. These are fine when we are communicating with people at work who have similar knowledge, but other sections or departments may not understand them.

ACTIVITY 5

How many of the following terms can you explain? They are taken from a range of different disciplines.

   (a)   DCF
   (b)   The marketing mix
   (c)   A byte
   (d)   Calibration
   (e)   The state of the art

You can check the answers at the end of the chapter.

We hope this proves the point but congratulations if you got them all right — or even most of them. An engineer often fails to think about the recipient if talking to an accountant and *vice versa*. One must deliver a message that people are capable of understanding.

Observing basic principles of good communication   Whoever the recipient may be and whatever method of communication is chosen *the six essential Cs of effective communication* should be observed. These are that communication should be:

▶ *Clear* — there should be one meaning only

▶ *Complete* — all relevant information should be included

▶ *Concise* — the relevant information should be presented as briefly as possible

▶ *Constructive* — the message should be positive and achieve the desired result

▶ *Correct* — the message should be accurate (in content and presentation)

▶ *Courteous* — the message should be polite.

You may think, of course, that you do all this already. Remember, however, that this is your viewpoint and it may not always be shared by others. Compare this with driving a car; we all think we are the best of drivers, a view not shared by other motorists, as their gestures sometimes make clear!

How many times have you said something like "Why didn't he do what I told him?" or "Why doesn't she ever listen?". However, did the fault lie entirely with the other person?

Decoding the Message

Before any message can be acted upon it must be received and understood. There are a number of barriers which can prevent the message from being received and understood, ie they create interference.

ACTIVITY 6

What factors have created interference in any message you may have given or received recently? One easy example is the noise of an aeroplane roaring overhead when you are engaged in a conversation. Note down your own experiences before reading on.

Such barriers tend to fall into two separate groups and can be listed briefly as follows.

▶ Factors in the working environment:

(a) *Noise:* open-plan offices are particularly prone to this

(b) *Organisation structure:* the formal lines of authority may cause delay or distortion

(c) *Separation of work sites:* between branches, offices, etc.

▶ Personal factors:

(a) *Language:* different level of vocabulary or lack of familiarity with technical terms

(b) *Ambiguity or vague usage*

(c) *Hostile attitudes and individual perception*

(d) *Contradictory body language*

(e) *Poor timing:* speaking as someone is leaving, etc

(f) *Poor approach:* being patronising or aggressive.

Most of these are self-explanatory; you can probably see the environmental factors every day. The personal factors, however, are rather more complex and are not always so obvious, so that you often run the risk of ignoring their impact.

Language If the sender has not observed the basic principles of good communication or if the language is inappropriate, the recipient may not decode the message properly. If the vocabulary is vague or ambiguous, it may be possible for him or her to misinterpret what it means.

Attitudes and perception   The recipient is an individual with his or her own range of attitudes and perceptions. We all have our own. Our attitudes and our perception of other people and the world around us develops from our personality and past experiences. It is not possible to say that one perception is right and the other wrong — they are merely different. It is important to recognise that people in other specialisms or from another generation or on a different level of authority may see things differently; in delivering a message one should not create hostile attitudes in the recipient through the use of inappropriate vocabulary or tone. Also, if one appears too dominant, submissive or patronising this may arouse negative responses such as anger, aggression or resentment.

ACTIVITY 7

What would be your attitude if you had asked someone to produce a report for you to take to an important meeting and they produced a scruffy, dog-eared document that was badly typed and full of incomprehensible jargon?

The perception of the person who prepared the document was obviously that content was more important than presentation. Your perception is likely to be that you do not want either to read or present it in its present form. The assumption that most people make is that if *appearance* is poor, content is likely to be weak or inaccurate.

Body language   Another major problem encountered in face-to-face communication is contradictory body language. Body language includes tone of voice, gesture, facial expression and posture. As both senders and recipients of messages, we depend heavily on body language to support and reinforce what is being said. (Chapters 2 and 15 also deal with the subject of body language in specific contexts.)

If a sender's body language fails to complement the spoken message, there is difficulty in interpretation. For example, if someone thanks you profusely for your help on a piece of work but will not look you in the eye and is nervously fingering his or her hair, your interpretation is that the message of thanks is not sincere. You should be aware that *when body language contradicts a spoken message, the recipient tends to pay more attention to the non-verbal communication.*

Likewise, it is possible to detect contradictions in written communication if the tone of a letter is at odds with its content. The recipient will "read between the lines".

Achieving understanding and response   In order to achieve understanding and a favourable response, there are some actions we need to consider.

(a) *Observe the basic principles*
     The receiver is more likely to understand our message properly if the use of vocabulary is precise, the language is direct and the sentence construction accurate and simple.

  (b) *Reduce the environmental barriers*

ACTIVITY 8

Do any of the environmental barriers listed on page 12 exist in your own organisation? If so, what can you do to contribute to overcoming them?

You might like to jot down some notes before reading on.

You may think that you can do very little about these problems as they lie outside your immediate control.

It might be helpful to discuss problems with those in authority — but only if you can make constructive and positive suggestions. Even if you cannot eliminate the problems entirely, you may be able to minimise the effects.

(c) *Improve the personal factors*
Being aware of potential hostility and the possible reasons for it is half the battle. Then it is necessary to consider a way of approaching others so that your method is acceptable to them. In face-to-face situations give some thought to the ways in which body language can be used to support communication. Make sure that what you say and the way you look, stand and gesticulate are all complementary.

Develop a good sense of timing. Do not communicate important messages when people are trying to concentrate on other work, or as an afterthought.

Likewise try to gauge the right emotional moment for giving a particular message, ie not when someone is angry or upset.

Feedback

Every communication process should result in some indication that it has been received, understood and interpreted correctly and, if necessary, acted upon. This is often referred to as feedback.

In face-to-face situations, a nod, or even a facial expression, can indicate understanding and acceptance. Conversely, a yawn or a glazed expression tells its own story. It is necessary to be alert to these feedback signals.

On the telephone it is necessary to listen carefully to the tone of the other person's voice in addition to being aware of pregnant pauses as indications of whether the message has been understood or not. Sometimes questions which are asked specifically to obtain feedback may be necessary, eg "Do you agree?" or "Is this action agreeable to you?".

When composing memos and letters it is important to state at the end the action required from the recipient to demonstrate that the message has been received and understood.

You have probably noticed in computer programs that once some information has been keyed in you will be instructed what function to perform in order to receive feedback; this is because programmers have recognised that good communication involves inviting a response. To get the right response, they have also recognised the need to be user-friendly — a valuable lesson to be applied in any communication.

APPLYING THE COMMUNICATION PROCESS

This section will provide a brief reminder of some of the most important factors in communication, both from the viewpoint of sender and recipient.

The Sender's Responsibilities

(a) To think about the purpose of the communication before beginning.

(b) To think about what to say and how to say it to achieve understanding and a favourable response.

(c) To select the most appropriate medium (or combination of media) to achieve the desired purpose.

(d) To ensure that the language is suitable for the recipient.

(e) To try to eliminate or reduce barriers to communication.

(f) To try to ensure that the message is not likely to be minsinterpreted because of inappropriate or poor vocabulary, lack of precision or inappropriate tone.

(g) To encourage feedback.

The Receiver's Responsibilities

(a) Not to be distracted by environmental barriers — concentrate on the message.

(b) Not to let personal barriers (one's own attitudes, perceptions, pre-occupations) distort the message.

(c) To ensure that the message is fully understood. If in doubt, seek clarification rather than risk misinterpretation.

(d) To provide the sender with feedback so that he or she knows that the message has been received, understood and acted upon.

CONCLUSION

Communication is a complex human process. We would therefore encourage everyone to be critical of their own communication. In doing this, undertake the last activity (below) which shows one means of recording and evaluating communications.

ACTIVITY 9

Select one day at work and during that day record your communications on a diary sheet similar to the one shown below.

Fill in columns 1–5 as follows:

  Column 1: enter a brief identification of the purpose of each of your communications.
  Column 2: give a brief identification of the content of the message.
  Column 3: enter the individual or group to whom the message was transmitted, eg superior, friend, work colleague, etc.
  Column 4: enter the method(s) used, eg memo or telephone.
  Column 5: enter whether the choice of method was pre-determined by the organisation or chosen voluntarily by you.

Once you have completed your diary entries, look back over them and analyse critically whether you selected the right method and how successful you were in achieving your purpose. Enter your comments in column 6. You should evaluate your total entries to see your general level of success in communicating. If you are dissatisifed with your performance, consider how you might improve the quality of your communication.

Communications Diary Sheet

PURPOSE	CONTENT	RECEIVER(S)	METHOD(S)	ORGANIS-ATION/YOU	COMMENTS

ANSWERS TO ACTIVITIES IN CHAPTER 1

Activity 3

(a) We would suggest oral communication in the form of a formal private interview to
  - (i) bring the matter to the technician's attention and
  - (ii) find out any reason for the lateness with a formal warning that it constitutes the first stage in a discipline procedure.

(b) We would suggest a combination of oral and visual communication, ie
  - (i) a face-to-face meeting with the whole group to explain the rule and the reasons for it
  - (ii) illustrations/symbols beside the machines as a visual reminder.

(c) We would suggest a combination of oral and written communication, ie
  - (i) telephone contact to establish the facts and to show personal concern
  - (ii) confirmation by letter of any action you are taking.

Activity 4

(a) Computer software often uses the method of asking questions. Usually you have to key in yes/no answers to show that you are responding.

(b) Letters and memos should have a heading which encapsulates the contents and the first paragraph should contain a statement of purpose.

Activity 5

(a) *DCF*
This abbreviation stands for discounted cash flow and is a term used in accounting.

(b) *The marketing mix*
This is a phrase used in marketing to refer to a decision which involves product, price, place and promotion.

(c) *A byte*
This term is used in computing to refer to a group of binary digits in a computer and is a measure of capacity.

(d) *Calibration*
This term is used in engineering to refer to the correct graduations of a gauge.

(e) *The state of the art*
This term is used in many disciplines that involve technology in some form to refer to the current level of knowledge and expertise, eg in engineering, graphic design, computers, other office technology.

2 Effective Self-Presentation

As you progress through your college and work career you will find that there is an increasing emphasis on both self-presentation and gaining the co-operation of other people. At present, you are probably beginning to develop these skills and will continue to do so through practice; however, some guidance on how to project an acceptable image can avoid some of the problems arising from trial and error.

This chapter, therefore, will indicate some principles which you can apply in a number of work and social situations. They will concern the skills of speaking, listening and non-verbal communication. In later chapters, we will see how these can be used effectively in a number of situations such as telephone techniques, interviewing, team work, oral reporting and meetings and in relating to people outside your organisation. Let us begin by looking at the fundamental speaking skills.

SPEAKING SKILLS

You have already listened to many others speaking to you for various purposes: to deliver lectures or conduct discussions. You must have noticed that some people are better than others at this activity; in some cases you are interested and/or gain valuable information and in other cases the opposite occurs.

ACTIVITY 1

Note down the factors which you think contribute to an effective oral presentation.

You may like to turn to the end of the chapter to see if your list is similar to ours.

We hope that this activity has focused your attention on what you already know about this very important skill. We will now look at some of these elements in greater detail.

Preparation and Planning

Remember the maxim *engage brainbox before opening mouth*. Whatever the situation the basic communication principles need to be observed. It is necessary to identify the nature of:

(a) the objective

(b) the audience

(c) the time and facilities available

(d) the message to be conveyed

(e) the methods best suited to *all* the above.

ACTIVITY 2

Perhaps you have experienced the following situation: you are being briefed in a group concerning a complex assignment. You ask for an extension of the deadline by which the task has to be completed in front of the rest of the group. The reaction from the person asked is negative.

How do you think the situation should have been approached to achieve a more positive result?

The answer to Activity 2 lies in:

(a) the timing of the request and

(b) the method of the approach.

Very little thought was given to the likely reaction or attitude of the person who could grant or refuse the extension. It is worth noting that preparation is not only desirable, it is also in one's own interests. Think how different the reaction might have been if one had negotiated privately so as to avoid putting someone in the situation where they had to react not only to the request but also in front of others who would become implicated in the decision. There would also have been an opportunity to put the request tactfully and with logical reasons.

Therefore to speak effectively:

▶ DO be systematic about planning and preparing

▶ DO NOT be haphazard in your approach.

Structure and Sequence

Sometimes, the communication required will be formal and/or quite complex. An example of this might be oral reporting (Chapter 12), briefing others (Chapter 10) or addressing a meeting (Chapter 9). In such cases it is important to extend the planning

19

process to consideration of the order in which information is to be presented to maximise understanding and achieve a favourable response.

After all, you know from personal experience how important it is to receive logical instructions which start with your existing knowledge and build up in planned, digestible stages rather than plunging into complex concepts immediately.

ACTIVITY 3

You are giving a friend a first driving lesson and are describing the first task — how to move off. This includes a particular sequence of operations.

Write down these operations in a logical order. Ask someone else to do this too. Then compare your results. Which of you would be the more effective instructor?

No answer is given for this activity; it is for you to decide. You may have discovered how easy it is to forget one important stage or to put the operations into the wrong order.

The principle to bear in mind here is that you need to think primarily about *what is already familiar to your listener(s)* and *what is then the logical order for them* (not for you!).

A very simple mistake to make in sequencing is to assume that what seems easiest to you is automatically logical for other people. So:

▶ DO think about a structure for giving information

▶ DO present information in a sequence which is logical for your listener(s).

When words are not enough

ACTIVITY 4

Consider the following:

(a) When someone is giving you a verbal explanation of a scientific experiment or a technical process, what other methods might he or she use to help you understand?
(b) If you had to explain to someone how to set out and understand a balance sheet, what methods would you use?
(c) Think of a situation where you might want to use a picture as well as words to convey your message.
(d) You are abroad and someone with a poor knowledge of English is trying to give you directions through the town. What methods would you find helpful to support his or her words?

There are many times when we need to support talking to people with other communication formats. Sometimes this may be by:

(a) demonstration (possibility for (a) above)

(b) diagrams/charts/graphs/maps (possibility for (a) (b) and (d) above)

(c) photographs, videos, slides are very useful to show your listener(s) the actual appearance of something you are trying to explain, especially when the object in question is not immediately available

(d) body language — expressions, gestures, etc (useful in all face-to-face situations).

So:

▶ DO consider support methods which will help other people understand what you are saying.

Delivery

We are now ready to think about the presentation itself. Whether it is a formal occasion or an informal one, there are certain principles to observe. The first is choice of language.

(a) *Language*
     Apart from choosing language which the listeners will understand and respond to well, it is also necessary to consider the characteristics which are special to spoken English.

     Spoken English is not full of multi-syllable words, turgid phrases or complicated sentences. It is:

     ▶ simple
     ▶ concise
     ▶ direct.

     We talk in *short, simple sentences* without long involved dependent clauses. We use *direct, familiar words* including slang. We have licence to break some of the rules considered important in written English, eg finishing a sentence with a preposition. We use the first and second person "I" and "you" instead of the more impersonal third person "he", "she" or "it".

     We also need to consider how we use our voices.

(b) *Voice*
     It is necessary to aim for:

     ▶ audibility

▶ clarity

▶ variety of tone.

Audibility and clarity mean a *firm voice with clear diction* and, in formal situations, a slightly slower pace than normal conversation. Keeping one's head up and maintaining eye contact with the listener(s) can help clarity because it means that the voice is projected forward rather than down. It is vital not to be labelled a mumbler.

Variety of tone is important. A monotone will send any listener to sleep, as you may have experienced yourself!

Practice on tape is invaluable here, even if you are horrified the first time you hear yourself. Speaking to a group of people often makes us feel anxious and it should be recognised that anxiety often induces an increase in the pace of talking. Gabbled speech can be both irritating and confusing for the listener.

There are also many communication techniques which are non-verbal and which are known as body language.

USING BODY LANGUAGE

Non-verbal communication, or body language as it is known, is an essential part of face-to-face self-presentation since it has a direct effect on the perception and attitudes of those about us. Body language will affect the credibility of what is said. It can either antagonise people or secure their co-operation. The ability to control our own body language so that it conveys the right image is therefore an important skill to master. When we are speaking, our listeners are using our:

(a) eye contact and movement

(b) facial expression

(c) gestures

(d) posture

(e) touch and proximity

to interpret what we say and are using body language themselves to respond to what we are saying.

Eye Contact and Movement

To maintain eye contact with a listener is extremely important as it is a means of establishing rapport as well as gauging his or her response. Eye contact can show:

(a)   a challenge if it is prolonged and fixed

(b)   lack of interest or lack of confidence if it is non-existent

(c)   intention to deceive if there is furtive eye movement

(d)   interest, recognition and friendliness if it is frequent.

Facial Expression

People respond to facial expression instantly if one appears enthusiastic, interested and motivated and one's expression is *alert and responsive*.

The English tend to have rather immobile faces which unfortunately convey lack of interest. Watch the French or Italians and even without knowledge of their language, it is usually possible to deduce what they are trying to convey.

Most successful presenters make *maximum use of changing facial expression* to show amusement, humour, fascination, horror, anger, anxiety.

Practising in front of a mirror may give you some idea of how you appear to others but if you get the opportunity to do a practice presentation which is video-recorded, the playback is the biggest eye-opener of all. A common reaction is to see oneself as stiff faced with a wooden expression.

Features you might note in yourself and others are how we adjust:

(a)   the set of the mouth

(b)   the angle of the chin

(c)   the position of the eyebrows

(d)   the appearance of wrinkles and creases.

All these can be controlled to convey particular messages so always try to use a range of facial expressions to reinforce words.

Gestures

Again there is a range of gestures which communicate different messages. Some of these are as follows:

(a)   Open hand gestures which convey honesty or invite participation.

(b)   Hands held closed across the body which show defensiveness, unwillingness to share opinions or withdrawal.

(c) A wagging or slicing finger which is directive and conveys an attempt to impose opinions on others. It often transforms into an aggressive gesture.

(d) Weak, downward sweeping gestures which convey an inability to complete a sentence or articulate an idea.

Many gestures can show unease or a desire to hide the truth.

It is very important to remember that gestures are interpreted differently by various ethnic or national groups.

ACTIVITY 5

Look at the picture below. What does this gesture convey to you?

Then look at the possible interpretations at the end of the chapter.

In any presentation gestures can be used to emphasise, explain and demonstrate, sometimes more effectively than words alone. However, remember that *in general gestures should accompany words and not act totally as their substitute*. A vague wave of the hand and a feeble phrase such as "You know what I mean" usually ensures that your listener does not understand.

Mannerisms

All of us are prone to make involuntary movements. Many of these occur when we are nervous; often they are repetitive so that they become personal mannerisms, for example:

(a) fidgeting with clothes, hair, jewellery or pens

(b) running a finger round the back of the collar

(c) scratching

(d) jingling money or keys

(e)   clicking finger joints or drumming fingers on a desk.

Feedback from other people or from a video-recording can identify particular mannerisms. Persistent mannerisms can be distracting for listeners, so it is a good idea to be aware of your own so that you can begin to control them.

Posture/Stance

Inexperienced speakers often find it difficult to adopt an upright and confident posture. They tend to:

(a)   slouch or stoop (which conveys lack of confidence or reluctance)

(b)   lean on the desk or wall (which can convey indifference or over-confidence)

(c)   stand on one foot

(d)   pace up and down

(e)   fidget.

The last three all convey nervousness.

The same thing occurs with sitting postures. One can convey hostility, obstinacy, superiority or enthusiasm merely from the way one sits.

Proximity

One of the concepts you need to accept is that all of us value our personal space. There is a sub-consciously recognised space around us that we consider our own and we become nervous or resentful if some other people invade that space.

However, we also convey information by the degree of space we maintain between ourselves and others.

If one keeps one's distance from another person it signals formality, caution or dislike. A closer pattern signals informality and liking. However, if one gets too close to other people, they become anxious and defensive, and probably start backing off physically! If one talks to them standing when they are sitting, it can convey an attempt to dominate. If one remains sitting to talk to someone who is standing, it is difficult to sound authoritative.

Try to achieve the right degree of proximity according to the situation and the person or people you are talking to.

ACTIVITY 6

Think about the last interview you attended — for a college place, for a job, etc.

Did the interviewer sit behind a desk with you placed in a chair facing him or her like (a)?

(a)

Or did your interview place you in a seating arrangement like (b)?

(b)

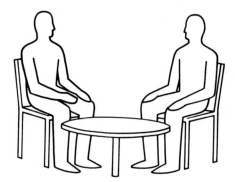

If so, what assumptions did you make from this about the degree of formality of the interview from this use of space?

Check your answer to this question with ours at the end of the chapter.

This has been quite a long section on body language but we make no apology because body language which complements speech is part of effective communication.

The last two sections have shown that speaking effectively is far from being a spontaneous activity; it is the outcome of all the following factors:

(a)   good preparation and planning

(b)   appropriate choice of methods and words

(c)   logical structure and sequencing

(d)   good diction, delivery and varied tone

(e)   controlled and complementary body language.

The other side of the coin is *effective listening* and this is a complex process too. For this reason, most people experience difficulty in listening and concentrating well. The evidence for this can be seen in the number of top organisations which send their staff, even at senior level, on courses designed to promote this skill.

LISTENING SKILLS

Sometimes, especially when you are new to the work organisation, you spend a great deal of time "on the receiving end" of other people's communication processes; they may or may not be successful at speaking. What can you do to promote effective communication as a listener, even if the message has not been clear in some way?

The first factor to identify is the need to *regard listening as a skill to be developed and not as an automatic process*. You will sometimes have heard the rather irritating phrase "I hear you", often indicating disagreement. Perhaps, however, this summarises what actually happens; we hear, but do not really concentrate, thus missing a great deal of the message. Listening is a skill we often neglect.

Barriers to Effective Listening

There are many barriers to good listening:

(a)   environmental noise

(b)   our own preoccupations

(c)   our attitude to the speaker and/or his or her message.

How, then, do we learn to listen? It is after all vital in the early stages of anyone's career in order to progress.

ACTIVITY 7

When you are on the receiving end, what faults do you exhibit which result in you failing to concentrate and/or understand?

List them briefly.

When you have done this, you might like to compare your list with the common faults which are given at the end of this chapter.

Supplementary activity
Before you read on, you might like to note down what you can do to overcome your own failings.

It is quite usual for people to find any number of faults in other people's listening or speaking skills. It is more difficult to be honest about their own! Poor listening should never be excused by blaming the speaker, although the temptation is always to do this.

Techniques for More Effective Listening

There are, in fact, several elements within one's own control. Some simple techniques, which may need to be adapted according to whether the situation is face-to-face or over the telephone, are:

▶ Focus eyes and/or ears and *give full attention to the speaker.*

▶ *Concentrate on the content* of what is being said without being distracted by physical appearance/mannerisms and/or oral characteristics.

▶ Deliberately *identify the main problems* or facts by noting key phrases, stressed words, pauses for emphasis.

▶ If the situation involves instruction, or one is required to remember later what has been said, take *brief* notes. Select only relevant facts when making notes by listening and summarising rather than by using verbatim reporting.

▶ Remember that the *speed at which one listens is greater than the speed at which the speaker delivers* the words. This should give time to summarise, select and subhead — not to daydream.

▶ *Question and clarify what is not understood*; even though one may feel embarrassed, it is better to appear a fool earlier than later when one's mistakes become only too evident.

▶ If on the telephone, remember that it is easy to mishear proper names and numbers, and both are very important (there is a significant difference between £15 and £50 to the payer) so check back (repeat one five or five 0).

▶ Try to *ignore distractions*.

▶ *Take note of the body language* and/or the *tone of voice* to help in understanding correctly.

Demonstrating Attention

Listening, of course, is not a passive activity. The other person needs to know that one is listening, particularly when using the telephone. *The recipient must demonstrate that he or she is listening.* This feedback process is vital to a successful dialogue.

But how can this be achieved without interrupting?

ACTIVITY 8

If you are listening to someone on the phone, what methods do *you* use to show that you are listening?

Jot down your ideas.

The answer is *paralinguistics*. Of course, you probably did not use this word but you may have noted what this means, ie using:

"Mm", "I see", "Got it", "Yes", "Uh-huh", "Oh, really"

— all noises or minor phrases which, when combined with tone, can convey agreement, disagreement, surprise, questioning, but in every case comprehension and reception of the information concerned. You often have to give this help so that the other person can deliver his or her message effectively.

Put yourself in the role of the speaker; it is much easier to tell a story or hold a conversation if the other person demonstrates that he or she is listening by encouraging words and facial expressions and an alert, interested posture.

INTERPRETING BODY LANGUAGE

One important aspect of listening and understanding a message correctly is being able to interpret body language. While it can be used to support speech, it can also be used to interpet the information other people are conveying.

The following activity should enable you to develop your interpretative skills substantially.

ACTIVITY 9

For at least one week, select any kind of interactive programme on the television, eg chat shows, interviews, live audience participation programmes — avoid fiction or drama. Turn off the sound for five minutes.

See how much of the message you can pick up by simply observing the body language. Try to arrange this experiment with a friend who can tell you whether your interpretation was correct or not.

Were you poor at this at first? Most people are! Did you improve as the days went by? The longer you train yourself to depend on body language, the more you can use your eyes as well as your ears for listening. After all, you are only developing the skill any deaf, or partially deaf, person *has* to acquire.

One of the main uses of this technique is to help us determine the validity of what is being said and assess the honesty of the speaker.

EXAMPLE

Recently during an interview involving the representatives of two sides in an industrial dispute, a trade union leader was heard to be making conciliatory, co-operative statements. Yet he was seen to be maintaining prolonged eye contact with the employer, adopting a forward crouching stance, had a set chin and was using his finger to emphasise points.

Clearly the body language contradicted the words.

We should observe combinations of body language signals (as in the above example) and not rely on any one signal alone. For example, taken alone, a finger touching the nose could mean nervousness or might simply mean that the person's nose is itching. We should look for clusters of signals which include eye contact, facial expression, gesture, etc.

CONCLUSION

We hope this has given some helpful, if fundamental, guidelines on successful speaking and listening, and the role played by body language in both these activities.

The danger is to label basic guidelines as "common sense". Often common sense is not all that common! Certainly the rules, however simple, are often totally ignored; hence the perpetual complaints about lack of communication skills in any organisation, at all levels.

The first two chapters in this book give the principles which need to be considered in any communication process. They can then be applied to the requirements of the specific situation, whether the methods ultimately chosen are oral or written.

ANSWERS TO ACTIVITIES IN CHAPTER 2

Activity 1

The factors you may have thought of which contribute to an effective presentation are:

(a)   an interesting voice

(b)   presenting information at an appropriate pace

(c)   using a clear structure which is easy to follow

(d)   making a lively presentation including plenty of facial expressions and gestures

(e)   using a range of examples and visual aids which help understanding

(f)   content and delivery is adapted to the needs of the audience

(g)   good choice of language and vocabulary.

Activity 5

If you are English this gesture is normally interpreted as everything is just right — it is OK. However, if you use this same gesture in some Eastern Mediterranean countries it would be interpreted as a rude gesture — much the same as our two uplifted fingers!

Activity 6

Diagram (a)   This is a formal seating arrangement where the interviewer is conveying his or her use of authority and defending his or her territory by sitting behind a large desk and placing a barrier between you. You can expect this interview to have a degree of formality.

Diagram (b)   This more relaxed seating arrangement, where you are closer together with no intervening barrier, is signalling the interviewer's intention to welcome you into his or her territory. You can anticipate that this interview will be more informal.

Activity 7

The most common faults in listening are:

(a)   allowing yourself to be distracted from the content by poor delivery

(b)   allowing yourself to be distracted by environmental factors — noises, other people

(c)   allowing yourself to daydream by staring out of the window or round the room

(d)   reacting emotionally to certain words or phrases so that you miss some of the content

(e)   not paying attention to body language and/or tone to reinforce what you hear

(f)   not checking back if you think you might have missed or misheard information

(g)   expecting the speaker to achieve thought transfer rather than regarding yourself as an active participant in the process.

3 Effective Written Communication

In written communication, the basic principles of preparation, planning and logical sequencing hold good. The difference lies in:

* (a)   the language used

   (b)   the fact that it is often a one way method of communication — or at least with delayed or limited feedback

   (c)   the fact that there is no body language to assist.

The guidelines for preparation, planning, structure and sequencing are therefore the same as those discussed in the previous two chapters; the techniques required in composing written communication, however, are different.

Most people recognise that a separate approach is required but misunderstand the methods by which this is to be achieved and often become passionately committed to the wrong methods. For this reason, bad practice in all business documents, notably letters, memos and reports, is widespread. It is also increasingly deplored. The most usual faults, as identified by the Plain English Campaign, are using:

   (a)   unfamiliar words rather than familiar ones

   (b)   jargon

   (c)   outdated and/or unnecessary phrases

   (d)   complicated sentence construction

   (e)   poor paragraphing.

In addition, there are, of course, the problems of inaccurate English usage, now the subject of so many complaints.

USING UNFAMILIAR WORDS

English is a difficult language to master. The longer Latinised forms are often used when we wish to present ourselves as important or knowledgeable; sometimes they are used to deceive. Generally, however, we use the basic Anglo-Saxon form in everyday speech and most people understand this without any trouble. The difference is illustrated by the phrase:

"Scintillate, scintillate, miniscule asteroid"

as opposed to:

"Twinkle, twinkle, little star".

In our business communication we should be aiming for clear, quick understanding. Anything else is not cost effective.

ACTIVITY 1

Find a more familiar word for the following:

(a) anticipate
(b) commencement
(c) despatch
(d) optimum
(e) utilise.

Compare your answers with our suggestions at the end of this chapter.

We are not suggesting that long words should be eliminated completely from written communication; merely that it should be recognised that frequent use of unfamiliar words can obscure the meaning of a message.

Although one should use familiar vocabulary to promote understanding, it is important to realise that, in written English, this should not deteriorate into slang or words which are so overused that they no longer mean anything specific. Examples of such overused words are "nice" or "things"; you can probably think of others. Also make sure that words that are familiar to you are also likely to be familiar to your reader; if you use technical terms or jargon — beware!

Use of Jargon

A scientist often has to communicate with non-scientists, financiers with non-financial people, engineers with salespeople; keeping the message clear should always be the overall aim. Technical terms used within a specialism should only be used when communicating with fellow specialists in the same field. Refer back to Activity 5 in Chapter 1 as this may remind you of how frequently we use jargon.

Stilted Outdated Phrases

For some reason, we seem to like using these types of phrase in letters and reports. This is usually because we have all learnt from practices which preceded our own, so we have copied bad habits.

ACTIVITY 2

See if you can find a more direct word or phrase for the following.

We acknowledge the receipt of . . .

Please do not hesitate to . . .

In the not too distant future . . .

At the present time . . .

Due to the fact that . . .

According to our record . . .

Check our suggestions at the end of this chapter.

We hope you will avoid using any of these phrases in future — remember to *be direct and concise.*

Equally inappropriate is the practice of including meaningless or unnecessary phrases; this is also an unfortunate relic of our past. Some examples of phrases which can be totally omitted are:

No doubt you are aware of the fact that . . .
(If they are aware, why say so?)

May we take this opportunity to say . . .
(You're going to anyway!)

I am writing . . .
(They already know that!)

For more examples, you might like to read Sir Ernest Gower's *Plain Words* in which he pleads with civil servants to abandon these meaningless phrases.

COMPLICATED SENTENCE STRUCTURE

ACTIVITY 3

Read the following sentence:

Since long complex sentences lend themselves to obscurity and are incomprehensible to many it is probably best to avoid them as most writers consistently advise, bearing in mind, of course, that it may be impossible to break some sentences down, although this is rare, since most sentences consist of numerous subordinate clauses which can usually be divided into separate sentences if you wish to observe the principle that one idea per sentence is sufficient for any reader to digest at any given time.

You will see that the sentence is both complex and inaccurately punctuated.

Now simplify it and divide it into short, easily digestible sentences which would be clear to any reader. You may need to change the order and the wording slightly to achieve this. Our suggested answer is given at the end of the chapter.

Although most of us believe that long sentences demonstrate a command of the English language, in fact the opposite is true. Many of us become grammatically incorrect when we attempt a long sentence with many clauses. Common errors are:

(a)   to omit the verb

(b)   to omit the punctuation which is vital to accuracy.

Even if grammar and syntax are entirely correct, the purpose of business communication is defeated. Remember, in business we want to achieve understanding and a favourable response as quickly as possible. Keep to shorter, simpler sentences so that the sentence construction is correct.

INCORRECT USE OF PARAGRAPHING

The common faults which are noticeable in business documents are:

(a)   *Failing to divide into paragraphs at all*
This often occurs when one is composing short letters or within main sections of a report. Although these are brief communications, they still contain different ideas or topics which need to be separated. By using paragraphs appropriately, the reader can follow the line of thought more easily.

(b)   *Using a new paragraph for virtually every sentence*
This is another common fault frequently found in letters and summaries. If a

new paragraph is used for virtually every sentence it can give the impression of the letter or report, etc being disjointed; there is a staccato effect if it is read aloud.

Written communication needs to flow if it is to be easy for the reader; paragraphs which vary in length help to achieve this flow.

(c)   *Indiscriminate grouping of points*
Paragraphs should bring together a number of *related* points, not a collection of random thoughts. Usually, there is one sentence, often the first one, which outlines the main idea on which other thoughts may depend. This is called the *topic sentence* or *key sentence*. It is a good idea to check that paragraphs are composed around a key sentence.

You will have noticed how usual it is that paragraphs begin with the topic sentence. Sometimes the topic sentence will come at the end of the paragraph. This approach is often adopted in newspapers or circular letters where an attempt is being made to build up excitement, expectation or interest.

Wherever it occurs in the paragraph, *the topic sentence should be clearly identifiable.* It is a signpost and acts as a guide to the reader.

ACTIVITY 4

Read through the passage below; underline the topic sentences and indicate where you think the paragraph breaks should occur.

The procedures for discipline at work are the concern of every employee. Although a new employee may not be immediately concerned in disciplining others, the rules which apply should be known. These are usually contained in the contract of employment signed on entry to the organisation. The employee also needs to realise the position of the employer in instituting disciplinary procedures. Some major issues concern grounds for dismissal. The factors which influence an employer's decision concern not only the behaviour which has led to dismissal procedures being initiated but how this might affect other employees. For example, where an employee had been convicted of a serious or violent crime, other employees night feel genuinely concerned about working with the employee again. Once again it depends on the job. If it is a responsible one supervising young immature staff it might be justifiable to dismiss, but the employer might consider transfer to another job where such responsibilities don't exist. If the offence is not really relevant to the job then the employer should resist any pressure by other employees to dismiss, certainly at the initial stages. If that doesn't do the trick, and the other employees are seriously worried, it may become necessary to dismiss. If that situation is likely to arise, the employee should receive a warning, confirmed in writing afterwards, that if relationships with other staff become intolerable dismissal will be inevitable. If it is a question of not trusting an employee because he or she holds the position of cashier and has been convicted of shop lifting at another store, this could form reasonable grounds for dismissal. The employer should consider, however, whether it is feasible to transfer the employee to other work that does not involve a position of trust and access to money or goods. If the employee's name is blazoned across the local paper for some very colourful behaviour it may form grounds for dismissal if it affects the employer's reputation. This is a difficult area and probably better ignored when it has no bearing on the job. What is news today is quickly forgotten tomorrow.

(Passage adapted from *Croner's Guide to Disipline* 1988.)
You can check your version against our suggestion at the end of the chapter.

All the common faults which we have discussed so far in this chapter contribute to the production of obscure communication, unfortunately only too common. It is often referred to as the art of "gobbledegook" or writing with a high fog factor.

THE FOG FACTOR

If complex, long words and complicated sentence construction are used in written communication, readers are unable to understand the information quickly and easily: it is difficult to find their way, just like entering a blanket of fog. It is possible to calculate the extent to which a written passage is clear and simple.

The "fog factor" can be calculated by:

(a) counting the number of words of three or more syllables on approximately half a page

(b) counting the number of sentences in the passage chosen

(c) dividing the number of sentences into the number of words.

The result is the fog factor:

$$\text{ie} \quad \frac{\text{Number of words of three syllables or more}}{\text{Number of sentences}} = \text{Fog factor}$$

The lower the fog factor, the easier it is to understand the passage. What is an acceptable fog factor depends on the level of understanding of the interested reader. For example, readers of the quality press are happy to accept a fog factor of eight or even slightly above. The tabloids aim for a fog factor of three or even below. You need to make similar decisions in your own business communication.

ACTIVITY 5

The following letter has a number of common faults as well as a high fog factor. Calculate the fog factor and then write an improved version of the letter.

Dear Sir,

We are in receipt of your communication of 5th June and note your dissatisfaction regarding the unsatisfactory situation which you have given in your commentary and which concerned our procedure in computerising your bank statements.

We note that following your perusal of your recent statement you were of the opinion that it was illegible and incomprehensible.

It will be appreciated that computerisation assists our organisation in the speed of its transactions. In the not too distant future we may, however, conduct an evaluation of the current situation and review the reactions both affirmative and negative of our customers.

Regretting our inability to be of service but assuring you of our best attention at all times.

Yours faithfully

You can then check your version against ours at the end of the chapter.

NOTE TAKING AND NOTE MAKING

Whatever task you may face in written and oral communication, an extremely useful skill is that of making precise and clear notes to summarise your thoughts or complex material. The ability to make or take good notes has a wide variety of applications and is rightly valued by employers. It is also a skill useful in any course of study.

Uses of Note Making/Taking Techniques

ACTIVITY 6

Try to identify for yourself the tasks within your chosen course of study or career for which notes may be essential and list these.

Generally, note taking may be required in the following situations.

Preparation for:

▶ making a telephone call

▶ writing a memo or letter

▶ composing a report

▶ attending a meeting or conference in which one is required to participate

▶ producing a summary of articles, experiments, documents, etc for other people's use

▶ producing an oral summary for other people's information, eg from a training course.

Recording:

▶ proceedings at meetings

▶ telephone messages for oneself and others

▶ condensed information drawn from a variety of sources

▶ information from an interview.

Studying:

▶ aiding recall of oral or written information

▶ condensing information drawn from a variety of sources (books, articles, lectures, seminars, experiments, practical workshops, etc)

▶ concentrating listening skills

▶ testing acquisition of knowledge.

From this list it is evident that effective note taking techniques can assist one's competence in much of one's work. For this reason, the relevant techniques are worth attention.

Note Taking

Note taking while reading   To some extent, this is easier than taking notes when listening, since the material can be reread as often as necessary. There are different ways of reading and we may not be aware that we do read differently for particular purposes. Some methods are:

(a) *Scanning:*
This normally involves looking for key words in reference books.

(b) *Skimming:*
This, on the other hand, means looking for the broad framework of ideas or facts within the material. It is here that subheadings can be invaluable in helping the reader to skim-read effectively. If there are no subheadings then it means identifying the key sentences in each paragraph.

(c) *Reading for studying or critical reading:*
This is a more concentrated activity and you will need to take notes not only to summarise but also to assess and evaluate what you read. By putting complex ideas in your own words, you ensure your own concentration; the process of interpretation ensures that you really understand the content.

Note taking from oral material   This is more difficult since the information is quickly given and the speaker moves on. Nevertheless, there are many occasions when it is vital to record what has been said. You will need to develop the ability to select what is important and to omit what is merely digression, elaboration, repetition, example or illustration.

Whether you are dealing with written or oral material, the original note taking is usually random — a collection of quickly jotted ideas and points. Too often we try to create orderly notes at this early stage. One technique for jotting notes down quickly is to use *patterned notes* or *mind maps*. An example of creating a mind map is shown on pages 42 and 43. Points can be jotted down anywhere on the page and the connections made between them. Mind maps may look chaotic but they do help in any initial planning or recording process.

ACTIVITY 7

Try this technique for yourself by recording the main points from a television or radio interview. As you watch or listen, take quick notes in the form of a mind map, selecting what is important only. Then convert your mind map into a formal set of notes in a logical sequence under subheadings.

Schematic notes   Formalised notes produced under subheadings and listed points following a logical sequence are known as *schematic notes*. They are particularly useful for summarising information gathered from a variety of sources. It is when the summary is for another person — a tutor or superior — that one needs to be particularly careful that the information is presented in a sensible sequence and can be clearly understood. The following section provides some guidelines on this.

EXAMPLE OF MIND MAPPING

You have recently attended a conference called "Job Search". It dealt with finding first jobs and job change. There were a number of speakers, some of whom were more competent than others. You decided to jot down points at random. Your page looks like this.

Researching job prospects: stage 1

On the way home from the conference on the train, you start to connect the related points. You begin to see that connections can be made on the basis of your own analysis, the analysis of others and sources of information. Your mind map when you reach home looks like this.

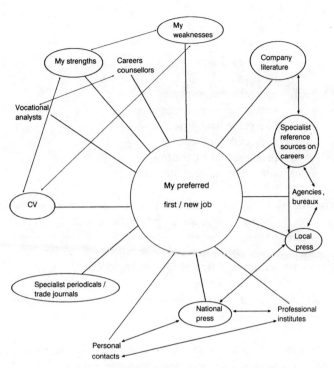

Researching job prospects: stage 2

However, if you are to make sense of these "jottings" at a later date it is important to formalise them and arrange them under relevant subheadings which clarify the outline of the material. The first stage is to link related points together.

The following morning you convert your mind map into a set of orderly notes under subheadings as follows.

(a) *Objective:*
This is to find the right job for me.

(b) *Self analysis:*
I need to list
(i) my strengths,
(ii) my weaknesses

and produce a *curriculum vitae.*

(c) *Analysis by others:*
This can be done by
(i) career counsellors,
(ii) vocational analysts,
(iii) specialist agencies/bureaux.

(d) *Sources of job information:*
These include
- (i) national press,
- (ii) local press,
- (iii) specialist/trade press,
- (iv) specialist agencies/bureaux,
- (v) company literature,
- (vi) personal contacts,
- (vii) professional institutes,
- (viii) specialist careers literature.

Now you have the relevant information grouped under subheadings, it can be used as a check list to undertake a systematic search for a job.

Techniques for summarising written information

(a) *Read the original information critically* to identify the subject, main facts and the development of ideas.

(b) *Write down a heading* which encapsulates the subject — this can be used later to check points for importance and relevance.

(c) Go through the written material to *identify topic sentences*. Use these topic sentences to decide on the subheadings for the summary. Underline the main points to use in each paragraph.

(d) Using the subheadings and underlined points as guidelines; *write out the summary*. Ensure related points are grouped together.

(e) Make sure that *information is presented consistently* in terms of numbering and degree of indentation.

(f) Check back to ensure *the balance of the original material is retained* and undue weighting has not been given to one part.

(g) *Check back on basics such as spelling, punctuation and use of vocabulary* so that it is written in clear accurate English

Note Making

This technique is necessary to prepare an oral or written report, brief a group of people, prepare for an interview or compose a letter or memo. Notes may be taken from a variety of sources to provide background information, but it is also necessary to go through the *creative activity* of building up one's own set of notes.

(a) *Consider the objectives and recipients*
As with any communication, *define the objectives and identify the readership or audience*. This will influence not only what to say but also the choice of vocabulary, approach and the sequence to use.

(b) *Collect data*
An essential area of preparation is to *collect together the necessary facts, ideas, figures, illustrations*, etc relating to the topic to be treated or the document to be composed. Once data has been collected, it must be sorted and organised.

(c) *Select and place the information in sequence*
Whenever facts are presented in writing, it is easier for people to understand if the order is clear. *Select those facts and ideas directly relevant to the topic* and then *group related points together*. Anything which is not relevant to the objectives or of interest to the readers or audience should be ruthlessly pruned.

(d) *Use subheadings and numbered points*
Notes need to be subheaded and numbered logically so that they can be referred to quickly and easily. If one is talking from notes, they will need to be written or printed in large letters so that they are easily legible and the subheadings emboldened or underlined so that they can be referred to at a glance.

(e) *Anotate the notes*
Sometimes *notes of this kind may need annotating*, ie a comment in the margin against a point or section. This can be used, for example, to give a time allocation for each section or a reminder to show a viewfoil or provide a handout at a particular point.

CONCLUSION

If the fundamental rules and basic techniques of good written communication covered in this chapter are mastered they can be applied to any written document. Specific forms of written communication will be dealt with in Sections 2 and 3 of this book.

ANSWERS TO ACTIVITIES IN CHAPTER 3

Activity 1

Existing word

anticipate
commencement
despatch
optimum
utilise

More familiar word

expect
start or beginning
send
best
use

Activity 2

Existing phrase

We acknowledge receipt of . . .
Please do not hesitate to . . .
In the not too distant future
At the present time
Due to the fact that
According to our records

More direct phrase

We have received . . .
Please . . .
Soon
Now
Because
We see

Activity 3

Most writers advise that long complex sentences lend themselves to obscurity and are incomprehensible to many, so are possibly better avoided.

Of course, it may be impossible to break down some sentences. However, this is rare, since most sentences consist of numerous subordinate clauses which can usually be divided into separate sentences.

This observes the principle that one idea per sentence is sufficient for any reader to digest at any given time.

Activity 4

The procedures for discipline at work are the concern of every employee. Although a new employee may not be immediately concerned in disciplining others, the rules which apply should be known. These are usually contained in the contract of employment signed on entry to the organisation.

The employee also needs to realise the position of the employer in instituting disciplinary procedures. Some major issues concern grounds for dismissal. The factors which influence an employer's decision concern not only the behaviour which has led to dismissal procedures being initiated but how this might affect other employees. For example, where an employee had been convicted of a serious or violent crime, other employees might feel genuinely concerned about working with the employee again. Once again it depends on the job. If it is a responsible one supervising young immature staff it might be justifiable to dismiss, but the employer might consider transfer to another job where such responsibilities don't exist. If the offence is not really relevant to the job then the employer should resist any pressure by other employees to dismiss, certainly at the initial stages. If that doesn't do the trick, and the other employees are seriously worried, it may become necessary to dismiss. If that situation is likely to arise, the employee should receive a warning, confirmed in writing afterwards, that if relationships with other staff become intolerable dismissal will be inevitable.

If it is a question of not trusting an employee because he or she holds the position of cashier and has been convicted of shop lifting at another store, this could form reasonable grounds for dismissal. The employer should consider, however, whether it is feasible to transfer the employee to other work that does not involve a position of trust and access to money or goods.

If the employee's name is blazoned across the local paper for some very colourful behaviour it may form grounds for dismissal if it affects the employer's reputation. This is a difficult area and probably better ignored when it has no bearing on the job. What is news today is quickly forgotten tomorrow.

(Passage adapted from *Croner's Guide to Discipline* 1988.)

Activity 5

Dear Sir,

Thank you for your letter of the 5th April. We are sorry that you find your computerised statements difficult to read and understand.

The bank uses a computer for a faster and more efficient service. Soon, however, we will review our service in the light of customers' reactions.

We are sorry we cannot change the situation immediately but assure you that we do note customers' comments.

Yours faithfully

(Reduced to a fog factor of two.)

4 Effective Visual Communication: Methods, Uses and Presentation

---

ACTIVITY 1

Try to list some brief answers to the following before beginning the chapter.

(a) Why do you dress up for an interview?
(b) What initially attracts you to another person?
(c) What attracts you to read a report?
(d) What helps you to understand complex statistical data or financial information?
(e) What helps you to find essential services or facilities in a foreign country?

You will have a range of answers, but the common factor you are likely to have is the *importance of visual impact*.

VISUAL COMMUNICATION

It is for this reason that organisations spend a considerable amount of money promoting and advertising their products and services through the mass media and even through sponsorship of events. They rely heavily on visual material for their impact.

Potential customers of any organisation are struck by the number of visual images which have been carefully designed by marketing and public relations personnel to promote an awareness of the organisation's identity and to encourage them to use its products and services.

All of these show the extent to which we depend on image for recognition. This is not, of course, a marketing text book but the examples do serve to increase awareness of the strong connection between memory and visual impact. Whatever your specialisation, you need to recognise and use visual methods effectively to secure positive acceptance of yourself and your work. The illustration at the bottom of the page shows the significance of visual communication in terms of memory retention and how important it may be in accompanying other communication media.

ACTIVITY 2

What products or services do you associate with the following?

(a)   A black horse
(b)   An old English sheepdog
(c)   A tiger
(d)   A labrador puppy
(e)   A kestrel

We think you will have identified all of these easily but in case any of them gave you trouble, the answers appear at the end of the chapter.

Let us now look again at the questions in Activity 1. Questions (a) and (b) will be taken together.

Personal Presentation

You probably realised the importance of personal impact in this situation. Of course, it does not just stop at interviews.

Seeing and hearing 50%

Seeing 30%

Hearing 20%

Reading 10%

How much do we remember?

The way in which one appears to others is vitally important. Many organisations are taking to the idea of corporate dress, even those which have never traditionally adopted a uniform. Building societies are some of the latest to do this. Even if there is no uniform, some organisations, consciously or unconsciously, expect a certain conformity in dress. This is because the appearance of employees affects the perception of clients and customers about an organisation.

When we are initially attracted to somebody think of the part played by their appearance. It may be colour of hair or eyes, the kind of clothes they wear or the body language they are using.

Visual Presentation in Written Communication

There are a number of techniques used by publishers of books, periodicals and newspapers which enhance the attraction of the written word. These include the use of:

(a) illustrations, diagrams and graphs to aid understanding and increase interest

(b) a variety of typefaces (size and characteristics) to signpost or emphasise

(c) space between paragraphs, or in margin size, to reduce the density of the text

(d) careful positioning of illustrations on the page to create a balanced appearance

(e) schematic layout to promote understanding.

These techniques can be used in handwritten documents and now can be easily incorporated when word processing using integrated business software or desk top publishing. Correct layout, whether in letters, reports or other business documents, also conveys an image of professionalism and efficiency.

In the case of a report and a discussion paper, the packaging — that is the binding, title page and cover — often dictates whether people are attracted to read the contents. A dog-eared, tatty appearance implies a haphazard approach to the content — whether this is actually true or not. If you find your project filed in the wastepaper basket or left in a pending tray, perhaps you should look again at presentation.

Graphical Presentation

The mass media have shown us that the general public respond more readily to the presentation of numerical information by visual means. For example:

(a) the "swingometer" is used at election time to show changing support for a constituency candidate

(b) the "clapometer" is used to register the level of applause for a contestant

(c)   mobile "bar charts" may be used as an alternative to the clapometer to show the level of support for a particular act in a talent contest.

Business charts and graphs   In business communication, graphics can play a similar role. In reports, commentaries, summaries and projects where there may be a variety of readers with differing levels of interest, some may wish to immerse themselves in detailed tables of statistics while others may merely wish to identify an overall trend. Charts and graphs are useful here.

As managers, readers will probably have to deal with statistics in some way — figures on profit, sales, production output, manpower employed, items purchased or consumed, use of equipment and so on. Many of these statistics will have to be presented in a form which can be easily interpreted by non-specialists.

Use of graphics may include:

(a)   *line graphs* to show trends over a period of time (see example on page 52)

(b)   *bar charts* to compare total quantities at different points in time. Bar charts may be drawn horizontally or vertically, be simple or compound (see example on page 52)

(c)   *pie charts* to show proportions — or relationships of parts to a whole (see example on page 52)

(d)   *pictograms* to show very general trends in a pictorial form (see example on page 53).

Other chart formats may be *organisation charts* to show the hierarchical structure of an organisation, similar to the examples in Chapter 5. Some organisations use *flow charts* to show how various stages in a procedure or process are linked (see example on page 53).

Simple computer graphics packages make it possible to convert tables of statistics into the first three forms of graphical representation mentioned above. More sophisticated packages will produce a wide range of visual formats. Remember — whenever graphs and charts are used:

▶ they should have an appropriate heading

▶ in the case of line graphs and bar charts, the axes should be clearly labelled

▶ a key may be necessary.

This section has only dealt with general business graphs common in many specialisations. Obviously, particular functions or specialisations may have a range of more

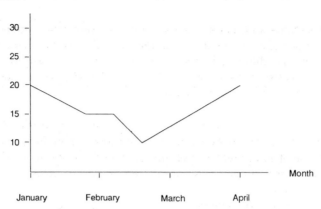

Line graph showing sales figures for three months

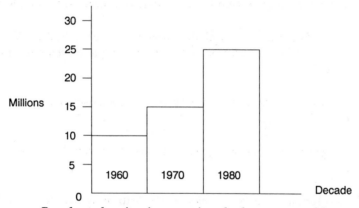

Bar chart showing increase in telephone ownership

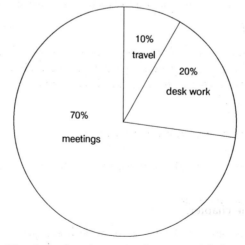

Pie chart showing use of managerial time

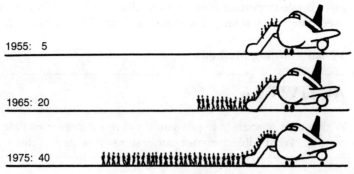

Pictogram showing increase in air passenger traffic (millions)

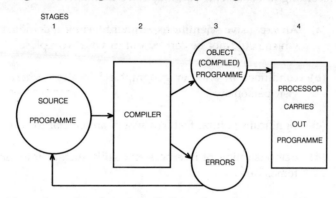

Flow chart showing compilation of a software programme

sophisticated diagrams, charts and computerised graphics (eg engineering drawings, animated graphs, cross-sections, layout plans, etc).

Visual Presentation through Symbols and Signs

Symbols and signs are a substitute for the spoken or written word. They are particularly useful when the meaning must be conveyed quickly and when language or noise barriers must be overcome. Road signs are a good example, as are symbols on packaging or at railway stations or airports. Remember that brightly coloured symbols are attention getters — they intrude on perceptive processes.

ACTIVITY 3

Look around your own organisation and note in what situations symbols are useful as a means of communication.

You might like to check your own research findings against our batch of symbols at the end of the chapter.

Although we have covered the visual presentation methods dealt with in Activity 1, there is one important area yet to be discussed — the many visual methods which are used today for training, instruction and briefing. Consider the following activity.

Visual Training Methods

ACTIVITY 4

Within your specialism or job, you may have experienced video used as a training method. What subject matter can best be presented in this way?

According to your field, you may have mentioned:

(a) An expensive scientific experiment/technical demonstration/operational process which could not be carried out in your workplace

(b) conditions in another geographical location where it would be expensive to visit personally

(c) significant natural features which are crucial to your study

(d) demonstration of interpersonal skills such as interviewing, negotiation or customer care

(e) simulation of actual operating conditions such as driving or piloting a plane where the video is the visual stimulus in a computer program.

There are, of course, many more examples. The video and the computer provide a number of interactive processes which are extremely useful and relevant in many training situations. Chapter 20 of this book lists some of the useful training videos on communication and interpersonal skills which are available.

CONCLUSION

This chapter has attempted to show that visual methods are at least as important as oral delivery or the written word. They may act as a substitute for or a support to both of these other forms of communication. They are very memorable, which is the reason that they are used so frequently in marketing or training. They also assist comprehension of complex material.

This concludes the section on basic communication techniques: oral, written and visual. The next two sections concentrate on the application of these techniques to specific forms of business communication.

ANSWERS TO ACTIVITIES IN CHAPTER 4

Activity 2

(a) Black horse associated with banking.

(b) Old English sheepdog associated with paint.

(c) Tiger associated with petrol.

(d) Labrador puppy associated with toilet tissue.

(e) Kestrel associated with lager.

Activity 3

SECTION 2: INTERPERSONAL SKILLS WITHIN ORGANISATIONS

INTRODUCTION

The first section in this book provided a general introduction to the fundamental communication skills which we all need to apply at work.

This section begins by looking at the first encounter between an individual and the employing organisation; Chapter 5 will therefore cover the communication structures designed by organisations within which any employee must operate. By examining a variety of such communication systems and the working environment which results from them, we hope to help you decide what kind of organisation might best suit you.

The choice is, of course, a two sided one and the organisation must, in its turn, select individuals appropriate to its needs. Chapter 6 will therefore give some guidance on how to present yourself effectively in applying for a job and at the selection interview.

Once you join an organisation you become a member of a department or a small section within a department, where you need to operate as part of a team. This involves participating constructively and making adjustments to other members of your group. Chapter 7 looks at the skills required in team work.

Team work involves good leadership and effective motivation of the team by the person in the leadership role; this is not an easy task. Chapter 8 will deal with the management skill of leadership and team building. Leadership and good teamwork is particularly required within the meetings, both formal and informal, which so frequently occur at work. As these are significant time wasters if not used properly, Chapter 9 will examine ways in which you can help to make meetings more productive. Chapter 10 will look at the very important area of instruction and briefing.

Section 2 will conclude with two chapters concerned with the application of written skills to particular internal documents such as forms, memoranda and reports. Some guidance will also be given on the oral presentation of reports.

5 Communication Systems in Organisations

When considering any organisation as a potential employer, it is very important to think carefully about the type of organisation it is: its size, history, its present structure and markets will all affect the working environment. If one is to operate effectively, which essentially means happily, it is necessary to choose one which is compatible with one's expectations, aspirations and personality.

FORMAL ORGANISATIONAL COMMUNICATION

As organisations develop beyond the very small venture, they develop organisation structures which provide a framework for the activities of employees and indicate the formal channels of communication which should be followed.

Vertical and Horizontal Channels of Communication

One way of beginning to look at organisation structures and the formal channels of communication is to look at a company's organisation chart. There are many kinds of these, but the most common type is the one which resembles a family tree.

Example of a vertical organisation chart

We have also included examples of the other kinds which may be found on pages 62 and 63.

The vertical chart is the most common in this country and gives the formal lines of authority and accountability, that is the channels through which communication must take place. Some communication, for example, will be passed downwards and some

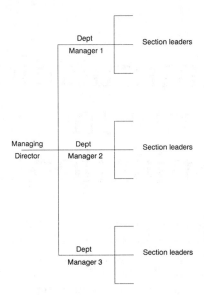

Example of a horizontal organisation chart

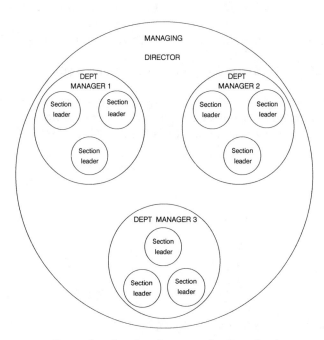

Example of a circular organisation chart

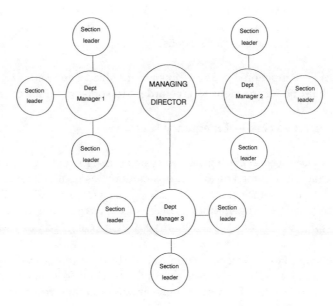

Example of a spherical organisation chart

upwards (vertical communication). People also need to communicate laterally, between departments and sections so that everyone can work towards achieving the common objectives of the organisation by co-ordinating their activities.

ACTIVITY 1

Try to obtain an organisation chart of your company or college.

Make a list of the types of communication which take place within it under three columns as follows. We have given an example for each column.

Vertical communication		**Horizontal communication**
Downwards	*Upwards*	*Laterally*
Instructions	Requests	Discussion

You might like to check your answers against ours at the end of the chapter.

One of the basic differences between vertical and horizontal communication is:

(a) vertical channels involve line relationships where one person holds authority and the other is accountable.

(b) horizontal channels involve functional relationships where neither of the people involved are directly in authority over or accountable to the other but both have a responsibility to inform each other about specific matters and to respond to one another's needs.

Where functional relationships are involved one needs tact and diplomacy; remember that one has no right to give orders to someone in another department.

Direct Access — Emergency Measures

All this seems very logical and systematic. However, we must not forget that communication is a human process. Consequently, as in all matters relating to people, emergencies arise which have to bypass the normal channels if disasters or delays are to be avoided. All organisations establish bypass systems to suit their circumstances. You can probably identify some in your own college or company.

Some bypass systems are official — they are recognised and used by management as part of a policy of direct access when they feel that this is necessary. One typical example might be a staff representative having direct access to a senior manager in the case of a collective complaint.

INFORMAL SYSTEMS OF COMMUNICATION

We now need to consider those bypass systems which we all know exist and which are not officially recognised (in common terminology "the grapevine"). The grapevine grows for a number of reasons and is used in a variety of ways, some of which are good and some not so good!

▶ *The grapevine allows official work to be carried out by methods which are more acceptable to employees than those laid down by the organisation.* For example, let us suppose you need some information quickly; the formal system (that is going to your boss/tutor) may be lengthy or you might want to demonstrate that you can find out for yourself. It is simpler to go directly to the source of the information. This may result in quicker and more efficient work.

▶ The converse of this is the *confusion which the grapevine may cause when it is a source of rumour spreading dissatisfaction.* Too often the information becomes distorted when it is passed around and this can have disastrous results.

THE SHAPE OF THE ORGANISATION

Tall and Flat Structures

You may have noticed during Activity 1 that your organisation chart had a certain shape. It may have had:

(a) *many levels* with each manager controlling a relatively small number of people — *a narrow span of control*; in this case, the shape would have been tall and thin.

(b) *relatively few levels*, with each manager controlling a large number of people — *a broad span of control*. In this case the shape would be flat.

Tall, thin structures tend to more typical of large private and public sector organisations. Here is an example.

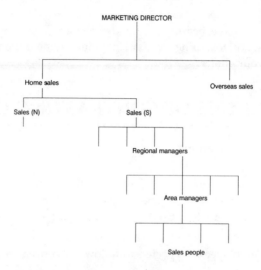

A simplified chart showing the levels of authority within a large marketing department

Short, flat structures, on the other hand, are more typical of small businesses. This might include professional partnerships, small construction or engineering concerns, independent hotels or restaurants, small specialist laboratories or agencies.

Example of a flat structure

Sometimes large organisations also design flat structures in order to gain the advantages which they have to offer.

ACTIVITY 2

1. What do you think might be the advantages and disadvantages of each kind of structure? List these briefly.

2. Compare your list with our suggested one at the end of this chapter. Make a note of any which you might have missed.

3. Which type of structure do you prefer and why?

Now you have begun to consider the reasons why you might prefer one type of organisation to another, we can introduce some more variables, which might ultimately affect your choice.

CHARACTERISTICS OF CONTRASTING ORGANISATIONS

Large Organisations

Organisations with many levels of authority are often described as hierarchies, they can also sometimes be labelled as bureaucracies. Characteristics which immediately spring to mind when thinking of employment in this type of organisation are:

▶ the employee is expected to follow set procedures

▶ appointments are made on the basis of expertise

▶ progress through the organisation is based on set criteria and grading systems are often used

▶ the employee is given only limited discretion and authority to make decisions and these are based on a clearly defined job description

▶ there is a tendency to rely heavily on written communication and formal meetings

▶ decision-making and communication can be delayed because of the number of levels

▶ such organisations tend to be resistant to change.

You may have reacted adversely to the above, but consider some of the advantages to the employee for a moment. They allow:

▶ each employee considerable personal security since expectations are defined and known and job descriptions are specific

▶ the employee to know the criteria by which he or she will progress, so it is possible to plan a career path

▶ authority to stem from the position held within the organisation so it does not depend purely on popularity

▶ decision-making to be directed and supported by procedures and by the immediate superior so it is rarely taken in isolation

▶ conditions and terms of work to be set and clear so no personal negotiation needs to take place.

These characteristics will be found to varying degrees in large organisations; they will be most prominent in organisations whose main objectives are to demonstrate permanence, stability and impartiality.

Small Organisations

Smaller organisations, with fewer levels of authority, have different characteristics. Those which are immediately apparent are:

▶ they are more flexible and can adapt to environmental change more easily

▶ they can offer greater variety of work

▶ there is more opportunity for the employee to use initiative in making decisions

▶ it is easier to identify with the whole work team

▶ it is often possible to negotiate your own terms and conditions of work

▶ progress depends more on your immediate performance than on set criteria.

You may feel that these characteristics are more attractive. However, there are some drawbacks such as:

▶ job roles are often not clearly defined and other people's expectations can be confused and conflicting

▶ appointments and promotions sometimes rest on subjective judgements

▶ decisions are usually individual and the effects can rebound on the employee who made them

▶ the power of the central figure is paramount and his or her decisions are often carried out in spite of disagreement.

We have admittedly drawn an extreme picture here; many small organisations recognise the dangers and overcome them effectively by deliberately adopting or incorporating some of the techniques of large organisations. So, in the most successful organisations of either size, they are designed to combine the most appropriate features to meet their needs and objectives.

ACTIVITY 3

Look again at the decision you made at the end of Activity 2.

What factors which have now been discussed might be important to you and might therefore affect your final choice?

List these briefly and keep your list safe — it may prove useful when you attend your next job interview as a basis for observation and questioning.

CURRENT DEVELOPMENTS IN THE DESIGN OF ORGANISATION STRUCTURES

Both small and large organisations reach a stage in their development when some form of adaptation from the original structure is necessary. This may come about because of expansion or contraction; it may occur because of a change in the market, economic climate or legislation.

In recent years, many organisations have realised the need for change and have adopted different structures as part of their corporate strategy. One major reason for this has been the recognition that they have reached a point where their activities and operations need to be regrouped in some way.

Regrouping of Activities: Matrix Structures

The most popular traditional grouping has been by function — marketing, production, research and development, personnel, accounts, etc. However, these departmental divisions can have distinct disadvantages when:

(a) operating in a rapidly changing environment

(b) diversification into multi-products or services has taken place.

One approach which has been widely adopted in these circumstances is known as the "matrix" organisation.

Characteristics of the matrix organisation The matrix organisation brings together people who have expertise in the different traditional functions into a multi-functional team. They are then able to pool their expertise to develop, resource, provide and promote a product or service. They also retain the support of their fellow specialists within their traditional function. The major commitment is to the task in hand. The following diagram shows how the matrix works in an organisation.

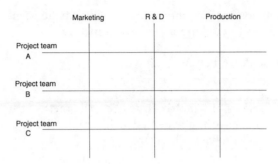

Matrix structure in industry

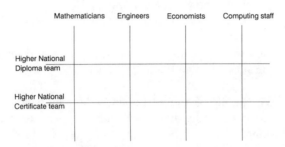

Matrix structure in education

As an organisation changes its products or services, specialists can be re-allocated to new teams.

Advantages of a matrix structure The advantages of working within a matrix system are:

(a) strong team commitment

(b) authority is related to expertise and contribution rather than to organisational position or personality

(c) there is an opportunity to overview the whole process

(d) there is immediate feedback of meaningful results

(e) there is the facility to retain a "functional home" and support system while enjoying the challenge of a multi-functional team

(f) there are possibilities of advancement and a career path related to two fields rather than one.

ACTIVITY 4

This all sounds like the solution — an idyllic scenario. Can you think of any drawbacks to working in a matrix structure?

Jot these down before reading on.

The problems of a matrix structure   The matrix structure has been much praised but those who have implemented it have experienced some practical problems, which need to be resolved. These are:

(a) There is dual accountability for the individual:

    (i)   to the work team and
    (ii) to the functional head of department,

and this can cause conflict of priorities and loyalties with little or no direction on how to solve them.

(b) As the life of a project is limited, some feeling of insecurity or instability may affect the individual, particularly in periods of cost cutting and staff redeployment.

(c) The more integrated the team, the more likely it is that it will be competing with other such teams for resources. This can prove counterproductive for everyone.

Regrouping Activities: Differentiation

Differentiation recognises that functional departments may need to be designed in different ways even within the same organisation. This means that it is possible to find small flat structures in one department while another may have tall, thin hierarchical characteristics.

As a general principle, functions which must relate to a dynamic external environment such as marketing and research and development need flatter structures than those which respond to the demands of internal organisations (eg production, office support services, management information systems). This can be seen in the example on page 71.

ACTIVITY 5

Look at your own organisation chart again. From what you have read in this chapter, are there now any changes which you think are desirable?

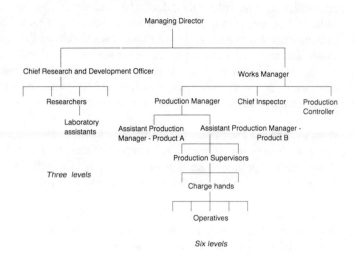

Organisation chart showing differentiation

Clearly, some organisations, whether they are large or small, are able to survive better than others. Widening markets and changing technologies will bring new challenges; economically and environmentally we are moving towards greater international activity. This will inevitably bring contact with approaches more typical of other cultures and nationalities which will affect our own work organisation. Indeed, with increased foreign ownership within the United Kingdom this is already occurring. Before we leave the subject of organisational approaches, therefore, we need to consider briefly the possible future influences and directions.

FUTURE DIRECTIONS

Many organisations within the United Kingdom today are owned by foreign investors such as the Japanese, the Americans and the French; these are probably the main influences at the moment, though there are many minor ones.

Each nation brings with it its own culture, applied to the work place. Today, we cannot afford to be isolationist or nationalistic — we need to adjust to them as they have to adjust to us.

The different approaches cover a very wide range, reflecting the beliefs and backgrounds of the countries or even the regions concerned. At one end of the spectrum, we may see the paternalism of the Japanese which demands long term organisational loyalty in return for family support with housing, schooling, health care and sponsorship. At the other end of the scale, we see the meritocratic American system which rewards success highly but is ruthless with incompetence.

From France and her European neighbours, particularly the Basque region and Spain, we have already experienced economically the effects of the strong agricultural co-operatives. In the United Kingdom, the concept of co-operatives is associated with the past. In Europe, it is a dynamic force which maintains such middle class institutions as banks and universities. As we move towards closer links with Europe, we will need to understand and respond to an approach which is common to them but a rarity to us; direct ownership of the means of production and resourcing has worked well elsewhere. To us, the idea of operatives as board members is either quaint or communistic; other countries have proved it can work.

With expanding employment opportunities within the EC and increasing job mobility, you may find yourself applying to organisations owned by other nationalities. If your chosen field has many foreign employers, it is worth researching their organisation structures and working environments before deciding to join them.

In any case, even if you are employed by a British organisation, you may well find that you need to meet and work with clients from abroad. If so, a knowledge of their organisational approaches can be invaluable.

CONCLUSION

We hope that this chapter has given you some ideas on the range of organisations which exist and how their structures influence the working environments of their employees. It should help you to realise that choosing an organisation suited to you is a vital but complex process. Once you have made your choice, however, it is up to you to convince the organisation that you are right for it. The next chapter discusses the process of applying for and obtaining a suitable job.

ANSWERS TO ACTIVITIES IN CHAPTER 5

Activity 1

Vertical communication		**Horizontal communication**
Downwards	*Upwards*	*Laterally*
Objectives	Progress	Information
Policy	Problems	Discussion
Information	Information	Consultation
Initiation of change	Reactions to change	Advice
Instructions	Grievances	Negotiation
Discipline	Requests	Requests
Advice	Suggestions	
Consultation		
Appraisal		

Activity 2

Tall thin organisations

Advantages	*Disadvantages*
Always a superior to refer to/fall back on when in doubt.	Individual feels closely supervised and restricted.
Limited span of control means chance of better dialogue between superior and subordinate.	Distortion of vertical communication as it passes through many levels.
Narrow span of control can mean smaller, more cohesive teams.	Decision making may be slow as may be response to requests.
Individual is likely to have a defined job role and know what to expect.	Very little initiative may be given to the individual.
Less competition for promotion, therefore promotional prospects better.	Feeling of separation between top and bottom of structure causing possible hostility, lack of motivation.

Flat organisations

Advantages	*Disadvantages*
Vertical communications are more direct and not so liable to distortion.	Horizontal communication can be more complex.

Quicker decision making — usually one person in charge.	Decisions can be imposed rather than agreed.
Job likely to be more autonomous because of difficulties of supervision caused by wide span of control.	Wide span of control may mean less support for individuals within the group.
Less separation between top and bottom of the organisation may mean better promotion prospects, so more motivation.	Wide span of control means more competition for time and resources.

6 Self-Presentation for Selection

The initial encounter that any individual has with an organisation is when he or she applies for a job. The first objective is to ensure that you are interviewed and you will only achieve this if you present yourself effectively in writing first. There are three ways in which this is usually done. These are in:

(a)   the application form

(b)   the *curriculum vitae* (CV)

(c)   the letter of application.

An organisation may require any or all of these. A well prepared CV can help applicants to fill in application forms properly, write a relevant covering letter and, if necessary, produce a new version of their CV appropriate to the specific job in question.

The second objective is to succeed at the interview. This requires self-presentation skills of a different kind; here appearance, manner, voice and fluency will all be important as well as the content of answers to questions.

ANALYSING ONE'S OWN ABILITIES AND APTITUDES

Before one can even begin to compile a CV or fill in an application form it is necessary to analyse one's own skills and knowledge. Organisations look at past achievements and behaviour in order to predict how useful people will be within the job they have to offer. Normally this divides into two areas:

(a)   *technical skills and knowledge*, ie the capability acquired in a chosen specialisation

(b)   *performance skills*, ie aspects such as self-organisation, ability to work with others and success in meeting deadlines.

The organisation normally begins with a written description of the job it has to offer, known as a "job description", and derives from this a list of skills and qualities which are required to perform it effectively. This second document is usually called a "personnel specification".

Analysing your own Strengths and Weaknesses

Each candidate will be assessed against his or her ability to fulfil the requirements of the job description and personnel specification, so it helps if one can systematically review one's own suitability. As you are likely to apply for a range of jobs in the first instance it is a good idea if you begin by trying to analyse your own capabilities on a general basis.

ACTIVITY 1

(a) List the specific technical knowledge which you have gained of subjects, skills or techniques; these may be derived from study, work or leisure. For example, even a part-time job in a bar could have given you cash handling skills; if you have been a club secretary, you may have developed your written documentation skills.

(b) List the performance or, if you prefer it, management skills, which you have had to employ in any of these areas. For example, a part-time job in a bar could have taught you problem-solving techniques to handle difficult people; if you have been a club secretary you may have had to organise others.

We hope you found this an interesting activity and that you were pleasantly surprised at how many skills you had acquired from a range of activities in your past experience. It may now help to categorise some of these in a more structured way so that you can draw on them when completing your CV or filling in application forms. You might like to base your own list on the one we have produced on page 77.

Range of Marketable Skills

All these skills are marketable; before you can claim to have any of them, however, you need to be able to quote specific instances when you have demonstrated them; otherwise, they will be perceived, probably correctly, as your own delusions of grandeur.

ACTIVITY 2

Produce a table of your skills. In the first column list the skills you have acquired; in the second column give specific examples of how you have demonstrated these against each; leave the third column blank — we will be coming back to it in Activity 3.

Skills	Demonstration	Preference rating

RANGE OF MARKETABLE SKILLS

Numerical skills	Ability to: keep accounts; handle cash; work out measurements and quantities; perform calculations.
Oral skills	Ability to: give instructions, use the telephone, conduct a structured discussion, conduct an interview, participate in a meeting, deliver a presentation, sell, negotiate.
Written skills	Ability to: write letters, memos and reports, check and edit written material, use appropriate illustrative material to support and extend the written word; complete forms; handle paperwork.
Visual and presentation skills	Ability to: present numerical data graphically; design illustrative material; use appropriate layout and design for written material; present self effectively.
Research skills	Ability to: gather data from appropriate sources; conduct investigations and/or experiments; observe results.
Analytical skills	Ability to: generate ideas, interpret data; use logical methods to solve problems and make decisions; evaluate solutions to problems.
Practical and mechanical skills	Ability to: perceive spatial relationships; operate equipment; identify and rectify faults in equipment; construct and design; create; assemble parts; install equipment or systems.
Organisational skills	Ability to: plan; schedule time; organise others; organise yourself; control; monitor progress; co-ordinate resources and people.
Team skills	Ability to: work constructively within a group; represent a group; lead others; give and enlist co-operation; give and take constructive criticism.

You are now armed with sufficient information about your skills to select those which are appropriate to the jobs for which you might apply. You should also consider, before applying for any job, those skills which you feel most confident and happy about practising. It may be that although you have acquired a certain skill, you would not be happy being asked to use it frequently.

ACTIVITY 3

Go back to your table from Activity 2 and give a preference rating in the third column. Give a mark out of five for each, five being reserved for the skills you feel happiest being asked to use.

You can now use your completed table to help you select the jobs which most suit your skills by comparing your list of preferred skills to those required in the advertisement or job description.

Personal Qualities

Before we have finished with self analysis, there is one more aspect to consider. This is the qualities which you bring to any activity you undertake. The next activity should help you to identify your personal qualities.

By persevering with this lengthy exercise you should have a list which shows those qualities which are most reflected in your behaviour. These are the ones you should emphasise in a letter of application or in an interview.

ACTIVITY 4

(a) Look carefully at the following list of personal qualities and tick those which you think you possess. I am:

adapatable	imaginative
aggressive	industrious
amiable	introspective
ambitious	loyal
assertive	objective
assured	open-minded
calm	orderly
cheerful	patient
considerate	persistent
creative	prudent
decisive	reliable
dependable	resourceful
determined	reticent
easy-going	self-confident
efficient	self-conscious
excitable	self-reliant
extrovert	shy
forceful	sincere
friendly	subjective
gregarious	submissive
helpful	tactful
honest	tenacious
humorous	trustworthy

(b)   Now show the list (without your self-assessment!) to someone who knows you well and ask them to carry out the same exercise from *their perception* of your qualities.

(c)   Finally, ask someone who experiences your behaviour at college/work but is not a close friend to carry out the same exercise.

(d)   Check through the three lists to see where there is consistency in perception. Note these qualities down.

MAKING AN APPLICATION

One often becomes interested in a particular job through a job advertisement. This is likely to ask applicants either to send in a CV with a covering letter of application, or telephone or write for an application form.

Analysing the Requirements

The first task is to look very carefully at the advertisement and "read between the lines" to determine the kind of person the advertiser is looking for. If you are attracted by an advertisement, it is a good idea to draw up a profile of the kind of person you think they are looking for in terms of:

▶ physical characteristics

▶ qualifications, work experience

▶ intellectual ability

▶ skills

▶ personal qualities

▶ special conditions, eg needs clean driving licence.

In other words, try to put yourself in the place of the person recruiting and decide what characteristics you would be looking for. Try Activity 5 on page 80.

Asking for an Application Form

If you are asked to write or telephone for an application form, remember that the first impression of you is from your letter or telephone manner. Some companies may even make notes on these as part of their initial selection procedure, so you should make

ACTIVITY 5

Look at the advertisement shown below. It appeared in *The Post* on Thursday 22 June 19 . .

Sales Trainees

We are a leading manufacturer of sophisticated communication equipment with a reputation for quality.

So that we can create and exploit new markets we are looking for sales trainees with the right skills and qualities to be part of our professional sales team. You will be set challenging targets to achieve but achievement will bring high rewards in terms of salary and benefits package, including a company car.

We are looking for men and women with a good level of education — degree or HND level in any academic discipline — who are aged 21 and over. Previous sales-related experience would be useful but is not essential as full training will be given. Since some trainees will be allocated to European Sales, an aptitude for a language would be an advantage. Other sales territories available include: North-East, Scotland and Wales.

Be a high achiever — with us! Letters of application, together with a CV, should be addressed to John Davies, Personnel Manager, Craven Communications plc . . .

Draw up a profile under the headings we have given above of the kind of person you think they want. Then look at our suggested profile at the end of the chapter.

sure you are effective. They may send you a job description with your application form. If so, you have a considerable amount of information on which to base the production of your profile.

DESIGNING A *CURRICULUM VITAE*

As part of your preparation for the job market, you should have a *curriculum vitae* which you can up-date from time to time as your circumstances change.

Purpose

If the advertisement asks for a CV the advertisers want a summary of personal details and experience so that this information can be used to eliminate those who are not suited to the job.

Layout

Since it is a record of essential facts about the application, it should be presented in a manner which is:

(a) clear

(b) concise

(c) complete and

(d) easy to read.

Unless the organisation specifies otherwise, the CV should not exceed two or three sides of A4 paper. This is because, for many jobs, there may be numerous applicants and the personnel department will not have time to read several pages of detail.

The various sections of the CV should be clearly headed and adequate spacing should be provided between the sections.

Content

The sections which should be included in a CV are shown in the example on the next page.

Since personal details and work history remain the same regardless of the job for which one is applying, a covering letter of application is needed so that the points about oneself that are important for each specific job can be stressed.

LETTERS OF APPLICATION

A covering letter is used to relate the applicant's particular skills, qualities and experience to the job offered. It is necessary to spend some time composing this as it is the opportunity to market oneself. This is where self-analysis and job profiling will be useful.

Although each letter of application is individually composed, there are some standard elements which should be included. These letters should be handwritten unless your handwriting is very untidy.

Structure of a Letter of Application

Opening paragraph
This should include:

(a) a clear identification of the post for which you are applying, including any reference number

CURRICULUM VITAE

Name:	Neil James Nokes
Address:	16, Kendal Avenue
	Wokingham
	Berkshire
	RG2 2AR
Tel. no.:	Wokingham (0739) 667857
Date of birth:	12.5.53
Nationality:	British
Marital status:	Married

Number and ages of children: 1 child of 1 year

Education:	St Edward's Primary School, Kirtlington	1958–1964	
	Fosters Grammar School, Kirkborough	1964–1971	
	Portland Polytechnic	1971–1974	

Qualifications:

GCE O level (University of Oxford Board)

English Language	Grade C	June 1969
Mathematics	B	June 1969
Physics	C	June 1969
Chemistry	C	June 1969
Geography	B	June 1969
History	C	June 1969
Economics	B	June 1969

GCE A level (University of Oxford Board)

Mathematics	Grade C	June 1971
Geography	B	June 1971
Economics	A	June 1971
Degree: BSc in Business Studies		June 1974

Specialist areas: Computer Studies and Marketing

Work experience:

1974 – 1975:	Management trainee:	Condor Business Systems Western Road, Bracknell.
1976 – 1978:	Marketing Assistant:	Condor Business Systems Western Road, Bracknell.
1978 –	Marketing Executive:	Silfax Software plc Frimley Road, Farnborough, Hampshire.

Interests:	Sailing, music, squash, motor sport.
Referees:	A. J. H. Porter, Marketing Manager, Condor Business Systems.
	F. L. Baker, BSc., General Manager, Silfax Software plc.

(b) where the job advertisement was seen

(c) a statement that you wish to be considered for the post.

Middle paragraphs
These should include:

(a) a selection from your achievements, skills and qualities which show that you can fulfil the job requirements

(b) an explanation of why you want to work in the organisation.

Closing paragraph
This should include:

(a) a clear indication of when you are available for an interview

(b) any special details concerning the company's reply to your letter, eg if reply needs to go to different address than that on the letterhead.

Style of a Letter of Application

Above all the letter needs to be *stimulating, positive and optimistic*. It should persuade the organisation that they must interview you. Perhaps you can see this from the two examples we have given in Activity 6.

ACTIVITY 6

(a) Compare and contrast the following two examples of letters of application responding to the advertisement that appeared in Activity 5.

(b) Which applicant do you think will reach the interview stage and why?

Applicant 1

Dear Sir/Madam

I am writing to apply for the post which was advertised in "The Post" on Thursday. I enclose a curriculum vitae. I can attend for interview at your convenience.

As you can see from my CV, I have an HND in Computing which includes the following subjects:

Programming
Computer Architecture
Systems Analysis and Design

> Project Management
> Quantitative Methods
> Computer Communications.

I would like to work for your organisation because you have a good reputation for quality. I feel I have the qualities needed to do the job well.

Thanking your for considering my application.

Yours faithfully

Applicant 2

Dear Mr Davies

Post of sales trainee

I wish to apply for the post of sales trainee advertised in "The Post" on Thursday 3 June 19... I enclose a copy of my curriculum vitae.

During my HND Computing course, besides gaining a basic knowledge of modern communications equipment, I have acquired a range of written, oral and numerical skills. I was involved in giving formal and informal oral presentations, both within my course and as president of the Students' Union. In my year as president of the SU, I negotiated with the Principal for improvement of student facilities on many occasions.

My part-time job in tele-sales for a frozen food manufacturer has given me the opportunity to develop my knowledge of sales techniques and the confidence to apply these. I have also been an enthusiastic traveller and consequently pursued a course in Business German as an optional subject at college.

I met a representative of your organisation at a careers fair earlier this year and I was impressed by the progressive policies of Craven and their commitment to creating career opportunities for young graduates with the skill and motivation to succeed.

I hope you will give me the opportunity to prove my suitability as a trainee at an interview. Apart from the weeks of 10 – 24 June 19.. when I am taking my final examinations, I can attend for interview at any time.

Yours sincerely

Enc   Curriculum vitae

Then check at the end of the chapter to see if your decision agreed with ours.

We will now continue by looking at some guidelines for completing application forms.

APPLICATION FORMS

Some organisations will ask applicants to complete their own application form in preference to submitting a CV. One reason for this is that it enables the organisation to compare applicants more easily because all the information is presented in a standardised format.

An application form should not be treated as "yet another form". Many intelligent, skilled people have been rejected for jobs at initial screening stages because of the poor quality of their application forms. If you are really interested in a job be prepared to invest time and effort in providing full, accurate information in a stimulating manner. Here are the stages for completing application forms.

Stages in Completing Application Forms

(a) Answer all the questions on another piece of paper first so that there is a rough draft from which to work. (An alternative is to photocopy the form.)

(b) Check the rough draft for *inaccuracies* (eg incorrect date), *incomplete information* (eg gaps in one's education/work experience), *poor sentence construction* and *incorrect spelling*.

(c) Check that the tone is positive.

(d) Copy out the edited version on to the application form carefully and legibly.

(e) Check whether any enclosures are needed, eg photocopies of certificates for qualifications.

These are the basic stages, but applicants may experience difficulty completing some sections.

Sections of the Application Form which may Present Difficulties

Below we have identified some sections which may be difficult to complete, together with some suggestions on how to complete them.

(a) *A section which asks the applicant to record any achievements or successes in his or her life.*
You should answer this by including any significant successes at college, at work, in leisure pursuits, in sport. Applicants should go further than this and identify the skills/knowledge used to gain these successes.

85

(b) *A section asking about previous work experience.*
This may seem difficult to answer if the application is for the applicant's first full-time job. However, employers are interested in part-time work, temporary work or work undertaken on periods of work experience/sandwich placements. Sometimes this can amount to quite a lengthy period. You should provide:

    (i)   the name of the organisation
    (ii) the job title
    (iii) the dates of employment, indicating whether part-time/sandwich placement, etc
    (iv) a brief explanation of the main responsibilities/tasks.

(c) *An open section.*
This usually comes in the form of a large blank space with one of several preambles:

    (i)   "Write your letter of application in the space below."
    (ii) "State, in your own words, the reasons why you have applied for this post."
    (iii) "Explain how you think your background and experience will help you if you are offered the job."
    (iv) "What personal qualities and skills can you bring to the job being offered."

This section is really asking applicants to match their knowledge, skills and qualities to the job being offered — once again self-analysis and job profiling will be useful for completing this section.

Once applicants have passed the initial test of making a good application for the job and are asked to attend an interview it is necessary to consider the next stage — preparing for the job interview.

PREPARING FOR THE INTERVIEW

There are three stages to preparing methodically for an interview.

(a) Carrying out research concerning the job and the organisation.

(b) Preparing answers to any general questions which might be foreseeable.

(c) Planning personal self-presentation — one's appearance.

Let us consider each of these stages in more detail.

Researching the Job and the Organisation

Gathering as much information as possible helps applicants to predict and prepare for some of the questions they may be asked about the work they may be required to undertake. It also helps in formulating the kinds of question applicants might want to ask.

This research stage is therefore very valuable; if it is completed thoroughly, applicants should be able to respond appropriately, feel more confident and appear intelligent and interested. All of these impressions are important — they are those which the interviewers will be seeking and can give the "edge" over other candidates.

ACTIVITY 7

Try to list the methods and sources which you might use to research a prospective employer and job. Compile one list concerning the job and one about the organisation. When you have finished compare your lists with those given at the end of the chapter.

When you have gathered all the information you can, try to foresee the questions you may be asked concerning the technical and organisational aspects of the job for which you are applying and prepare some appropriate answers.

You might like to note any questions you would like to ask — there is no reason why you should not take these with you and refer to them; it demonstrates that you have taken a serious and thoughtful approach.

Preparing for General Questions

Apart from specific technical questions about the job, there are often general questions which are asked by interviewers for which applicants need to plan replies if they are to appear fluent and competent. Some of these present a problem if applicants are not prepared and often have the effect of flustering or causing them to "dry up".

ACTIVITY 8

Here are just a few classic "problem" questions. Try to write a brief answer to each one which you think would be acceptable and promote your image in the eyes of the interviewer(s).
(a) What do you consider are your strengths and weaknesses?
(b) What do you think you can contribute to this job?
(c) Where do you see yourself in five years' time?

None of these are easy questions and they are often sprung on the candidate; it is difficult to answer them without sounding either submissive or boastful. *So what should your approach be?*

(a)(b) In answering these questions, your previous preparation should be invaluable. You could even begin your answers by informing the interviewer(s) that you have tried to analyse your strengths and weaknesses methodically before you applied for the job. In your answer, you should *select the strengths which you think are appropriate to the job,* state what they are and give examples of when you have demonstrated these strengths. This type of honest approach should avoid giving the impression either that your choice is haphazard or that it is a conceited reply.

If asked about *weaknesses,* you should *choose those which will not prove too damaging to your ability to carry out the job* while being clear-sighted about your own drawbacks. Again, your previous analysis should help you to appear structured and perceptive.

(c) The last question is, in many ways, the most difficult. After all, few of us know what the next five years will bring in terms of job opportunities or personal circumstances. Perhaps the best way to answer this is to ask the interviewer(s) to clarify a little more about the prospects, career development and further training which is offered in their organisation. You will then be more able to assess where you might reasonably expect to be in five years' time. At least it will open up the discussion and give you time to formulate a more informed answer.

In addition to these "problem" questions, candidates often seem to answer what should be very easy ones badly! You are likely to be asked about:

(a) the content of any course(s) you have undertaken

(b) your past work experience

and you should have full answers ready. Nothing gives a worse impression that someone who apparently can remember nothing about the last two years of his or her life or, alternatively, rambles on irrelevantly about inappropriate aspects of it.

Once you have completed these preparations, you need to plan the last details — your appearance and personal presentation.

Planning your Self-Presentation at the Interview

It has been said that selection interviews are decided within five minutes of the candidate entering the room! While this may seem a little extreme, it is certainly true that we all respond to appearance, voice, manner, expression and body language more than we do to what is said. The picture which presents itself gives an immediate visual impact which directly governs our perception of and reactions to an individual. Refer back to Chapter 1 where this was discussed in detail.

Here are a number of suggestions which may help with systematic preparation.

Clothes The old rules about wearing a good suit or a smart dress still largely hold true. Dress codes are not as rigid as they were, of course, but in most "office" jobs the way one dresses will represent the company's image. Whatever one wears it should be neat, clean and tidy; as far as possible one should avoid wearing jewellery — there is a temptation to fiddle with it if nervous and it can be distracting in sunlight. Interviewees should wear clothes that will increase confidence so that they feel that they look their best but also make sure that what they wear is comfortable.

Hair Hair seems to be a major factor in conditioning our view of someone. It affects our perception of someone immediately, and often arouses bias. The most important principle is that hair should be clean and neat; the length is less important although one should try to conform to the likely expectations of the organisation. It is a pity to risk a rewarding career because of a passing obstinacy over a fashionable hairstyle. It is helpful to adopt a hairstyle which at least does not tempt one to play with the odd loose strand.

Although there is not much more that can be planned in advance, there are a number of important points to bear in mind when attending the interview. The main points are listed below.

CONDUCT DURING THE INTERVIEW

At the Beginning of the Interview

Interviewees should:

(a)   have an upright, confident yet relaxed posture

(b)   provide a handshake that is firm (but not crushing)

(c)   give a smile of greeting as well as saying "I'm pleased to meet you"

(d)   wait until a chair is indicated before sitting down

(e)   settle into a suitable seated posture — avoid defensive crossing of arms (a barrier gesture) or sitting on the edge of the chair (a nervous gesture); find a position which feels comfortable, but look confident and professional.

During the Interview

Interviewees should:

(a)   maintain eye contact with the interviewer who is asking the questions; the expression should be interested and alert but not a fixed stare.

(b)   be audible and articulate clearly when giving answers. If candidates have pre-pared well there should be no need for frequent use of "um . . . er".

(c)   use gestures which are open and help to emphasise words.

(d)   check their understanding of the questions if they are in doubt. This is far better than taking the wrong tack through misunderstanding. Candidates should try never to look as though they are "thrown" — even if they are!

(e)   say that they need a few moments to consider an answer if they are asked a tricky question.

(f)   ask the questions they think are needed to enable them to assess the suitability of the job; it is always better to raise a question related to a specific point when it arises — it could be overlooked if left until the end. Questions about training, opportunities for advancement and the future policy of the organisation should be asked; candidates should clarify aspects of conditions of work as well as querying salary.

At the End of the Interview

Interviewees should:

(a)   check that the interview is at an end

(b)   check that they have asked about everything they need to know

(c)   check what the next stage should be and within what timescale

(d)   shake hands firmly and leave with a smile and a polite closing phrase. One's exit is as important as one's entrance since first and last impressions remain longest.

CONCLUSION

We hope this chapter has proved a helpful one and has demonstrated that a systematic approach to job applications is not only sensible but advantageous. If you take such an approach there is no doubt that you will feel better prepared and thus appear more confident than if you have given the matter little prior thought. Self-presentation is vital in acquiring the right job for you — and will continue to be so if you are to be successful in gaining promotion in the future.

ANSWERS TO ACTIVITIES IN CHAPTER 6

Activity 5

Physical characteristics:	Must be physically fit since there is a large area to cover involving extended travelling.
Qualifications:	Degree or HND; possibly consider HNC.
Experience:	Some previous sales experience desirable but not essential.
Intellectual ability:	Good general intelligence; no special areas of aptitude.
Skills:	Ability to communicate orally — basis of selling/negotiating. Written communication skills — likely to be sales reports to compile.
	Ability to communicate in a foreign language important if interested in European sales. Self-organisation skills — after training will have to organise own work schedule to meet targets.
	Interpersonal skills — will have to be able to relate to customers and other people within organisation.
Personal qualities:	Adaptable — the environment for communications equipment changes rapidly.
	Ambitious — it is necessary to have a desire to succeed and get on.
	Assertive/self-confident — must be able to look and sound confident at all times.
	Determined/persistent — closing sales can often be difficult.
	Extrovert — the job demands getting on with a wide range of people.
	Resourceful/self-reliant — a salesperson can only draw on his or her own resources when dealing with a customer face-to-face despite the back-up of the organisation.
Special circumstances:	A clean driving licence. No family ties which prevent reasonable mobility.

Activity 6

The better letter is from Applicant 2. The first letter provides inadequate information, merely repeats information from the CV or the advertisement, is poorly sequenced and is written in poor English. The second letter makes a conscious effort at relating skills and past experience to the demands of the job. We have annotated the letter from Applicant 1 with some critical comments.

Applicant 1

Dear Sir/Madam (*does not use name, though given in the advert*)

I am writing (*redundant phrase*) to apply for the post (*which post? — they may be advertising several!*) which was advertised in "The Post" on Thursday. (*Which Thursday?*) I enclose a curriculum vitae. I can attend for an interview at your convenience (*sounds like a meeting in a toilet!*).

As you can see from my CV I have an HND in Computing which covers the following subjects: [extract from college prospectus] (*This is mere repetition from the CV — nothing new*) I would like to work for your organisation because you have a good reputation for quality. (*This is pure repetition from the advertisement.*) I feel I have the qualities needed to do the job well. (*But what are those qualities?*)

Thanking you for considering my application. (*Incomplete sentence.*)

Yours faithfully

Activity 7

Job	Organisation
Job advertisements.	Company literature — it is worth requesting this from the personnel department. This might include the annual company report, company newsletters, publicity material, recruitment literature.
Other advertisements concerning similar jobs.	
Job descriptions — it is worth asking if there is one available (if it is not sent with the application form).	The media — newspapers, journals, TV, radio where these have run special items on the organisation or a similar one.
People one knows who have held a similar job.	

Careers literature in the local/college library.

Trade/professional journals relating to the organisation's business to gain a general impression of the main issues concerning the industry.

Company directories, eg *Who Owns Who, Kompass.*

7 Working Effectively in Groups and Teams

THE IMPORTANCE OF TEAMWORK

Today, organisations often emphasise "the ability to work effectively in a team" in their job descriptions and advertisements. They do so because people are being required to work together — to co-operate and pool expertise in order to achieve objectives. This is true whether one works in a computer or engineering project team, as a member of a specialist work group in marketing, accountancy, etc or whether one is part of a team providing catering or leisure facilities.

Although we often use the words "group" and "team" interchangeably (eg project group, project team) we can sometimes ascribe a special meaning to the word "team" for a group whose *members are working harmoniously and effectively towards achieving objectives*.

This is one aspect of work about which people are nervous. Working as a member of a group means measuring up to the expectations and standards of one's peers as well as superiors. However, everyone has some experience and expertise in group working on which to draw.

ACTIVITY 1

Can you think of any groups/teams of which you have been or are a member?
Try listing these briefly before reading on.

You will probably have realised by doing this activity that people have always lived and worked in groups. Teamwork has been vital to our survival and still is. Man is a pack animal, psychologically adapted to working in this way, so we have many natural advantages which we can use in the workplace. Your list in answer to the activity is likely to be quite long, including such groups as family, friends, sports teams, social clubs, religious groups, class, work teams, etc. However, before we go any further in our discussion it would be useful to define the word "group".

WHAT IS A GROUP?

A useful working definition of a group is a *"number of individuals who share interests and common goals,* who *interact with one another* to achieve these goals, are aware of one another and *perceive themselves to be a group".*

Look back to the list compiled for Activity 1; this definition can probably be applied to all of them. In some cases group cohesion and interaction is so strong, they could be called a team. We now need to consider why organisations and individuals tend to develop their activities in groups.

THE PURPOSE OF WORKING IN GROUPS

The purposes for which groups are established are different for organisations and individuals.

Organisational Purposes

Obviously, formal organisations create groups to help them achieve their overall aims and objectives. Groups can do this in a number of ways by enabling:

(a) a range of different skills, knowledge and aptitudes to be brought together, eg committees, project teams

(b) people with similar expertise to be brought together to facilitate the allocation of work, eg specialist work groups

(c) information and ideas to be collected from more than one source in order to solve problems and make decisions, eg investigatory groups, research teams

(d) progress to be monitored or adherence to procedures to be checked, eg inspection teams, work study teams.

The individual, too, has a personal interest in participating in groups.

Individual Purposes

As individuals, most of us have a desire to become group members because they are a means to:

(a) gain help, support and advice in order to achieve our work or personal goals

(b) satisfy our social needs by providing security and friendship

(c) reduce risk and therefore stress in the decision-making process.

Both the organisation and the individual therefore have a stake in developing teams which perform effectively and give personal satisfaction and motivation. One of the most important functions in supervisory or management positions at work is to make decisions and in this function, both organisations and individuals can benefit from teamwork.

GROUP DECISION-MAKING

There is considerable evidence to suggest that group decisions are of better quality than individual ones.

ACTIVITY 2

Try listing two advantages and two disadvantages of making a decision within a group rather than as an individual. You can check your answer with ours at the end of the chapter.

Basically, groups should be able to produce better ideas through pooling their expertise as well as reaching more logical decisions through the process of discussion. It is extremely important, however, that there is agreement — a real consensus — once the decision has been reached. If not, there will be little commitment to the decision. Lack of consensus and commitment is likely to occur when one or two group members have "bulldozed" the others. This kind of pressure is strongest when the issues are not really clear cut and an individual feels that he or she lacks support. If this kind of dominance is exerted within a group, the individual may react in one of several ways.

(a) *Compliance*
    The individual will apparently "go along" with the others, although his or her support will lack conviction (eg "Oh, all right then" or "Anything for a quiet life"). The result of this is often that the decision is not carried out at all or is carried out badly. Once the decision has failed, it may well be followed up by "I told you it wouldn't work".

(b) *Internalisation*
    The individual conforms to the group and completely accepts their ideas. The individual is prepared to submerge, or give up, his or her individuality and ideas. However, it also means that the group member is not making a positive contribution.

(c) *Rejection*
    The individual will either withdraw his or her efforts and become a silent (often resentful) member or physically leave the group.

(d) *Adopting a negative role*
    The individual may adopt a specific role in order to preserve his or her identity.

Often this involves negative behaviour in terms of aggression, blocking ideas, playing the joker.

Clearly, if the group decision-making process is successful, it will provide satisfaction and support for the group; if not, it will reduce confidence and productivity.

The purposes of the organisation and individuals in establishing teams will evidently only be achieved if groups of people are prepared to perceive themselves as a team and to make that team effective. As teams are so central to work activity, a great deal of research has been carried out to identify the factors which characterise effective teams. It is necessary to be aware of these if one is to build a constructive and successful team at work or at college.

CHARACTERISTICS OF EFFECTIVE TEAMS

ACTIVITY 3

Think back to groups of which you have been a member and which you would judge to be effective. What do you think are the main factors which made those groups effective?

The term "effective" in this context means achieving the group's goals. We doubt whether you had much difficulty listing the factors; the difficulty comes in applying these. Care has to be taken from the outset to plan a team to encompass the most favourable set of variables. Let us look at these in more detail.

Size

Size contributes substantially to the effectiveness of a team. However, it is impossible to state a given size to cover all circumstances. For example, a football team is considered to need 11 players to be effective, all with a specialist skilled contribution to make to winning a game. However, a group of 11 would not be effective in a work situation for a scientific research team where a high level of participation and interaction is needed. A smaller group of four or five would be more appropriate.

The main points to remember in relation to size are that:

(a) small teams allow better communication, interaction and participation

(b) large groups enable a wider range of knowledge and skills to be used; more ideas or perspectives can be contributed.

Working Environment

It is clearly very difficult for a team to be effective in achieving its goals if members cannot meet sufficiently frequently because they are physically separated, working in different parts of a building or even on different sites. If you have attended a multi-site college, you may already have experience of this. Other barriers may be set up by different lunch or tea breaks. A shared working environment with places to meet, even if these are crowded and noisy, are necessary where people need to work as a team. It has even been suggested that shared discomfort can increase group productivity and co-operation.

ACTIVITY 4

Can you think of any working groups where unpleasant or difficult working conditions resulted in a close-knit, highly supportive team?

You have probably drawn on your own experiences to answer the above question. However, there are some common examples we can use, eg oil rig workers, those serving on submarines, firemen, nursing and medical teams — all occupations where arduous or unpleasant physical conditions produce highly supportive teams.

Group Maturity

Just as no individual can be expected to be an expert at a job on the first day, no group can be expected to become productive or perceive themselves to be a team immediately. There are several learning stages and a number of mutual adjustments to be made before a group can work well together. This development usually takes place over four stages which can be categorised as follows.

(a) *Forming*

A group first needs to clarify its purpose and objectives, sometimes even its title. It will also need to establish the roles of each member and the methods by which it can proceed with its tasks. At the first stage, an individual is put into the group or seeks membership and must establish the necessary links with other members.

(b) *Storming*

This is an emotive word and very representative of what happens at this stage. In order to establish objectives, roles and relationships a considerable amount of discussion, argument, testing out of roles takes place. Individuals will have their own personal objectives which they want to achieve through membership of the group (known as hidden agendas). Conflict is likely to be a feature of this stage but gradually, with mutual respect, the group can work towards agreement.

(c) *Norming*

At this stage the group is beginning to mature and to agree common objectives, procedures, practices and roles. Trust and confidence is being built up among members as tasks are tackled. It is at this stage that commitment is tested and this needs to be present if the group is to move to the final and most satisfying stage.

(d) *Performing*

This is when the team becomes fully productive and is able to achieve its objectives.

All groups need to grow in this way before they can achieve success and work together well. The process will be more rapid and less painful if the characteristics of all the group members are balanced and complementary.

Membership Characteristics

The members of an effective team need to have some characteristics in common. These include:

(a) sharing the same values, priorities and objectives

(b) caring about the task, the team and the individuals within it

(c) an ability to listen and be open-minded

(d) an ability to use disagreement to develop better ideas

(e) an ability to resolve conflict rather than avoid it

(f) an ability to give and receive frank, constructive criticism and retain mutual respect.

If the above characteristics are not present within a group, the results will be that important ideas are over-ridden or ignored with consequent resentment, withdrawal of effort and lack of commitment.

However, it is also important that group members should differ from one another in some respects. These include:

(a) members should have a range of skills and knowledge relevant to the tasks the team must perform

(b) members should be prepared to play different roles within the group. A simple way of categorising roles is into "thinkers, doers and carers", ie those who are concerned with thinking through the consequences of certain actions, those who are prepared to get on with the implementation of the action and those whose main concern is to hold the group together as a cohesive unit to get the task done.

Development of Positive Individual Roles

The last sub-section mentioned some broad categories of constructive roles which can be performed within teams. Every individual will adopt a role, positive or negative, which reflects his or her personality as well as his or her attitude towards the group, the task and towards other group members.

We have identified some specialist group roles which readers might recognise from their own experiences.

(a) *Initiator*
This person suggests ideas and is not afraid if some of them are not accepted. The rest of the group may react negatively or positively to his or her suggestions but in either case this individual will act as a catalyst.

(b) *Information/opinion seeker*
This person asks for facts and ideas from others. This is useful in following up the ideas of the initiator and is also helpful in involving the quieter members of the group who may have valuable information to give. He or she helps the others to listen and to build on the initiating idea.

(c) *Information/opinion giver*
This can be a constructive role if the person provides facts and well-evidenced opinion. He or she can be particularly valuable if offering relevant experience and knowledge to the group. The outcomes will directly help the group towards an informed decision. Long term, the individual will help to develop the knowledge of the group about the work concerned.

(d) *Observer/commentator*
This person will listen and interject comments and suggestions to help the group move forward towards achieving its objectives. The role assists the discussion and keeps the communication flowing.

(e) *Evaluator/monitor*
This person will summarise and evaluate the group's progress and set standards. Sometimes this is the role taken by the leader of the group and it is valuable if this is the case. Every group needs an individual who can stop the discussion becoming stagnant, repetitive or trivial.

(f) *Communicator*
This person will monitor and assist the communication processes. Normally, the individual will help to limit over-talkative members and involve those who are less certain or find it difficult to be outgoing. He or she is valuable in

directing and co-ordinating discussion and ensuring that the group is not dominated by one or two extroverts at the cost of the ideas of the others.

(g) *Encourager/harmoniser*
This individual praises and supports contributions from others, is friendly and outgoing and will try to reconcile disagreements and reduce tension.

These types of role behaviour are all helpful to a team in achieving its objectives. Any team member may undertake one or more of these roles at different times. Collectively these roles help the tasks to be undertaken while the group works as a co-operative and happy unit. Unfortunately there is another set of roles which may have the opposite effect.

It is necessary to recognise these negative roles and develop coping strategies within a group if these are to be prevented from upsetting the work of the group.

The negative group roles are:

(a) *Attacker*
This person expresses constant disapproval of other members' ideas. He or she may attack one or two individuals or the whole group, criticising not only the ideas but also the objectives of the group. Sometimes personal criticism is made. This individual is likely to cause resentment, low morale and provoke anger and/or withdrawal. It is a dangerous role which threatens the effectiveness of the group.

(b) *Blocker or rejector*
This person resists the progress of the group by returning to issues already rejected by the rest of the group and by, in turn, rejecting new ideas. The individual has a tendency to make remarks such as "That won't work" or "It's been tried before". This role discourages, demotivates and irritates the rest of the group and delays progress.

(c) *Detractor*
This person refuses to be involved, ridicules the ideas of others and makes flippant remarks. Such an individual can make the group lose its self-confidence and respect and is very unhelpful.

(d) *Help-seeker*
This person constantly seeks enlightenment, help and support from others; he or she expresses confusion and bewilderment and communicates these emotions to the rest of the group. This is a gentler role than the other negative ones but it still causes delay and succeeds in clouding issues.

101

ACTIVITY 5

Can you think of any methods by which a group could cope with the four negative roles? Your strategies should be socially acceptable, not violent or abusive, since you will have to work with these people again. Jot down any strategies that have worked successfully in the past or any ideas that come to mind now. Also discuss your ideas, if possible, with other people who have attempted the same activity. You can also check against our suggestions at the end of the chapter.

Discussion on how to deal with difficult members of a team is never wasted. If your own attempts have failed in the past, you should now have a number of new strategies to try. Group pressure from the majority in a group, if used tactfully and skilfully can often be very successful in encouraging individuals into more positive roles.

There is one role which has not appeared under either the positive or negative categories. This is the one called the "clown" or "playboy". You are probably all familiar with this role; it is adopted by the individual who makes jokes and is generally lighthearted in his or her approach to the work of the group but is not as negative as the detractor.

ACTIVITY 6

In what group situations have you seen the playboy role make a positive contribution to the group? Are there instances that you have witnessed where the playboy role was negative in its impact?

Obviously people's experiences are likely to differ. Generally the humour of the playboy can lighten the atmosphere when a group is becoming too heated in its discussion. A joke can often put the issue into perspective again. Sometimes the person who is being over-lighthearted in his or her approach can develop cohesiveness amongst the other members — they are brought together in their desire to make him or her take the matter seriously. However, if people permanently play the playboy role, they can become stereotyped in that part so that any good ideas they contribute are not taken seriously.

Whatever roles occur within a group, it is clearly essential that communication must continue between the members if problems are to be solved. Some of the channels which can be established for group communication are discussed in the next subsection.

ACTIVITY 7

Now we have identified the kind of roles performed in groups it is useful to observe people's role behaviour in the next group decision-making/problem-solving activity in which you are involved. We suggest you use the observer sheet shown on page 104 to note the kinds of behaviour that members of your group exhibit. Each time a member demonstrates a particular kind of behaviour record a tick in the appropriate column.

Once you have completed your observer sheet, it can become a basis for discussion about group roles. You will be able to pinpoint:

(a) some people's concentration on particular roles
(b) other people's ability to exhibit behaviour across a number of roles
(c) positive group roles which may not be performed by anybody within the group
(d) negative behaviour which may have inhibited the decision-making or affected the harmony of the group.

Communication Patterns

If teams are to be effective, communication channels must be appropriate to the task. Particular patterns suit different activities.

The wheel

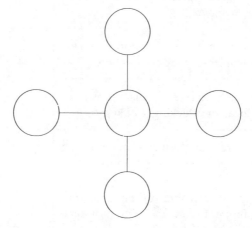

Here the members communicate through the leader. It is suitable where problems are relatively simple and speedy results are required. However, the person at the centre of the wheel needs good communication skills. It is particularly appropriate where one member of the group is allocating relatively simple, repetitive tasks to others. A head waiter or waitress might use this for his or her team of restaurant staff or a sales manager with sales representatives.

ROLE ANALYSIS SHEET — OBSERVING INDIVIDUALS

ROLE BEHAVIOUR	MEMBERS			
	1	2	3	4
Initiating — suggesting ideas				
Information/opinion seeking — asking for information or opinions from others				
Information/opinion giving – volunteering information and opinions				
Evaluating — supplying standards of accomplishment, measuring group progress				
Encouraging — praising and supporting contribution of others, being friendly				
Harmonising — attempting to reconcile disagreements, reducing tension				
Communicating — keeping channels of communication open, eg limiting over-talkative members				
Observing/commenting — offering suggestions to help the group to function				
Attacking — expressing disapproval of others' ideas or attacking whole group				
Blocking — resisting progress by returning to issues rejected by rest of group				
Detracting — refusing to be involved, making flippant remarks, being mundane				
Rejecting — refusal to agree with anything				
Help seeking — constantly seeking help or support, confusion and bewilderment, generally delaying the group				

The star

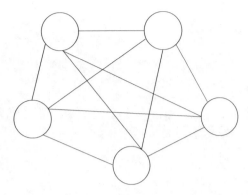

Here all the members can interact more directly, so it is particularly appropriate for experts working closely together on complex problems where discussion and agreement is important. This is therefore the type of network you would expect in an advertising team for brainstorming a new product name, slogan or for policy-making bodies at the top of an organisation.

However, as deadlines approach or emergencies arise it sometimes re-forms into a wheel to enable faster decision-making to take place. You have probably witnessed this changeover if you have undertaken group assignments at college or participated in teams at work. At the beginning of the task, the star pattern works effectively because it enables everyone to contribute. As the deadline grows closer, one member is likely to emerge or be appointed as co-ordinator to structure the tasks so that everything is ready on time.

In co-ordinating the various roles within the team, the central figure, that of the manager or team leader, will be the ultimate factor in determining success. Leadership is a subject of its own which will be explored at greater length in the next chapter. However, we cannot omit it completely from a consideration of the factors which make an effective team, so a brief summary of the functions a team leader is expected to perform are shown below.

ACTIVITY 8

Here is one further pattern often found within organisations. It comes with certain variations.

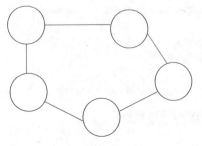

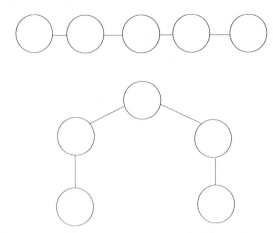

Three versions of the chain

Each individual only interacts with one or at the most two others, often for organisational reasons such as a strong hierarchy or divisions between locations or departments.

Can you list the probable outcomes of this pattern?

Our answer appears at the end of the chapter.

Team Leadership

One's experience of appointed leaders may have been good or bad. Consider the characteristics of leaders who have "emerged" naturally to lead a group:

A good team leader:

(a) is accepted and respected by the group; his or her status/expertise is perceived by them as being high

(b) demonstrates a balance between concern for the task, the group as a whole and for individual members

(c) sets a good example, showing personal commitment to the objectives and avoiding favouritism or victimisation

(d) allocates work fairly and logically according to the abilities and motivation of each indvidual

(e) clarifies what results and standards are expected

(f) is flexible and open-minded

(g) gives adequate feedback on progress

(h) gives encouragement and recognition

and lastly, he or she helps the team to evaluate their performance.

We have discussed the factors which contribute to effective teams at some length. However, success in working in teams comes from the individual and collective efforts of group members. We have therefore finished this chapter with some reminders of actions which should be taken to build effective teams.

PERSONAL CONTRIBUTION TO EFFECTIVE TEAMS

The checklist we have given below should cover the most important points.

(a) When involved in the formation of a group for the first time, try to negotiate with the body that is creating it (tutor, manager, etc) so that its size, location and the characteristics of its members are all suited to the objectives it must achieve.

(b) Whether you have actively chosen the other people working in the group or whether you have been "put" into it, the first priority is to *agree objectives*. Harmony as a team cannot be developed and the tasks set cannot be achieved unless objectives are agreed.

(c) Whatever you may privately think about other members of a group to which you may have been allocated, you should adopt a positive attitude to that group, ie an active, positive contribution, a commitment to meet deadlines set and a willingness to resolve group problems.

(d) Recognise that the early stages will be "stormy" because people will want to establish particular roles and may have different ideas about how the objectives should be achieved. This is a natural stage of development and should be treated as such. Your own participation at this stage can help the group if you can:

   (i)   use *assertive behaviour* rather than being submissive or aggressive (for more details see Chapter 15)
   (ii) *listen attentively* and carefully evaluate the ideas of others as well as putting forward your own views
   (iii) *accept criticism* from others without an emotional reaction.

   This type of behaviour will enable the group to move on to the norming stage of development more quickly.

(e) Evaluate the group processes that are happening and have sufficient flexibility to adopt behaviour associated with positive roles that are needed for the group to perform effectively.

(f)   Recognise that communication channels within a group may need to differ according to the nature of the task, the expertise and the attitudes of members of the group and the timescales for task accomplishment.

(g)   Deal with problems that are inhibiting harmony within the team — do not avoid them. Frank, open discussion about differences in perception, the adoption of negative roles by group members, lack of commitment to the group or task deadlines is better than building up resentment or lapsing into apathy. Conflict resolution is difficult but necessary.

(h)   Do not assume that negative behaviour within a group is totally the fault of the individual exhibiting it. Groups often alienate individual group members unwittingly and are then surprised when the individual exhibits negative behaviour, eg a withdrawn member may have been attacked by the group earlier; a blocking member may have had his or her ideas rejected without due consideration by the group. Sometimes the behaviour dates back to experiences in previous groups. Try to establish the cause for the behaviour and deal with that rather than reacting to its manifestations.

CONCLUSION

This chapter has concentrated on identifying the elements which make a good team; recognising these help you to build one. Team-building is now a major concern for most organisations and they will look critically at the ability of any entrant to participate well in group work, in whatever environment that work may be taking place.

Effectiveness should never be measured merely in terms of completing a task or reaching a decision. A team must also review its own strengths and weaknesses and be aware of the processes by which it operates. Some organisations have entered into large-scale *organisation development programmes* to accomplish this throughout all their work groups.

ANSWERS TO ACTIVITIES IN CHAPTER 7

Activity 2

Advantages of group decisions	Problems of group decisions
Enables people to pool their expertise.	Can be slow, so that in emergencies it is unacceptable.
Provides mutual support for the decisions taken.	Group pressure can be exerted from one or two dominant members and people may not support decisions if this occurs.
Allows full discussion so it is more likely to gain commitment to a decision taken.	

Activity 3

An effective team has:

(a) clear objectives which have been agreed

(b) members who are committed to these and contribute fully to achieving them

(c) a good "mix" of people who can contribute relevant ideas and/or skills

(d) a supportive atmosphere where people can give and take criticism which is constructive and say what they really think

(e) a leader who can keep their attention on the task, direct well but keep a harmonious working atmosphere

(f) a commitment to hard work but the ability to enjoy this

(g) an ability to listen to each member and to communicate

(h) respect for each member

(i) a high success rate

(j) members committed to the task and the group as a whole.

Activity 5

You can try the following strategies:

The attacker: If the attacker criticises an individual he or she must be given an opportunity to reply. Driving resentment underground only results in withdrawal. If it looks as though the two people are heading for a major confrontation, the rest of the group should be invited to comment to take the heat out of the issue. If the group is attacked, then again time should be given for a reply and *each* individual should be asked to comment.

The blocker: You might ask this person to rationalise. For example, if the statement is made "It won't work" then ask "Why?" and explore the possibilities. He or she needs to be moved towards making *constructive* suggestions.

The detractor: This person needs to be given a really demanding task quickly. It stops him or her viewing the group and tasks as unimportant and occupies him or her sufficiently to prevent flippancy. The detractor will become concerned with proving himself or herself.

The help seeker: This person is an attention getter. Explain once and suggest that he or she writes this down. Then suggest that he or she refers to the written explanation when in doubt. Do not let such a person carry on appealing to the group — this will only result in a confused and frustrated group.

Activity 8

Outcomes of chain pattern of communication within a group

(a) Since access by one member to others is limited to one or two, it may create feelings of lack of involvement or frustration.

(b) Those at the ends of the chain may feel particularly "left out".

(c) It may result in some distortion or vetting of information as it passes along the chain.

(d) It may be a relatively slow method if decisions or problems are complex because messages will have to pass frequently up and down the chain to clarify points.

8 Leadership and Motivation

In the previous chapter, we noted how often today the emphasis is placed on ability to work in a team when companies are recruiting staff. For those wishing to seek a career at a supervisory or management level, they include something else — the necessity for leadership qualities. It is very difficult for candidates with limited experience to assess whether they have these or not. Their testing grounds have been very limited; they might have chaired a club, run a charity event, led a voluntary group of workers or captained a sports team. All this is valuable experience, but how far does it really help us to assess whether we have these elusive "qualities" or not? Did we really analyse what had occurred during our period of authority and why?

"In any case", you may ask, "if I enter a company as a management trainee, won't it be a very long time before I am actually asked to lead people?"

LEADERSHIP AND MANAGEMENT

The answers to these questions may help to clarify the position.

(a) Past experience in any kind of leadership position is helpful, because it gives at least one experience which can be analysed and used as a building brick to consider what leadership is about.

(b) Quite often, management trainees *are* put in a position of responsibility over other people quite early. It will depend on the nature of the organisation, of course. However, in people-oriented environments like leisure, catering, retailing, conservation management and the service industries, it is likely to come sooner than in other areas.

(c) In all cases, however, the organisations which are seeking management staff are looking for potential — whether people show the behaviour and characteristics which might be developed later for the full managerial role. It must be admitted that some companies are still rather hazy as to what exactly they are trying to identify in terms of leadership qualities.

This is not surprising. The concept of leadership and the nature of power have always fascinated people, but have remained rather intangible and difficult to analyse.

111

Nevertheless, different types of power and contrasting styles of leadership have been the subject of a great deal of investigation.

There is a very practical reason for this; whether they understand the exact nature of what they seek or not, societies, armies, industrial, commercial and leisure companies have long recognised that effective leadership and the skilful use of power are essential to success. It is for this reason that the qualities associated with them are mentioned in their recruitment literature.

This chapter, therefore, offers a brief guide to the ideas which have developed concerning different kinds of power and the characteristics of effective leadership. We all encounter the exercise of power at an early age, so let us begin with the familiar.

ACTIVITY 1

So far, who has been able to exercise power over you? Can you identify the differences in the kinds of power you have experienced?

You might like to list your thoughts on these questions before reading on.

TYPES OF POWER

There are several different kinds of power which are exercised within society and organisations. They can be categorised briefly as follows:

Customary Power

This is the *power derived from custom and practice* — in other words, from tradition. Aristocrats and priests exercise this kind of power, regardless of their actual wealth or income. At a different level, parents exercise customary power over their children.

Any of these examples may have appeared on the list in Answer to Activity 1.

Position Power

This is *derived from the post to which a person is appointed or elected.* Company directors, generals, Members of Parliament and policemen/women hold this kind of power; so do managers and supervisors.

Expert Power

This means the power which is *derived from knowledge, experience and skill.* Research scientists, artists, plumbers and solicitors have it, as does anybody whose expertise is valued by others and is thus in demand.

Resource Power

This power is *gained from control over resources within society or within an organisation* and can be considerable. Think of the Bank of England, the treasurer's department of a local authority or the chief accountant within a company. At other levels, the stock controller or even the person who holds the key to the stationery cupboard exercises a considerable amount of influence over others! Power derived from personal wealth could also be included in this category.

Personality Power

This is really the most mysterious quality, though few of us would deny its existence. People can quite clearly *influence others through the force of their personal characteristics or their magnetism*. This quality is sometimes called "charisma" and it may be the first word which springs to mind when we consider the idea of leadership.

There are problems associated with this kind of power however.

(a) Any manager or leader who has it is not easily replaced. For example, one cannot easily teach it to his or her successor and the departure of a charismatic individual can have a traumatic effect on the people left behind.

(b) It is possible for charisma to be used for undesirable ends — to dominate others and to compel them to take actions which are uncharacteristic of them and which they would not normally undertake. Leaders of gangs may fall into this category.

(c) Unlike the others, it is uncontrollable power possessed only by the individual, not by the organisation which employs the person concerned. So while it is often sought and admired, it can bring attendant drawbacks.

It is important to realise that, in many instances, there is more than one type of power present. Each will serve to reinforce the others. Those people who are able to combine various forms of power will be able to exert considerable influence over others.

While we have concentrated on thinking of power belonging to individuals, consider that that power is also exercised by groups.

ACTIVITY 2

Below is a list of four influential occupations. How many kinds of power are exercised by each?

(a) Doctors
(b) Teachers
(c) Actors
(d) Pop stars

Our suggested answers appear at the end of the chapter.

Different kinds of power also characterise our accepted leaders. In our society, a good example is the position of the Prime Minister, who exercises power of position, resources and customary power; some Prime Ministers also possess power of expertise and charisma — perhaps Sir Winston Churchill is the best illustration of this. Within our organisations, too, managers at all levels usually have at least two methods of influencing others — the power of position and the power of expertise. However, there is more to the concept of leadership than the possession of power and these other aspects need some detailed consideration.

CONCEPT OF LEADERSHIP

There are many ideas concerning what constitutes leadership, partly because people's experience of it differs. Most believe it has something to do with charisma, but on a working basis, the power of personality is not the only factor to take into consideration. Perhaps it would be useful to provide a working definition.

Leadership is the ability to inspire people towards a common goal.

While this is a simple definition, it is not at all simple to find those who can achieve it, or to train people to do so. It is this aspect which has proved so problematic for organisations, since they all require their managers or officers to possess leadership qualities. This has led to many years of research, the outcomes of which are summarised below.

THE SEARCH FOR A LEADER

Trait Theory: A leader can be selected for the "right" characteristics

The belief which underlies this theory is that "a leader is born and not made". If this is so, there must be common characteristics (or traits) which are evident in all leaders. Therefore, if we could identify what these traits are, it would be easy to write them into a personnel specification for a manager or officer and simply select the person who is the nearest match to them.

ACTIVITY 3

Below are the names of several prominent historical leaders. You might like to add others. What personality traits did they have in common?

Hitler, Napoleon, Churchill, Ghandi

Write these down before moving on.

When this exercise has been done in the past, it has shown that there were too few relevant shared traits to be useful for selection purposes in companies. The common characteristics are:

(a) most leaders are more intelligent than the groups they lead — although this does not mean they are intellectuals but that they have relevant specific knowledge

(b) most leaders have immense self confidence

(c) most leaders have a conviction in the rightness of their beliefs and decisions

(d) most leaders have the ability to "overview" a situation, ie to grasp all the variables pertinent to their situation; this is sometimes called the "helicopter" approach.

The inability to find many common traits amongst leaders has led theorists to undertake studies into the style which leaders adopt to see if a specific leadership style is effective.

Style Theory: A leader can be trained to adopt the "right" approach

Through research carried out into management attitudes, it was found that a number of different styles existed. Three very distinct styles were initially identified as:

(a) *autocratic leadership* — in which the manager takes all the decisions and informs his or her subordinates what they are

(b) *democratic leadership* — in which the manager identifies the problem to be solved and invites suggestions from the working group before making a decision

(c) *laissez-faire leadership* (in English "leave them alone!") — in which the manager permits the subordinates to make their own decisions.

Initially, it was thought that the "best" style was democratic leadership and much time was spent trying to train managers to adopt this style.

ACTIVITY 4

(a) Can you think of any situations you have already experienced or that you might experience in your intended career in which a democratic style would not be effective? Why?

(b) Can you think of any groups of people with whom you have worked for whom a democratic style would not be suitable? Why?

We have made some general suggestions at the end of the chapter.

As you may have seen from this activity, you can experience problems if you try to adopt one style in all situations and with all groups.

Further research also identified that the three general styles mentioned above were too limited to explain the variations that actually existed.

It was recognised that variations in the situation and the group affect style; so do the attitudes of the managers themselves, and the type of organisation in which they operate. Structure, size, nature of work and ethics all contribute to the organisational factors which must be taken into account.

The most recent approach has therefore been to examine a greater range of styles and the possibility of using these flexibly according to circumstances. This is sometimes called "the contingency approach".

Contingency Theory: A leader must adapt his or her style according to circumstances

The choice of styles open to a manager is more varied than was originally supposed. A diagram showing more distinctions between styles appears below.

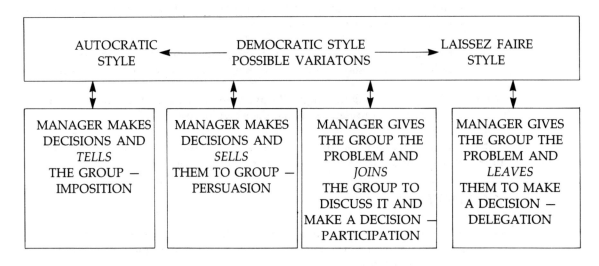

AUTOCRATIC STYLE	DEMOCRATIC STYLE POSSIBLE VARIATONS		LAISSEZ FAIRE STYLE
MANAGER MAKES DECISIONS AND *TELLS* THE GROUP — IMPOSITION	MANAGER MAKES DECISIONS AND *SELLS* THEM TO GROUP — PERSUASION	MANAGER GIVES THE GROUP THE PROBLEM AND *JOINS* THE GROUP TO DISCUSS IT AND MAKE A DECISION — PARTICIPATION	MANAGER GIVES THE GROUP THE PROBLEM AND *LEAVES* THEM TO MAKE A DECISION — DELEGATION

A range of leadership styles

When a manager decides which of the above to adopt at any given time, several interacting variables need to be taken into account. These are:

(a)   the nature of the task

(b)   the composition of the group

(c)   the individual skills and attitudes within the group

(d)   the constraints and opportunities offered by the organisation

(e)   the manager's own personality and attitudes.

All these will need to be balanced carefully; the manager or leader should be able to meet any contingency (set of circumstances) by being flexible. The essential question to answer is "What style of leadership will get this group to perform at their best for this task?"

A table showing each style — its characteristics, advantages and disadvantages is provided below.

Chart showing advantages and disadvantages of different styles of leadership

Characteristics	Advantages	Disadvantages
TELLING STYLE		
Manager controls decisions and information.	Members of group are protected from making the wrong decision.	Manager is not benefiting from ideas of others.
Manager is clear about what is needed and how to achieve it.	Manager is protected from mistakes made by the team.	Those who wish to make a contribution may feel frustrated.
Meetings are used for briefings and instruction.	Decision-making is not subject to delay.	Decisions are only as good as the manager.
		The group members are receiving no development; this will affect the competence of the organisation as a whole long term.
SELLING STYLE		
Manager feels the need to sell decisions.	Group is more likely to give support to decision.	Group may see the manager as manipulative.

117

Manager believes it is important to get decisions accepted.	Group likely to feel manager cares how they feel.	Individuals may feel one is being played off against another.
Knowledge of individuals and work group used to manoeuvre so that potential support/ opposition is known.		
Manager still retains full control of the decision.		

JOINING/PARTICIPATING STYLE

Manager takes the role of a discussion leader.	More information or ideas available to the manager.	Potential problem of control for the manager.
Manager takes final decision after hearing views of group.	Involvement of the group likely to produce high level of commitment.	Group may not want to be involved or may lack skills or knowledge.
Group know they can influence decision.	Free and frank atmosphere created.	Decision-making may be delayed.
Meetings used to invite information and comment.	Group likely to feel valued by the manager.	

LAISSEZ-FAIRE STYLE

Manager leaves subordinates to make decision.	Group is highly motivated and involved, feeling valued for its expertise.	Manager has very little control, which can be a problem if deadlines are not met.
Can operate with highly expert groups, eg doctor's practice, social workers, university staff, scientists.	Decisions are likely to be made with everyone making a contribution.	
Meetings would be used for discussion on progress and feedback.		

Ultimately, it is up to the manager to choose the method of leadership which will provide the best balance between sufficient control and the meaningful involvement of the working team. This balancing act has often been illustrated by the diagram which appears below.

Keeping the balance
(adapted from John Adair)

If we break down the actions which the leader needs to take in order to be effective we have a checklist as follows:

(a) *Achieving the task*
   (i)   Define the task clearly for everyone.
   (ii) Set up and agree objectives.
   (iii) Make a plan (in consultation with the group when appropriate).
   (iv) Allocate work and resources rationally.
   (v)   Control the quality, speed and quantity of work.
   (vi) Check progress and performance against objectives and plans.
   (vii) Adjust and modify as necessary.

(b) *Maintaining the team*

   (i)   Set achievable but challenging standards and targets.
   (ii) Maintain fair discipline and set a good example.
   (iii) Ensure effective communication within the team, using appropriate channels (see Chapter 7).
   (iv) Consciously foster team spirit.
   (v)   Train and develop the team in relation to the tasks.
   (vi) Encourage and give a sense of purpose.
   (vii) If the tasks are large and disparate, appoint acceptable sub-leaders.

(c) *Developing the individuals*

   (i)   Praise individuals for work well done.
   (ii) Recognise and use individual abilities.

      (iii)   Train the individual when needed.

      (iv)   Give status and reward where possible.

      (v)   Attend to any personal problems.

All these factors need to be combined to motivate the team towards better performance. Motivation is the prime concern of any manager or leader, so we now need to examine the perennial question of what motivates employees and why.

MOTIVATION

Motivating people is essential to the management process, which has been defined as "taking decisions which have to be implemented through other people".

The aim is to obtain optimum performance from them — realising and using their potential to attain the desired goal. So we need to ask what motivates people to work? Is it different for individuals and groups?

ACTIVITY 5

Below is a list of 12 factors which are known to affect the response of people at work. Try ranking them in the order which you think would be most important to you. If you can do so, ask one or two of your friends or work colleagues to carry out the same activity.

MOTIVATION FACTORS

Factor description	Own ranking	Rankings *Others*		
		1	2	3
1. *Recognition*: Receiving recognition from peers, superiors, and/or subordinates for one's good work performances.				
2. *Sense of achievement*: The feelings associated with successful completion of a job, finding solutions to different problems, or seeing the results of one's work.				
3. *Advancement*: The opportunity for advancement or promotion based on one's own ability.				

4. *Status*: Being according various position-based privileges such as a well-appointed office, selected parking place, or other prestige elements.

5. *Pay*: A wage that not only covers normal living expenses but provides additional funds for certain luxury items.

6. *Supervision*: Working for a superior who is both competent in doing his or her job and looks out for the welfare of subordinates.

7. *Job itself*: Having a job that is interesting, challenging, and provides for substantial variety and autonomy.

8. *Job security*: Feeling confident about one's security within the company.

9. *Co-workers*: Working with co-workers who are friendly and helpful.

10. *Personal development*: Given the opportunity in one's job to develop and refine new skills and abilities.

11. *Fringe benefits*: A substantial fringe benefit package.

12. *Working conditions*: Safe and attractive conditions for doing one's work.

Then compare your rankings and discuss why there are differences.

This is an interesting experiment to carry out *before* you read on and see what has emerged from the research carried out on motivation in the work place.

There are no answers given in the text this time, since the factors which motivate people differ according to the individual.

Before we go any further, there is one more question we need to ask — "What is motivation?".

Motivation — A Definition

It is easy to confuse motivation with the word "movement". We can get a donkey to move by using a carrot or a stick; with people we can use incentives or threats and reprimands. However, these only have a limited effect; they work for a while and then need to be repeated, increased or reinforced to secure further movement. A working definition of motivation is

enabling people to perform tasks willingly and to the best of their ability.

Motivational factors are those which, as one motivation expert put it, make us give "more than a fair day's work — and that is usually only about 65 per cent of a person's capacity". Clearly every manager should be concerned with releasing 100 per cent of an individual's effort to maximise performance for the good of the organisation *and* to enable the individual to develop his or her potential and gain satisfaction.

Motivation Factors

We will now examine some of the research which has revealed the factors which induce us to release that effort.

(a) *Maslow's hierarchy of needs*
Abraham Maslow found that all employees had a series of needs which should ideally be satisfied at work. He also found that usually, as one need was fulfilled, the next level of need tended to become the prime motivator, hence the idea of a hierarchy or series of five steps. These were:

Maslow's identification of needs

Need:	*Mainly satisfied at work by:*
Physiological needs (food, warmth, shelter)	Salary/wages
Safety/security needs (safe conditions, job security)	Good working conditions and benefits
Social needs (belonging, appreciation)	Harmonious teams
Esteem needs (need for status/power)	Promotion and respect for position/expertise
Self-actualisation needs (need for self-fulfilment)	Challenging work which realises an individual's potential

Sadly, the research showed that all too often, the first two levels of need were the only ones satisfied within the work place. The others were often sought outside, with consequent detrimental effects on performance. The ideas of Maslow are now widely familiar in management circles and enlightened companies do make efforts to provide for the top three levels, with varying degrees of success.

Perhaps even more influential, however, has been the two factor theory put forward by Herzberg. We will now look at this briefly.

(b) *Herzberg's motivation and hygiene factors*
Frederick Herzberg carried out widespread surveys to find out what gave people satisfaction at work. Two sets of factors emerged which affected behaviour differently.

The first set *prevented* dissatisfaction, ie they prevented high labour turnover, absenteeism and industrial disputes. He called these "hygiene factors" because they prevented an organisation's ill-health. The second set were those which *actively motivated* people to give a committed performance. He called these "motivators".

He stressed that both sets of factors are important. If hygiene factors were missing, people felt they were being treated unfairly and this led to a revenge psychology. He also promoted the idea of job enrichment and developed his most well-known statement that "Every job should be a growth experience". His factors are listed in the table below.

Herzberg's hygiene factors and motivators

Hygiene factors	Motivators
Company policy	Achievement
Administration	Recognition
Supervision	Nature of work itself
Salary	Responsibility
Relationships with others	Advancement
Working conditions	

The two factor theory has resulted in much more attention being paid to building-in job satisfaction and creative elements to work tasks.

ACTIVITY 6

Your first experience of trying to motivate others will probably be as the leader of a small working team. Try to identify which of the above factors would be under your control. In each case, suggest in what ways you could improve these factors for the people within your group. We suggest you make out lists using the following headings.

Factors I could control   *What I could do to improve motivation*

We have made some general suggestions at the end of the chapter.

There was one factor omitted from both these studies which we included as one of our variables which must be considered in successful leadership. This is the attitude of the leader or manager towards the working group. Some interesting results emerged when a research programme was undertaken to explore what the effects were of different management attitudes on the output and morale of working groups.

(c) *McGregor's Theory X and Theory Y*
    As we have seen, the style of leadership adopted by a manager will have a major impact on the working group. Douglas McGregor found that style was an outcome of how the leader perceived his or her team. Two quite different perceptions with sharply differentiated attitudes emerged. He labelled these different attitudes Theory X and Theory Y. They are explained briefly below.

Managers held the following different sets of beliefs about their subordinates:

Theory X	*Theory Y*
People dislike work and will avoid it if they can.	Work is necessary to people's psychological growth.
People must be forced or driven to put in the right effort.	People can be interested in their work and enjoy it.
People would rather be directed than accept responsibility.	People will direct themselves towards an *accepted* target.
Money motivates.	People will seek and accept responsibility *under the right conditions*.
Anxiety about security motivates.	Self-imposed discipline is more effective than external control.

People have very little creativity.

People are motivated by the desire to realise their own potential.

Creativity and ingenuity are widely distributed and grossly under-used.

ACTIVITY 7

Before you read on:

(a)   Which of the above seems closest to your own beliefs?
(b)   What do you think the effect on group behaviour and performance would be of each theory?

A manager who believes in Theory X, will have the tendency to:

(i)   closely supervise staff because he or she cannot trust them
(ii)   devise control mechanisms to chase progress
(iii)   delegate simple tasks to subordinates and check back frequently to see that they are completed correctly.

This looks like a recipe for increased productivity.

If a manager believes in Theory Y, he or she is likely to:

(i)   delegate responsibility for the task to subordinates and check occasionally
(ii)   delegate tasks which will make their jobs fuller and more demanding
(iii)   devote time to training and briefing.

This looks very time-consuming, fraught with risk and unlikely to increase output.

In fact, the findings from research contradict what one might expect. Productivity in teams managed by Theory Y managers was greater than those managed by believers in Theory X. If we apply our own experience to this, we can probably see why. The reaction of most of us to being watched constantly and given routine jobs is to work grudgingly and only when watched. Theory X becomes a self-fulfilling prophecy!

If we are given responsibility and the work is made interesting it becomes a learning experience and we become more committed to it.

Although the above theories have been applied widely in all kinds of organisation, recent research has indicated that motivation is a more complex process than this.

125

(d) *Process theories of motivation*

While the above theories stressed the common elements in human motivation, the process theorists have stressed *the differences in motivation between individuals and even in the differences for one individual at varying points in time*. Motivation is subject to an organic process.

The important elements in determining an individual's motivation are:

(a) effort
(b) performance
(c) reward.

If people are to be motivated they must see a strong connection between these three elements and management needs to help them establish these links. If an individual invests effort in performing a task but the manager does not consider this to be a "good performance" and the reward is low, that individual is likely to become demotivated. Those readers still at college could think of this process in relation to completing assignments! Those at work may have been disappointed in their last appraisal. Effort often needs to be assisted by help and guidance from management if performance is to show an improvement.

Better rewards also need to be linked to improved performance, whether the rewards are money, benefits, promotion, etc. However, managers should also recognise that if the reward on offer for good performance of tasks does not equate with the individual's own priorities in needs satisfaction, effort invested will be low. *People do not place the same values on the same rewards*. Some people, for example, may value money more than their leisure time and *vice versa*. Neither are we static in our expectations — we re-establish our priorities frequently.

Another complication in the process is that the individual must believe that good performance will lead to the promised reward if effort is to be invested. Experiences of false promises in the past may well lead to reduced effort.

ACTIVITY 8

Try answering the following questions about your own motivation processes.

(a) Look back at some of the items mentioned under Maslow or Herzberg. What would you place most value on in a job at present? Why?
(b) Has this been different in the past? Why?
(c) Can you envisage a time when your priorities in values might change? If so, why?

There are obviously no right answers to these questions. However, it should enable you to realise that any individual bargains with work and the organisation about using his or her energy. One makes a psychological contract, putting in the required effort to obtain the outcome which is preferred at that stage.

Any manager or leader, indeed any organisation as a whole, will need to recognise that this process is ongoing and changing and will need to respond to it. The principles which need to be consistently observed if high motivation is to be maintained are:

(a) Changing goals and values within the working group need to be systematically and continually re-assessed; this can be done through meetings, discussions, appraisal schemes and day-to-day conversations — lately this has become known as MBWA — Management by Walking About.

(b) People need to acquire the skills necessary to perform their jobs well so that effort leads to performance and rewards become less subject to chance. This can be achieved through good briefing, training and development.

(c) Rewards must follow from performance and also be responsive to the individual's particular needs; this is not easy, but it is possible if one takes time to discuss them with each individual.

CONCLUSION

All the aspects we have discussed in this chapter — effective teamwork, successful leadership and a high level of motivation — are inextricably linked. They are also essential criteria for the achievement of individual and group goals and company objectives. They cannot be separated and you will find as you progress in your career that although sometimes one area will assume more importance than another, together they ensure that human resources are used to the best possible advantage to everyone concerned.

ANSWERS TO ACTIVITIES IN CHAPTER 8

Activity 2

Doctors
Teachers
} You may have thought that both these groups exercise *power of expert-ise* — professional knowledge gained through their training as well as *power of position* — in their practice, school or college. They also exercise a degree of *customary power* — especially in social gatherings. It is particularly evident in traditional communities.

Actors
Pop stars
} Your first thought was probably that they exercised *power of personality* — the elusive but influential charisma which guarantees them their public. They also demonstrate *power of expertise* however — their acting or musical ability and knowledge on which initial and continued success will be based.

Activity 4

You may have identified the following possible drawbacks to the democratic style.

(a) It will only work if the members work well together and can genuinely accept or give constructive criticism.

(b) The leader must have a high degree of trust and members would have to be knowledgeable and expert, otherwise a greater degree of direction and control would be necessary.

(c) It could lead to delayed decision-making.

(d) The leader would have to be strong and highly respected if he or she is not to be over-ruled.

Activity 6

You will probably have realised that many of the hygiene factors, eg company policy, determination of salary, working conditions, may not be within your direct control and that even administrative procedures may have been decided by those above you. We have therefore concentrated our answer on those factors over which we think you have greatest control.

Factors I could control	What I could do to improve motivation
Supervision	Choose style of management which suits the tasks, the group and the individuals within it.
Relationships with others	Arrange activities so that people who are known to work well together continue to do so.

Actively attempt to maintain good communications and harmonious relationships within the team using the carers, communicators and encouragers.

Achievement   Allocate tasks according to the skills and talents possessed by individuals.

Set goals and sub-goals that are achievable by the group and the individuals.

Recognition   Give constant feedback on progress achieved.

Give praise for work well done.

Responsibility   Ensure that the group recognises the importance of their work.

Ensure that everyone has a chance to develop by delegating tasks within their existing capabilities and giving training in new tasks. Keep a check.

Ensure that those given responsibility also have the authority to make appropriate decisions.

Advancement   You may or may not control this but it links with all the above.

Certainly fair and accurate appraisals should help those who deserve promotion to secure it.

9 Meetings

In the previous two chapters we discussed group decision making, team work and leadership at some length. Perhaps the most frequent application of these at work is within the framework of meetings.

Research has shown that attendance at meetings increases as people rise to managerial positions and, on average, they may spend more than 50 per cent of their time in this activity. This makes it an expensive process in terms of the hours involved.

It is all the more unfortunate, then, that many regard meetings as unproductive and a waste of time. This may be for one of two reasons:

(a) the meeting may not have been necessary (the decision could have been taken by one person)

(b) the meeting may have been run inefficiently, so that the participants became bored and frustrated.

It is for both of these reasons that the reaction to a meeting being called is often an explosive "Meetings, bloody meetings" (the title of a training video on the subject).

REASONS FOR UNPRODUCTIVE MEETINGS

ACTIVITY 1

Think of any of the meetings you have attended so far — at college, at a social club, at work. If you have experienced this kind of reaction, why was this?

Try to list some of the faults you have noticed, before reading on.

You may have noted any of the following faults in your own analysis.

(a) *Feeling ill-prepared for the meeting*
You may feel you were given insufficient information in advance; conversely, you may have been given too much so that you did not have time to digest it all. In either case, it will mean that you will have felt ill-prepared and unable to contribute properly.

(b) *Poor chairing of meeting*
You may have identified that the fault lay with the chairperson or discussion leader and that the meeting was out of control. This may have been because of:

    (i) repetitive or irrelevant discussion
    (ii) dominant speakers who prevented others from contributing
    (iii) conflict between two members holding up the discussion.

(c) *Participants were merely expected to rubber-stamp a decision*
Sometimes you may become frustrated because a meeting has been called yet the decision seems to have been made already.

These recurring faults often raise the question of "Do we really need to have meetings?" The fact is that these faults only occur if meetings are badly organised and conducted; if they are efficiently run, they can make a significant contribution to an organisation's communication system.

PURPOSES OF MEETINGS

An organisation must operate through people; decisions must therefore be made in consultation with those who must implement them or who will be affected by them. Their acceptance must be secured; they must be briefed and informed if commitment is to be obtained. Meetings are an important method by which this can be achieved. There are, of course, a range of meetings which take place at work, from the very formal at board level or in local authorities, at council level, to the informal meeting between managers and their staff. The purposes of meetings — what they are meant to achieve — are common to all levels however.

ACTIVITY 2

Think back again to some of the meetings you have attended. What were their objectives?

Jot down what you think they were intended to achieve before reading on.

Meetings can fulfil a number of different purposes. They can be used when people want to:

(a) consult with all those concerned with a decision to be made to sound opinion and to exchange views

(b) arrive at a decision which is agreed by those who will implement it

(c)   pool ideas and expertise to solve problems and arrive at recommendations

(d)   plan and/or monitor work in progress

(e)   brief or train people for new procedures or work

(f)   inform people about decisions or new policies

(g)   negotiate agreements between individuals or groups

(h)   share the responsibility for a decision

(i)   allocate responsibility and authority for carrying out an investigation

(j)   discuss results of investigations.

No single meeting will be likely to fulfil all these purposes, as each will have specific objectives of its own.

There are many different kinds of meeting and it is useful to be able to identify these in order to be clear about their purpose within the organisation.

TYPES OF MEETING

Most people are likely to be required to participate in a number of different types of meeting early in their work lives and will need to decide what is required of them in each case. They will need to know not only what meetings are for but also about their conduct and procedures. In simple terms we can categorise meetings into formal and informal. In reality the range is very wide. The diagram below gives an indication of the spectrum of meetings one might expect to find in the workplace.

Range of meetings to be found in organisations

Most formal	Some formality	Least formal
Board meetings	Project meetings	Problem-solving meetings
Council meetings	Progress meetings	Brainstorming meetings
Staff association meetings or employer/trade union meetings	Departmental or section meetings	Briefing meetings

The procedures and conduct expected in each type also vary.

ACTIVITY 3

One of the procedures which will vary considerably is the documentation which will be expected for the type of meeting to be held.

What kinds of documentation might you expect, for example, for the most formal types of meeting given above?

List as many as you can before reading on.

This activity will have led you to give some thought to the differences in conduct between the various kinds of meeting you may have attended. Listed below are a number of areas which may differ and will help you distinguish between formal and informal meetings.

Characteristics of formal and informal meetings

Formal	Informal
A written constitution which determines rules, procedures.	No formal constitution: members decide rules and procedures

Documentation

Set requirements for the provision of: 　notices of meeting 　agendas 　motions 　minutes 　officers' reports.	No formal documents are required. Meetings are called by telephone, memo, personal contact. Someone may be asked to take notes or participants and leader may make their own.

Special officers

These vary in number and type but there is always: 　a chairperson 　a secretary 　and usually a treasurer.	There are no special officers; the person calling the meeting, usually the manager, acts as a discussion leader.

Decision making

There is a formal method of decision making — the vote.	Decisions either arise out of common agreement or the manager takes a decision after consulting the other participants.

133

Terminology

Special terms are used.	There is no special terminology.

At first, one is likely to attend informal meetings most frequently; all the principles we have discussed in previous chapters concerning teams and their leadership will be relevant here, so we will summarise only briefly what is expected of people at this kind of meeting.

INFORMAL MEETINGS

Participating

The first role one is likely to take in a meeting is as an ordinary participant. This does not mean, however, that one has no responsibilities. If the meeting is to be productive, it is important for every participant to come prepared, behave constructively within the meeting and afterwards follow up any actions which have been allocated to them.

ACTIVITY 4

Together with other management trainees, you have been asked to attend a meeting to discuss your progress on a management training programme operated by your organisation. The meeting is with your immediate superior and the management training officer.

What will you need to do in terms of preparation for the meeting?

Check your own ideas with ours at the end of the chapter.

We hope that the above activity will have demonstrated how important it is that participants are well prepared if they are to give a good account of themselves in the meeting. Below is a checklist of dos and don'ts for participants which may be used as a reminder each time one attends an informal meeting.

Do	Don't
Preparation	
Check on the meeting's objectives.	Turn up at a meeting without prior thought and preparation.
Know your own objectives	
Collect together relevant papers, information and ideas.	

Make notes as a reminder of the main points to raise.

Within the meeting

Play a positive and active role within the meeting — task and/or group maintenance behaviour.	Assume your own interpretation of the meeting's objectives is correct.
	Indulge in role behaviour which is counter-productive.
Contribute to effective time management.	Waste time in fruitless argument.
Listen to other members' points of view.	Revel in the sound of your own voice.
Follow any protocol appropriate to the type of meeting — even in informal meetings there may be some formalities.	Alienate other members by ignoring appropriate protocol.
Make notes for future reference and/or action.	Trust memory alone.
Voice any reservations about decisions *within* the meeting, not afterwards.	Indulge in silent resentment within the meeting but complain afterwards and/or sabotage the decision.

After the meeting

Act on decisions within the time scales required, using the notes made at the meeting.	Forget to act on decisions or claim ignorance.

Later on in your career, you may well be asked to lead a meeting and indeed may have already done so at college, in work or in outside clubs. Again, as we have discussed the techniques and approaches of effective leaders in the previous chapter, we will consider this only briefly in the context of controlling a meeting.

Leading

Apart from the basic principles, here are some brief guidelines for controlling meetings.

(a) *Preparation*

The leader needs to:

(i) clarify the objectives of the meeting

(ii) write down what he or she wants to achieve

(iii) draw up a relevant attendance list, so that the right people are involved to achieve results and no-one is asked to be present unnecessarily

(iv) inform people about the purpose, time and location

(v) ask people to bring with them any information which will be useful in the meeting and clarify what they will be expected to contribute

(vi) prepare any information or notes which will be helpful

(vii) arrange an environment which will be free from interruption and provide refreshments (if necessary)

(viii) work out approximate timings for each item based on their importance

(ix) work out a speaking order related to this in terms of who needs to contribute on each item and to avoid dominance by extrovert members.

(b) *During the meeting*

As in any leadership situation, the discussion leader needs to balance the needs of the task, the group and the individuals within the meeting. Below is a summary of the activities which will help the discussion leader to achieve this.

Task functions: ie to keep the participants working on the tasks relevant to the meeting.

(i) *Initiating* — by proposing tasks and goals; defining problems, suggesting procedures or ideas.

(ii) *Information seeking* — requesting facts; seeking relevant information, asking for suggestions, ideas.

(iii) *Information giving* — stating a belief; providing relevant information.

(iv) *Summarising* — pulling together related ideas; re-stating suggestions after discussion; offering a decision or conclusion for the group to accept or reject.

(v) *Clarifying* — elaborating, interpreting or reflecting ideas and suggestions; clearing up confusion; indicating alternatives and issues; giving examples.

(vi) *Consensus testing* — checking to see how much agreement has been reached.

Group maintenance functions: ie to make sure the participants work as a team to achieve the meeting's objective.

(i) *Encouraging* — being friendly and responsive to the participants; accepting contributions; giving opportunities for recognition.

(ii) *Expressing group feelings* — sensing feelings, moods and relationships within the group; sharing one's feelings with others.

(iii) *Harmonising* — attempting to reconcile arguments, reducing tension; getting people to explore their differences.

(iv) *Modifying* — when the leader's own ideas or status is causing conflict, modifying own position, being able to admit error and maintain self-discipline for the sake of group cohesion.

(v) *Keeping the channels of communication open* — ensuring participation by providing procedures/protocol for discussion.

Individual motivation functions: ie to make sure that each individual participant makes a contribution to achieving the objective and does not feel overwhelmed by the group.

(i) *Recognising* — individual expertise and experience.

(ii) *Encouraging* — the individual to contribute on the basis of experience and expertise.

(iii) *Accepting* — individual suggestions and contributions.

(iv) *Eliciting contributions* — from those who are quiet or withdrawn.

(v) *Responding* — to feelings expressed by individuals.

(vi) *Controlling* — those individuals who threaten to dominate (without alienating them).

In addition, throughout the meeting the leader will need to note what actions have been decided, by whom they are to be implemented, how and by when. Lengthy minutes are not needed but a quick action list of this kind is invaluable.

(c) *After the meeting*
The leader will need to:

(i) confirm his or her action list in writing to the people concerned in case they have not taken notes

(ii) check on outcomes to see how implementation is taking place

(iii) help with any problems which may arise.

If these checklists are put into practice, meetings should be cost-effective and productive for all concerned.

There may also be occasions when one is asked to attend a more formal meeting. Certainly as one progresses through a career, there are likely to be more of these. The rest of this chapter will therefore be concerned with this type of meeting.

FORMAL MEETINGS

These are usually necessary when

(a) the participants represent groups of people, as in a social club committee, a local council or committee meeting, or a negotiating meeting; or

(b) powerful sectional interests are present as in the board of a company, a shareholders' meeting or an inter-departmental committee.

Because so much is at stake, formal meetings either have a full legal status or at least perform an executive role within an organisation. For these reasons, it is important that their procedures have an official standing. This is often reflected in the written constitution which states the rules and procedures by which such meetings must operate. In all cases, it is essential that a formal meeting should be:

(a)   properly constituted

(b)   properly convened

(c)   properly conducted

(d)   properly recorded.

In this way it is analogous to a court of law; it conforms to regulations, has a professional place and must formally note all the decisions made.

ACTIVITY 5

There may be many formal meetings or committees which affect your life at present; certainly some of these will be within your local council; some may be work based. Try to take time to attend one that allows observers (eg local council meetings) so that you can observe the protocol and procedures and/or ask to see the written rules or constitution. This will help you to put this part of the chapter in context.

Properly Constituted

To be properly constituted, a formal meeting will normally have:

(a)   Written terms of reference, giving its purpose and limitations. These are normally derived from standing orders or a memorandum given by the parent body who set up the meeting(s) concerned. In the case of a central or local authority, it will be derived from statute. If a meeting tries to discuss matters outside its terms of reference, its right to do so will be challenged. The term "ultra vires" is used for this and is included in our glossary later in the chapter. The constitution also states whether the meeting has an "executive role" (ie it can authorise the implementation of its decisions) or is advisory only (can only recommend its decisions to a higher body).

(b)   Written regulations concerning the documentation required, timescales and the procedure for electing and/or appointing officers.

(c)   Rules governing the right to attend. Usually this right applies only to authorised members. However, exceptionally, an outside person may be co-opted to a meeting because he or she has particular expertise which is relevant to the matter under discussion. He or she will then be known as a "co-opted member".

(d) Rules concerning the minimum number who must attend before a decision can be made. This is usually two thirds of the total membership and is referred to in meetings terminology as the "quorum".

Properly Convened

A meeting must conform with its constitution. This will govern the rules concerning the documents needed to call the meeting as follows.

(a) *The notice of meeting*
Sometimes this is called a "summons". It is usually circulated 21 days in advance of the meeting but the time varies according to the constitution. It will state:

    (i)   the title
    (ii) the date
    (iii) the time
    (iv) the venue

of the meeting and must be circulated to every member.

(b) *The agenda*
This is usually circulated with the notice of meeting; clearly members need to prepare for the meeting for it to be effective and will therefore want to know what topics are to be discussed. The agenda often has a specified order of business, although detailed content will vary. The normal sequence is given below.

MODEL AGENDA

Apologies for absence
Minutes of last meeting
Matters arising
Correspondence
Officers' reports
Motions or special items for discussion (will vary)
Any other business
Date of next meeting

It is also normal for the chairperson to have his or her own agenda, although this is not mentioned in the constitution. However, it is an essential tool to help him or her to lead and control the meeting. It is a special version of the agenda showing additional information which will be of value to the chairperson during the meeting.

ACTIVITY 6

Before reading on, you might like to think carefully about what kinds of information a chairperson might need to conduct a meeting efficiently. List these briefly before referring to the example chairperson's agenda given on page 142.

Such a document can help the chairperson:

(a) to allocate the time available in the best way to meet priorities

(b) by acting as a memory jogger for the contributions which can be made by participants and/or for the information which he or she needs to bring to the meeting personally.

Examples of the first part of the document cycle, all those papers needed before the meeting, are given on pages 141 and 142.

Properly Conducted

The officers appointed need to be clear as to their duties and perform them efficiently and well. The most important of these are the chairperson and the secretary. They need to work in very close consultation with one another and know the constitution and its requirements well. Two checklists are given below concerning their duties, which may be helpful if one is asked to carry out either of these roles.

1. *Role of chief officers of a meeting*

    (a) *Chairperson*
    A chairperson is needed to direct and control proceedings; the constitution will define the exact powers and duties as well as how the chairperson is to be elected or appointed. Main points to remember are that this person should:

    (i) prepare for the meeting by checking the agenda and drawing up a suitable chairperson's agenda
    (ii) check any points of procedure and ensure that they are carried out
    (iii) ensure that the meeting is properly constituted and that a quorum is present
    (iv) keep order and keep discussion within the terms of reference and within reasonable time limits
    (v) ensure that proposed motions and amendments are correctly

Example notice of meeting

WORTHINGTON'S plc

NOTICE OF MEETING: HEALTH AND SAFETY COMMITTEE

A meeting of the above committee will take place on Friday, 10th May 19. . at 10.30 am in the Board Room. All members are asked to attend if possible. The agenda is attached.

Signed

P L Pearson
Secretary

Example agenda

WORTHINGTON'S plc

AGENDA: HEALTH AND SAFETY COMMITTEE
Meeting 10th May 19. .

1. Apologies for absence.

2. Minutes of the last meeting.

3. Matters arising.

4. Correspondence: replies concerning previous queries to the Local Authority Fire Department.

5. Report of the Safety Inspector.

6. Discussion of the motion "That a series of courses should be run in conjunction with the local college on the safety responsibilities of supervisors".
    Proposed: Mrs L T Young   Training Officer
    Seconded: Mr J D Clint   Senior Supervisor
                        (Maintenance)

7. Any other business.

8. Date of next meeting.

Example chairperson's agenda

Time	Item	Notes
Time	*Item*	*Notes*
10.30	Apologies for absence	Lucy King is on holiday. John Tredvers is on a course.
10.32	Minutes of last meeting	Have been circulated. To check and sign only.
10.35	Matters arising from minutes	Loose tiles — have already been relaid. Fire hazards — see correspondence.
10.40	Correspondence	Secretary to present Fire Officer's replies. Date for his visit to be checked with members.
10.50	Report of the Safety Inspector	J Harmer to present the salient points. Actions need to be allocated and confirmed with S Lyons and R Treadgold.
11.05	Motion "That a series of courses be run in conjunction with the local college on the safety responsibilities of supervisors."	Ask proposer, Laura Young, to speak for the motion and suggest costs/time rota. Ask for other reactions. Ask seconder — John Clint to reply.
11.20	Any other business	—
11.25	Date of next meeting	Suggest Friday 12th June 11.00 a.m.

worded, proposed and seconded and are in order, where these have been submitted in advance

(vi) formulate discussion and decisions, questions and/or new motions or amendments which have been moved for consideration during the meeting

(vii) decide on points of order and other incidental matters which require decisions at the meeting

(viii) move the procedure of the meeting forward by putting relevant questions and summarising, thus preventing irrelevant or repetitive discussion

(ix) take the vote and, where authorised, give a casting vote; take a poll, where necessary; declare result

(x) get approval for the minutes and sign them

(xi) convene, adjourn, and declare the meeting closed, where necessary; decide on the date of the next meeting.

NB Sometimes a vice-chairperson may be elected or appointed to assume the role of the chairperson if absent.

(b) *Secretary*

The committee secretary is effectively the administrator of the committee. He or she carries out the following duties:

(i) supervises and carries out all administrative activities associated with the document cycle

(ii) keeps the records and minutes and takes notes at the meeting from which the minutes are formulated

(iii) helps the chairperson to prepare the agenda and sometimes the chairperson's agenda

(iv) conducts communication including correspondence on behalf of the meeting

(v) checks any reports and prepares any other information which may be needed at the meeting

(vi) supervises all administrative preparation for the meeting including booking room, etc.

However, according to the constitution, the secretary usually acts as an observer and recorder only and does not participate in the meeting.

In addition, both the secretary and the chairperson need to know the terminology of meetings and the regulations concerning each of them. As these are very lengthy, a glossary is given at the end of this chapter for reference.

Properly Recorded

All of what has transpired is recorded by the secretary at the meeting and summarised afterwards. This summary is known as the "minutes". The minutes usually follow the order of the agenda and copies are circulated to all members before the next meeting for their approval. Sometimes they are also entered in a minute book. The minutes must be agreed by all the members at the following meeting at which time the chairperson signs them. Once he or she has done so, they become a legal document and can only be changed by a resolution taken in a full meeting.

There are two kinds of minutes which may be kept.

(a) Narrative minutes — these are very full and record most of what people said at the meeting as well as decisions and action.

(b) Resolution minutes — these give the decision with, possibly, very brief reasons. Sometimes they also have a column for action. This can be very useful for reference after the meeting.

ACTIVITY 7

Below is a narrative minute based on item 6 of the agenda on page 141. Try to reduce it to a resolution/action minute. Jot down your answer and compare it with ours at the end of the chapter.

"Mrs Laura Young supported the motion by saying that the supervisors she had talked to had very little idea as to their safety responsibilities under the law. She said that she had investigated the college courses locally and had found that they were reasonably priced and could be run at dates and times which suited the company. The other members of the committee asked that she should present them with costs and, on her doing so, were able to approve. Mr John Clint supported her statements. It was resolved unanimously that the courses should go ahead and that she should liaise with the supervisors to arrange dates and times for training to take place before the next safety inspection in July."

CONCLUSION

Meetings can be a very effective method of communication if conducted efficiently. If not, they can be a costly waste of time and effort. We hope that this chapter has clarified some of the ways in which the leader, the officer and the participants can contribute to their success.

GLOSSARY OF TERMS

Types of meeting

Ad hoc committee	Sometimes called a special, or special purpose committee. It will be appointed to deal with one particular issue.
Advisory/consultative committee	A committee which refers advice to a main executive committee.
Annual general meeting	A meeting of all the members of an organisation or shareholders of a company that must be held each year.
Executive committee	A committee which has the authority to act on its decisions
Extraordinary general meeting	A meeting of all members of an organisation or shareholders of a company to discuss some matter of importance for which the consent of all or the majority of members is necessary.
Standing committee	One which has no finite time span but meets regularly during this indefinite period.
Sub-committee	A group appointed by a main committee to undertake specified work on its behalf. It must report to the main committee periodically.

Documents

Agenda	A list of items to be discussed at a meeting.
Attendance record	The book in which each member present at a meeting signs his or her name.
Chairperson's agenda	The agenda prepared for use by the chairperson.
Constitution	The document which states the rules and procedures which govern the conduct of the meeting.
Memorandum	A document setting out information to enable a committee to make a policy decision.
Minute book	A book containing a signed copy of each set of minutes.

Narrative minutes	A summary of all the points raised in discussion together with resolutions and votes.
Resolution minutes	A summary of all the resolutions passed.
Notice of meeting/meeting summons	A notification to members of the time, date and place of a meeting.

Conduct of meeting

Addendum	An amendment which *adds* words to a motion.
Addressing the chair	A member wishing to speak on a point must rise and address the chairperson saying "Mr/Madam chairman . . ."
Adjournment	The chairperson may, with the consent of the members, adjourn the meeting in order to postpone further discussion or because of shortage of time.
Adjourned by consent	This means that the unfinished business of one meeting will be discussed at another meeting by consent of those present.
Adjournment sine die	The unfinished business will be discussed at a future meeting but no date has been specified.
Co-option	The power given to a committee to allow others to serve on the committee.
Ex officio	A person may be a member of a committee *ex officio*. This means "by virtue of his or her office".
Intra vires	**This means that the topic is within the powers of the person or committee concerned.**
Lie on the table	A matter is said to "lie on the table" when no action can be taken on it.
Motion	A proposal that certain action be taken.
Next business	A motion "that the meeting proceed with next business" is a method of delaying the decision on any matter brought before the meeting.
No confidence	When the members of a meeting disagree with the

chairperson they may pass a vote of "no confidence" in the chair. In this situation the chairperson must vacate the chair in favour of the vice-chairperson or some other person. There must be a substantial majority in favour of this motion.

Point of order   A question regarding the procedure of a meeting or a query relating to the standing orders or constitution.

Postponement   The action taken to defer a meeting to a later date.

Proceedings   The business discussed, the main points of discussion and the decisions and agreements taken at a meeting.

Proposer   The person who recommends a particular motion.

Putting a question   To conclude the discussion on a motion it is usual for the chairperson to "put the question" by announcing "The question before the meeting is . . .".

Quorum   The minimum number of members necessary for a meeting to be held.

Reference back   This is an amendment referring a report or other item of business back for further consideration to the body or person submitting it.

Resolution   A formal decision carried by a meeting. A resolution cannot be cancelled (rescinded) at the meeting at which it was adopted.

Rider   An additional clause or sentence added to a resolution after it has been passed. It differs from an amendment in that it adds to a resolution instead of altering it. It has to be proposed, seconded and put to the meeting in the same way as a motion.

Right of reply   The proposer of a motion has the right to reply when the resolution has been fully discussed.

Seconder   A person who supports the proposer of a motion.

Standing orders   These are the rules compiled by the organisation to regulate the manner in which its business is conducted. May be called the "constitution".

Substantive motion   A motion altered by a previously agreed amendment.

147

Take the chair	This means that someone does the work of a chairperson during the meeting.
Terms of reference	A statement of the work to be done by a committee.
Ultra vires	When a matter is *ultra vires* it is outside the power or authority of the committee or organisation.

Voting

Ballot	A written vote which preserves the secrecy of each individual's vote.
Casting vote	An additional vote, usually held by the chairperson to enable a decision to be taken in the case of an equal number of votes being given for and against the motion.
Going into division	The physical division of members for voting purposes.
Majority	The greatest number of members either for or against a motion. The rules will define the majority of votes required to carry a motion.
Nem con	(Nemine contradicente) The passing of a resolution without opposing votes but with some members abstaining.
Nem dis	(Nemine dissentiente) Sometimes used instead of nem con.
Poll	This is the term used for the method of voting at an election. In a meeting this usually takes the form of a secret vote by ballot paper. The way a poll is conducted is usually laid down in the constitution.
Proxy	A person authorised by a member to vote on his or her behalf.
Scrutineer	The person who counts and examines closely the vote at an election.
Teller	The person appointed to count the votes at a meeting.
Unanimous	When all members of a meeting have voted in favour of a motion, it is said to be carried unanimously.

Vote   To express, either verbally or in writing, whether one
                        is for or against a motion.

ANSWER TO ACTIVITIES IN CHAPTER 9

Activity 4

You might have thought of any or all of the following.

Check and bring with you:

(a) log book or diary

(b) notes on previous meetings held on this topic

(c) any special project you may have completed as a trainee

(d) any notes you have made on your work progress, work problems.

Prepare:

(a) any points you wish to raise about the above

(b) the facts, ideas, arguments related to your point of view.

Activity 7

''L Young had investigated supervisors' knowledge of safety under the law; this was minimal. Suitably priced courses were available locally at appropriate times. She was supported by J. Clint.
Resolved: L Young should arrange courses with supervisors/college before July.

Action: L Young.''

10 Giving Orders and Instructions: Briefing and Training

Quite early in their career people may find that they are asked to supervise other people including those who may be older than them; this means that they will need to be able to give instructions and to brief a small work group.

Another situation which may arise is that they may be required to train someone who is new — either new to the whole organisation or to a particular task.

Sometimes people feel uncertain how they should go about this aspect of their work; especially when faced with it for the first time; so in this chapter we will suggest a few guidelines which we hope will be helpful in tackling the business of giving instructions, briefing or training.

IMPORTANCE OF GOOD INSTRUCTIONS

There are a number of reasons why one should aim to give good instructions to staff. Clear, accurate, complete instructions:

(a) save time because staff will know exactly what to do

(b) improve the quality of their work because it will be accurate and contribute to the section's objectives

(c) improve staff's motivation because they will know exactly what is expected of them, how to do it and why

(d) reduce the need for close supervision and one will be able to rely on staff to do a good job.

GIVING INSTRUCTIONS AND ORDERS

In any managerial job, giving instructions and orders is an essential activity, yet very little training is ever given in this area. Managers are expected to know how to do it and to be able to issue clear instructions and orders which meet with the required actions. They need all their communication skills to help them. There are three initial questions for a manager to answer:

(a) *What* do I need to tell them?

(b) *Who* do I need to tell?

(c) *How* should I go about it?

What Instructions Need to be Given

Here it is essential that the manager is clear in his or her own mind as to exactly what orders need to be conveyed. It may require a check on facts first, if necessary with a superior or a more experienced colleague. So it is necessary to be clear about:

(a) why the instruction is necessary and what it is to achieve

(b) what the staff are required to do — precisely

(c) what outcome or action is required from the person receiving the instruction.

Lack of clarity and accuracy in giving instructions will have the inevitable consequences of poor performance and lack of respect for the person issuing them. The next important factor is the people to whom the instructions are given.

Who Needs to Know?

A great deal of resentment is often caused by either leaving out someone who needs to be given an instruction or by approaching people in the wrong way. It is therefore important to consider who needs to be given instruction. Instruction-giving should be tackled differently for individuals and groups.

HOW TO GIVE INSTRUCTIONS AND ORDERS

One needs to consider three things here:

(a) getting the procedure right

(b) getting the method of instruction-giving right

(c) getting the right behavioural response, by thinking about possible reactions.

The Right Procedure

There are four basic facts which anyone needs to know when receiving an order or instruction if he or she is to carry it out properly and feel fully briefed. These are:

(a) *what* they need to do — the precise facts

(b) *how* they need to do it — the method

(c) *why* they need to do it — the reasons and the objective

(d) *when* it needs to be done — the timing.

ACTIVITY 1

Look at the following instruction:

"Everyone must submit their stationery requirements on form 66 by 1st March 19. . for administrative reasons."

Does this instruction fulfil the above four factors?

Could it be improved in any way? If so, how?

Jot down your answers before reading on.

At first glance the instruction above complies with the rules — it states what, how, why and when. However, do you think this instruction would receive a 100 per cent response. In fact, it received only a 45 per cent return. The problem lay in the reasons given. The phrase "for administrative purposes" is vague and does not relate to the concerns of the people reading it. If the final phrase had been "so that we can order new supplies before the end of the financial year and give you your stationery before April" the reaction might have been different.

This highlights the point that good instructions must take into consideration how to approach the people concerned.

Getting the Method Right

In some situations, one may have a choice between giving oral or written instructions. It is important to make this choice according to the nature of the facts, the importance of an accurate response, etc.

(a) *Oral instructions* are time consuming but they give the opportunity to respond to queries, misunderstandings and to use the other person's body language to gauge the reception of and response to one's instruction.

(b) *Written instructions* provide a permanent reference of the essential facts but there is no feedback as to whether the member of staff has fully understood them or has any commitment to them.

153

Where they are complex, oral instructions may need to be backed up by written information.

Approaching People in the Right Way

Any instruction-giving situation requires one to be aware of the likely reactions of the other person and to phrase a message so that effective communication takes place. Some people are easier to communicate with than others. We mentioned earlier that some people for whom a manager may be responsible will be older than him or her; clearly this may pose a challenge in making the right approach.

ACTIVITY 2

What reaction do you think an older employee might have when he or she is given orders or instructions by a younger member of staff?

(a)   How do you think he or she might perceive the person concerned?

(b)   How do you think he or she might react to the situation?

Jot down your ideas before reading on.

Approaching an older person   Often the initial attitude of an older person in a work group to a younger superior, however highly qualified or trained and whatever his or her job title, is one of scepticism; although the older person recognises that the theory may have been learnt, he or she reasons that the practice and the experience is missing — whereas his or her experience has been accumulated over a period of time.

The older person's reaction may be to question at best, or at worst, to oppose. This does not always take the form of open defiance — it can sometimes be much more subtle. The person concerned may seem to agree — to go along with the instruction. However, if he or she does not really agree, or wants to make the superior look incompetent, the older person will make sure the instruction does not achieve its objective.

ACTIVITY 3

A technical problem has arisen which you know how to solve from your training. You have to instruct an older man to do this and you know he has a great deal of experience. How would you approach him? Think carefully about this before comparing your answer with our suggestions at the end of the chapter.

The approach which we have suggested is often known as the "implied order" — because it is not imposed but arrived at by consultation. It is much more likely to obtain co-operation and a willingness to try the solution which at least appears to have been jointly agreed. One should always recognise someone else's experience and how it may help, or that person will inevitably see one as a conceited know-all and react accordingly!

Checking for commitment   In any instruction-giving situation, one should also check for commitment to carrying out the order. Ask the person concerned to re-cap on the agreement. If he or she is not committed it will become fairly evident from what he or she says at this point and, of course, how he or she says it. Body language will very often reveal when a person is simply compliant rather than committed.

Beginning and ending instructions   These are two very important points in the instruction-giving process. In opening the instruction, whether it is written or oral, focus the attention of the member of staff. No-one gets into gear straight away, so do not start on the major points first. In a spoken instruction, you can focus attention by mentioning the topic, eg "John, can we talk about the Wilson contract; you remember the situation was . . ." This helps the person concerned to switch his concentration from what he is doing to what you are saying. In written instructions, focus attention by a clear heading and an introductory sentence which defines the purpose.

Equally, it is not a good idea to give further important points whilst walking away from the other person or as an afterthought — he or she may not be listening and the point is likely to be ignored. Bring the instruction to a close by recapping on the action agreed.

Once instructions have been given, do follow up and ensure that they have been carried out correctly and that no problems or misunderstandings have arisen. This is particularly important in written instructions where you are not immediately observing the person's response.

To summarise, in an instruction-giving situation:

(a)   *Switch people on* — attract their attention with an introductory sentence.

(b)   *Discuss the task* (if it is an oral instruction) so that the four basic facts can be explained:

what, why, how, when.

Invite suggestions from the other person and offer your own.

(c)   *Agree the action to be taken* and ensure that the person both understands the instruction and is committed to it. If it is a written instruction, be careful to follow it up personally to check commitment.

(d)   *Check that the action is being carried out* and whether there are any problems.

155

Apart from giving orders and instructions, which is a fundamental managerial task, one may also need to give training to a new entrant to the organisation or to someone who must tackle a specific task for the first time. While many of the principles we have discussed so far are still relevant, the preparation and conduct of training is a more complex process.

TRAINING PEOPLE AT WORK

Most training does not take place by sending people away on courses. Some of the most relevant and important training takes place at work, with an experienced employee helping one who is new to a task.

Induction Training

When someone joins an organisation he or she has a good deal to learn before performing adequately. A new employee will need to know about:

(a)   the organisation itself — its structure, rules, procedures

(b)   the job — its content, method of operation

(c)   the work team — their roles, expertise.

It takes some time for a person to "settle in" and to become functional, so it is to the advantage of the organisation that the employee receives help quickly and competently. Most organisations now provide an "induction training" period in order to achieve this.

The first part of induction training is usually concerned with the organisation as a whole, so it is often conducted by the personnel department or a senior manager. The second stage, however, which involves an introduction to the team and some initial training for the tasks involved in the job itself, is almost always carried out by the direct supervisor. This is one instance when one may be required to undertake training quite early in one's career.

On-the-Job Training

Once one has been with an organisation for a few months and become familiar with tasks and procedures, one may be asked by the manager to assist new members of the work group to acquire some skill. Again, one will be undertaking a training role.

Since this involvement in training could occur at an early stage, the remainder of this chapter will provide some guidelines on the training process. The term "process" is used deliberately because training tends to be an on-going activity. Training needs to be undertaken at frequent intervals if an individual is to develop and progress.

THE TRAINING PROCESS

Training boosts the confidence of the employee, improves his or her performance and is therefore of great value to the organisation. However, it needs to be systematic if it is to be effective. The process is probably best seen as a cycle, as shown in the diagram below.

The training process

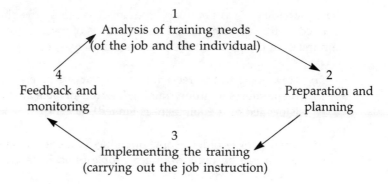

1
Analysis of training needs
(of the job and the individual)

4
Feedback and
monitoring

2
Preparation and
planning

3
Implementing the training
(carrying out the job instruction)

Analysis of Training Needs

There are two separate categories of facts that are needed as part of this analysis:

(a) those which concern the job itself

(b) those which concern the individual(s) to be trained.

The job   Analysis of the job means establishing:

(a) the main tasks to be performed

(b) the methods by which they are usually performed

(c) how the tasks can be broken down into manageable packages for training or learning purposes

(d) which areas are likely to create problems of learning, safety or costs.

No-one can train well until this kind of analysis has been carried out.

ACTIVITY 4

If you had to analyse a job for training purposes, what sources of information might you consult?

Note your answers to these questions before you continue.

You might, of course, know the job very well, so one important source of information could be your own experience of carrying out the job or observation of someone else in the work team who is either doing an identical job or a similar one. You would check the job description to identify the main tasks which need to be accomplished. There may also be written method sheets or work manuals, procedures or specifications to which one can refer. Whatever the sources, it is necessary to be clear about the nature of the tasks to be performed before one can prepare training instruction.

The individual   It is necessary to examine carefully the characteristics of those to be trained. Before deciding on the best methods of training to use you will need to know a number of things about the trainees themselves, eg:

(a)   How many will be receiving training at one time — it may be necessary to limit the numbers in group training if a considerable amount of one-to-one attention is needed or if equipment is limited.

(b)   Their ages — older people often have experience on which they can build and which can be used; younger people often have quick reactions so it may be possible to accelerate the pace of training.

(c)   Their existing knowledge and skills — this becomes the starting point for instruction; it is the foundation on which you will build their training.

ACTIVITY 5

We have mentioned three facts which you need to know about your trainees if you are to plan your training appropriately. Can you think of any other factors which you may need to take into account and why?

Our suggestions are given at the end of the chapter.

You may have thought of many more than we have suggested, but we hope you will now realise the importance of this initial process if you are to undertake the next stage successfully.

Preparation and Planning

There are a number of stages involved in planning training. These are:

(a)   *Define the purpose and context of the job*
       The trainees will need to know

         (i)   where the task fits into the work of the section
        (ii)   what its purpose is
       (iii)   why it is important

if they are to see a reason for and a meaning to the task.

(b) *Break down the job into easy stages*
It is easier for people to learn tasks a little at a time — to master part of it, build on that and then move on. Beware of giving too much instruction too fast as it confuses trainees and often makes them fail — a demotivating effect. So, set sub-objectives at each stage, then trainees can see themselves progress.

(c) *Sequence the instruction carefully*
Begin with the knowledge of the trainees and build "bricks" of instruction on that. Remember that it is easier to understand if an instruction is given in a logical order.

(d) *Identify any areas which may need particular attention*
These might include safety aspects or areas of difficulty. It will be necessary to emphasise these as they are key points on which one must give careful advice.

It is often helpful to use forms in planning so we have included a suggested form for planning training in a task.

Task breakdown sheet	
Job title _____	
Steps	Key points (eg safety aspects, areas of difficulty)

(e) *Plan the time and the location*
Make sure that sufficient time has been allocated to instruct adequately and that a location which is free from interruptions has been chosen. Failure to do this can be very damaging; neither the trainer nor the trainees will be able to concentrate. It is also likely that the trainees' perception will be that the task is seen as unimportant or that the trainer is not interested in them.

(f) *Assemble all the material and equipment needed in advance*
Remember to check that the equipment is working before the session begins.

Careful preparation and planning helps to make the learning process quicker and easier and is thus cost-effective for the organisation and motivating for the trainees.

Implementing Training — Carrying Out Job Instruction

This stage needs to be very carefully structured. There are six parts to successful job instruction:

(a) introduction

(b) explanation

(c) demonstration

(d) participation

(e) correction

(f) reinforcement.

Before we look at this in more detail, try the next activity.

ACTIVITY 6

Think back to a time when someone instructed you in a task.

How was the instruction introduced?

How helpful was this introduction?

Once you have thought about this, perhaps you would like to list what *you* think should be included when you introduce a task to a new trainee before reading on.

Introduction   The most important elements of an introduction are:

(a) to explain the purpose of the job

(b) to put the job into its context

but also

(c) to put the trainees at their ease

(d) to introduce the trainer if this is the first meeting

(e) to talk about the trainees' past experience

(f)   to establish a rapport.

At the beginning of any instruction, the trainees are often nervous, so a friendly approach is essential to allow them to relax and become receptive.

Explanation

(a)   Explain the job carefully in the sequence prepared.

(b)   Invite questions *en route*.

(c)   Emphasise key points.

Demonstration

(a)   Demonstrate the task in stages.

(b)   Explain again whilst going through the stages.

(c)   Remember to engage the trainees' visual sense as well as their hearing.

Participation

Invite the trainees to try the task. This is a vital component. Remember the saying:

What I hear, I forget;
what I see, I remember;
what I do, I understand.

Correction

It is extremely important to correct quickly — we all form habits very rapidly and to continue to do something wrongly is damaging.

Reinforcement

(a)   Allow time for practice.

(b)   Continue to watch and correct.

(c)   Give recognition and encouragement when trainees are successful.

(d)   Question specifically on difficult or important aspects.

(e)   Leave trainees with a written method sheet to refer to at the end of the instruction.

There is now only the last stage to consider — the follow-up stage where feedback needs to be noted and the trainees' progress monitored.

Following Up Training — Feedback and Monitoring

In addition to the written method sheet for the trainees' reference one also needs to keep an eye on their progress. This does not mean standing over them for a week but being accessible and approachable so that they will be happy to seek advice and guidance on any problems.

It also involves keeping an unobtrusive check from time to time. After all, if one teaches a child to swim, one does not get out of the pool and go home after the first few strokes. If it is not always possible to be available, it is a good idea to ask another experienced person to help trainees with any difficulties.

CONCLUSION

Lastly, it is worth repeating that the whole process of training should be a continual one if people are to gain job satisfaction and personal development at work. A manager's ability to provide systematic instruction and training will be an asset to the organisation and to the work group. It is also a skill which he or she will need to exercise more frequently as his or her career progresses and responsibility for the development of people increases.

ANSWERS TO ACTIVITIES IN CHAPTER 10

Activity 3

The most constructive approach in this situation with the older employee is to discuss the problem jointly — to consult. Try asking if he has come across the problem before and, if so, what solutions were tried. If one of these relates to or coincides with the one you were going to propose, *suggest* that this might be tried to see what results occur.

If a similar solution has not been tried before, offer it as a suggestion and ask what he thinks. You might need to try two possible solutions and monitor what happens. The important points are:

(a) to *ask* him what he thinks

(b) to *recognise his experience*

(c) *not to impose* your own solution.

Most people respond to being asked for their advice and it helps them not to see you as an arrogant newcomer.

Activity 5

You may have mentioned any of the following:

(a) *Attitudes and motivation*
     Clearly these will affect their interest in what they are being told. If they have a favourable attitude and high motivation, your task is easy but demanding, for their learning rate will be very quick. If not, you may have to think of methods to stimulate their interest and give incentives to learn.

(b) *Intelligence level*
     Again, this is likely to affect the pace of the training you give.

(c) *Vocabulary*
     This will affect the terms you can use. Any new terms will need to be clearly defined and explained.

You may have thought of other examples.

11 Internal Written Communication: Forms, Memoranda and Notices

People within organisations communicate in many different ways; we have already discussed the variety of oral interaction which takes place within teams and meetings in an attempt to meet joint objectives. There are also many written methods, the most common being the form, the memorandum and the notice. Although these are frequently used, they are often a source of frustration, resentment or communication breakdown. This may seem surprising, since they are routine and should present few problems. This is clearly not the case, so in this chapter we will consider each of these methods in turn.

THE FORM

Purpose and Uses

Forms are used in a variety of ways by any organisation, but in all cases the purpose is the same — to gather accurate and sufficient information on the basis of which informed decisions can be made.

ACTIVITY 1

(a) List the different kinds of form which are used within your organisation and which you have been required to complete.

(b) What kinds of information were they designed to collect and why?

Your lists will have varied according to your own experience. However, your attempt to answer the second question may have shown that your forms tend to fall into certain categories related to their function within the organisation. Here are the main categories with some examples under each.

(a) *Forms used as a basis for selecting and assessing personnel*

   (i)   application forms
   (ii) college report forms
   (iii) appraisal forms.

(b) *Forms used for record keeping*

   (i)   work progress forms
   (ii) laboratory report forms
   (iii) stock record forms
   (iv) record of number of visitors/clients/customers
   (v)   records of usage of facilities.

(c) *Forms used for monitoring*

   (i)   forms for placing, collecting, progressing orders
   (ii) questionnaires to potential or existing customers or clients
   (iii) petty cash forms and other forms for monitoring expenditure.

(d) *Forms used for recording critical incidents*

   (i)   accident report forms
   (ii) breakdown/fault report forms.

Importance of Accurate Design and Clear Wording

In all the above cases, it is extremely important that the design and the wording of the form are planned very carefully to elicit accurate and full information.

ACTIVITY 2

Collect a variety of forms together. Those which might be easily accessible are forms sent out by catalogue companies, forms used within your own organisation or college, forms at the post office or bank, etc.

Make a list of any aspects of design or wording that might result in inaccurate, inadequate or irrelevant information being presented.

Compare your list with ours at the end of this chapter.

The faults which you will have noted yourself and those which we have given are only too common. They result in frustration and possibly carelessness in the form-filler and in inadequate or inaccurate information for the organisation: both are unconstructive outcomes.

Importance of Presentation and Tone

There is one further aspect which deserves consideration and that is the public relations function often performed by these forms which are seen and used by the public (customers, clients, intending entrants, suppliers, etc).

Here, the presentation and clarity of layout will affect the image of the organisation itself. Therefore, the forms need to give the impression of professionalism and efficiency. The layout should be attractive and provide suitable space for entries to be made; the questions should be clear and the tone of the questions and/or instructions should be helpful and friendly, not aggressive, demanding or officious.

Remember that internally, a form produced in one part of the organisation for completion by another department, section or individual needs the same attention to presentation and layout.

Responding to Poor Design and Presentation

Clearly as a customer or client one can respond to a poor form by refusing to complete it or complaining to the organisation concerned. If one is working *for* an organisation and is faced with a form which one knows might cause:

(a) inaccurate or inadequate information to be passed on

(b) frustration or misunderstanding in those required to complete it

(c) irrelevant or superfluous information to be circulated

the situation is more difficult. It is, nevertheless, vital to take action.

ACTIVITY 3

You notice that on the appraisal form which your manager is required to fill in to assess your performance at the end of a six monthly work period, the following questions appear:

	Below average	Average	Above average
Is this employee's enthusiasm			
Is this person's honesty			

(a) What is wrong with the design and wording here?
(b) What will be the result?
(c) With whom should you raise the issue?
Please compare your answer with ours at the end of the chapter.

This activity and its answer should demonstrate the importance of good form design. It also indicates that when forms do not achieve their intended purpose, each employee has a responsibility to identify the faults and raise the issue with his or her manager or the originating department.

Forms seem deceptively simple; we hope this sub-section has demonstrated that they are an important part of the communication process and need to be well-designed to fulfil their overall purpose.

MEMORANDA

Memoranda are the most common form of internal communication used by the members of an organisation. They are usually written, typed, word-processed on pre-printed memo forms, although some organisations have already introduced the exchange of memoranda by electronic mail.

Purpose and Uses of Memoranda

Usually known as the "memo", the full name for this document is memorandum; as its name suggests its prime purpose is to act as a reminder to take action. Today, the memo is used to fulfil a number of functions beyond this. It can be used for any of the purposes shown in the answer to Activity 1 in Chapter 5 for communicating up and down the lines of command or communicating between departments and sections.

Problems of Memo Writing

The first and most important problem is that we cannot see the reaction of the receiver — or hear it! We may have used the wrong words or the wrong tone and the reaction may well be that our memo ends up in the pending tray indefinitely or screwed up in the waste paper basket.

(a) *Avoiding common faults*
It is therefore particularly important to avoid the following faults. These are:

   (i)   sending too many memos
   (ii) using an illogical sequence or structure
   (iii) using inaccurate, ambiguous or wordy language
   (iv) providing insufficient or inaccurate information
   (v)   providing superfluous or irrelevant information
   (vi) using a tactless or undiplomatic tone.

(b) *Determining when to use a memo*
Another major problem is using a memo in the wrong situation.

ACTIVITY 4

How would you feel if you received only a memo in the following circumstances?

(a)   You have put in a considerable amount of effort in recent weeks, including extra hours, to help your department develop a new service/project/procedure. Your superior sends you a formally worded memo expressing gratitude.

(b)   New methods of work are being introduced within your section, involving complicated new procedures. You receive a two page memo from your superior explaining these.

(c)   Your top management announce that they are closing down your section of the organisation by a circular memo to all staff.

Jot down your likely reactions before reading on.

Clearly each of these memos would result in an emotional reaction from staff; they are likely to be annoyed, resentful and upset that someone has not taken the time and effort to speak to them personally. Although the memo may eventually confirm the discussion about the above matters and would be acceptable in that context, most people would prefer face-to-face contact first.

(a)   We like to hear good and bad news from the people concerned; we can judge sincerity from facial expression and gestures as well as words. We only respect people who have the courage to face us with an unwelcome message rather than hiding behind bits of paper.

(b)   In situations of change, we like to have explanations and be given the opportunity to ask questions or voice our fears or reservations.

Designing a Memo

Length   The memo is a concise form of communication and the most usual length is that which can be contained on an A5 sheet. These are normally three or four line messages. Usually there is also an A4 size provided within the organisation for longer messages. If a message is likely to be longer than one side of A4 it is better to choose another form of communication such as the report.

Topic   A memo should contain information relating to one topic only. Never try to combine two or more messages in a single memo. It is a false economy.

ACTIVITY 5

Before reading on, identify two reasons why it is unwise to cover more than one topic in a memo.

You may have noted the following points for not covering more than one topic per memo.

(a) People are selective in the attention they give to information and tend to prioritise it. If more than one topic is included, the reader may pay attention and respond to only one part of the memo and ignore the rest.

(b) If the memo needs to be filed and it covers several topics, this may create decision-making problems for the filing clerk or create difficulties with cross-referencing or photocopies.

Layout All the memos have a heading which provides the basic background or reference information. It is important to be conscientious about filling these in, otherwise important information is denied to the reader concerning dates, senders, topic, etc. The headings are shown in the example memo layout on page 170.

If copies are to be sent to a number of readers, a circulation list is usually attached to the memo. Occasionally, a memo may be confidential, in which case it should be put in an envelope and marked "confidential". If there are enclosures to be sent with the memo, the letters "Encs" will appear at the bottom left of the memo with an indication of the nature of the enclosures.

NB: The following do *not* appear in memos:

(a) a salutation, ie "Dear Mrs . . ."

(b) a complimentary close, ie "Yours faithfully".

Normally the writer initials (rather than signs) the memo at the end. There is an example memo layout on page 170 which shows all these aspects.

Sequencing A memo, like any other written communication, should present information in a sequence that is easy and logical for the reader. There should be:

(a) An introductory sentence or paragraph stating the purpose of the memo. This enables the reader to focus his or her attention on the topic.

(b) The main points or facts set out in simple, direct sentences in numbered points whenever possible. Longer memos should be set out in clear, subheaded paragraphs, each paragraph dealing with a specific aspect of the topic.

(c) A concluding sentence or paragraph identifying what the reader needs to do about the information and by when.

Example of memo layout

```
            Name of organisation

                  MEMORANDUM

FROM:  (name and position)         DATE:   (in full)

TO:    (name(s) and position(s))   REF:    (if relevant)

SUBJECT:   (topic heading)

Introductory sentence giving purpose, background information.

   1.  Numbered points giving information required.
   2.
   3.


Concluding sentence defining action required of receiver.

                              (initials of sender)
```

Choosing a Style

While good layout is one important element in enabling the reader to understand and act on the message, another factor is style. Style covers the use of sentence construction, vocabulary and tone; one needs to adapt the style of a memo according to each new situation. The factors which influence style are shown in the table below.

Factors determining the style to be used in memo writing

Receivers	Are they	— superiors
		— subordinates
		— people on same level of authority
		— people in other parts of the organisation?
Message	Is it	— information giving
		— information seeking
		— persuading
		— reprimanding
		— praising?

Immediate situation	Is it	— routine
		— crisis
		— positive
		— negative?
Organisational style	Does it encourage	— formality
		— informality
		— autocratic style
		— democratic style?
Action needed	Is it	— simple
		— complicated
		— routine
		— new
		— critical?

Selecting the appropriate style can produce a positive response. An inappropriate style can produce an unwelcome reaction!

ACTIVITY 6

Using the list shown above, consider the following content and style of a memo sent by electronic mail. (NB the headings have been omitted.)

> Thanks for the info. on CL17. What about meeting over a drink to talk about the problems? Say 7.00 at the "Pheasant" tomorrow — OK?
>
> KL

In what circumstances do you think this style of memo would be inappropriate?

Check your response with ours at the end of the chapter.

NOTICES

Notices, like memos, suffer from the limitations of being a one way method of communication — the sender has no idea whether the notice has remained unread, or the message has been ignored, or whether it has aroused resentment which was not foreseen. Therefore, it is necessary to take care with the composition, layout and position of notices.

Functions of the Notice

Notices should only be used:

(a) When there is a need for mass communication *and* where the message it contains is either important to everyone in the organisation (as in the case of safety) or is a matter of selective interest only (for example, advertising a social event) which people will either want to read or not.

(b) When the message lends itself to visual display techniques. (Yellowing notices of closely typed information which have remained unread for months are only too common.)

Notices should not be used where the message is specific to a small number of identifiable people and/or is sufficiently vital to require everyone who is concerned to read and act on the information.

There are some documents which are displayed on notice-boards which are not strictly notices at all. They are reference documents which have been sent to everyone but need to be displayed as well, eg lists of extension numbers, organisation charts or travel allowances. These, although they need to be displayed, are not covered by the principles discussed below.

Composition of the Notice

Basic principles are more often neglected in notices than in other methods of communication. Because they are brief, they are also often abrupt, if not arrogant and can therefore arouse reactions which range from indifference to anger.

ACTIVITY 7

Consider the following:

JUNIOR PERSONNEL MUST NOT PARK THEIR VEHICLES IN THE PARKING BAYS MARKED A–F

Signed: . . . .

(a) What is wrong with the above notice and what behaviour might result from those reading it?

See if your reaction is the same as ours, which is given at the end of the chapter.

(b) Think of a legitimate reason for the basic message and then recompose the notice.

We have given a possible version at the end of the chapter.

Displaying the Notice

Location of the notice   Notices should be located either in direct proximity to where they are relevant, eg "Please switch off the lights" above the light switch, or in a well-lit central position which everyone passes daily and where they have time to linger, eg next to the coffee machine, in the cloakroom, by their lockers.

Initial attraction   Because a notice may remain unread unless it attracts attention, it is important to employ all the techniques possible to draw attention to it. This may be through wording, eg one desperate person composed his notice as follows:

SEX!

Now I've attracted your attention
I have the following car for sale . . .

It is not, of course, advisable on a formal notice-board to go to this extreme but the message should be clear.

Other methods of attracting attention include:

(a)   provision of a clear heading

(b)   size of notice and of the lettering

(c)   a first phrase which acts as a stimulus

(d)   coloured paper and/or use of coloured pens

(e)   signalling techniques such as underlining, capital letters

(f)   use of space around words or illustrations

(g)   an overall polished, professional appearance.

Remember that some messages lend themselves to pictorial devices — health and safety notices designed to shock, themes for social events. Others are relatively formal and must appear in a fairly conventional, if somewhat boring format.

Since the latter are often composed by higher management, and are therefore important, it is sensible to read them — however boring they are!

OTHER FORMS OF VISUAL DISPLAY AT WORK

There are a number of other forms of visual display which are employed within a work organisation. Many of these were mentioned in Chapter 4 (eg planning charts, statistical graphs and charts, diagrams, etc). Often these are on display within the organisation — on office walls, notice-boards, etc and therefore the same attention to composition and design needs to be considered.

CONCLUSION

As this chapter has shown, there are several methods which are available for communicating between people within the workplace. The major principle involved is to choose carefully which method is appropriate in the light of:

(a) what is to be conveyed

(b) why the message is needed

(c) to whom it is addressed.

Choosing should be a conscious and careful process. These routine methods of communication should never be treated lightly if they are to be effective and are to gain the required response.

ANSWERS TO ACTIVITIES IN CHAPTER 11

Activity 2

The usual faults associated with forms are:

(a) lack of space to give adequate information

(b) irrelevant questions to the purpose of the form leading to the circulation of pointless information

(c) ambiguous, misleading or unclear questions

(d) instructions which confuse the person filling in the form, thus leading to inaccurate information.

You may have found more than this in your collection, of course!

Activity 3

(a) It is very difficult, if not impossible, to assess "average" enthusiasm or honesty. These qualities are not quantifiable and therefore cannot be assessed in this way. A person is either honest or dishonest.

(b) The result is that meaningless information will be forwarded or that the person filling in the form will give up! He or she may leave this section blank, or worse, put a random tick.

(c) You should raise the matter with your manager and/or the personnel department since the form was probably designed or issued there.

Activity 6

This style of memo would be inappropriate if:

(a) the organisation in which you worked favoured a more formal style

(b) you were making assumptions about the level of familiarity between yourself and the receiver

(c) there was any possibility that the receiver was unfamiliar with "CL17" or might not know which public house you were referring to.

Activity 7

(a)   The notice shows very little understanding of human reaction; it certainly does not give any attention to the important communication objective: obtaining a favourable response. You might have noted the following points:

   (i)   The notice begins by discriminating against a particular group of employees and is thus liable to produce a rebellious response — "Why us?". Some will probably try parking in these bays to see what happens.

   (ii)   It is a direct order which is abrupt and very autocratic; nobody responds well to this approach.

   (iii)   As the notice gives no reason why people should not park in these bays, it poses a challenge.

The net result is that people will be compelled by a combination of curiosity and anger to have a go — not the response that is required!

(b)   An example of the reworded notice is:

SHORT-TERM CAR PARKING SPACES

The bays marked A–F have been reserved for short-term visitors from Head Office and other branches. They may also be used by specific members of this branch who are required to travel on company business daily and have been issued with CREAM PERMITS to display on their windscreens.

Other staff are therefore requested to leave these spaces free.

12 Report Writing: The Need for Clear, Accurate Reports

One of the most important documents which one may be required to produce is a report. Although some reports are simple and routine, others are quite complex. Whatever the type of report, however, it needs to be:

(a) *clear and accurate* — so that the correct information is provided for those who need it to make decisions

(b) *as concise as possible* — to ensure that it is read and the contents easily digested

(c) *complete* — to ensure that it contains all the facts that the reader needs.

The balance between being concise but complete is actually quite difficult to achieve and there has been considerable criticism of report writing standards from employers who are either faced with long, rambling accounts from which it is difficult to extract the relevant facts or brief general statements with no detail or justification.

In the early stages of their careers people will probably only be involved in oral reporting or in completing short routine report forms. However, as anyone's career develops, report writing is likely to become an increasingly frequent activity and therefore everyone needs to have the necessary skills.

ACTIVITY 1

Consider the following questions for a few minutes.

(a) What kind of reports have you read to date?
(b) What were their purposes?
(c) For whom were they written?
(d) How were they laid out?
(e) How successful were they in conveying information to the reader quickly and easily?

We will be covering all these topics within this chapter.

PURPOSE AND FUNCTIONS OF REPORTS

We need to be clear on two points:

(a)   what a report is

(b)   what it is intended to achieve.

Definition

A report is a document which conveys facts and ideas on a given subject for a specific purpose so that an informed decision can be made.

Often it will contain an evaluation of the facts and sometimes, but not always, it will give recommendations which advise action. Reports are therefore an important communication method which can assist or impair the management process.

Purposes of Reports

There are many types of report and their purposes may differ slightly according to the nature of the work they concern. Generally, reports will fulfil any of the following purposes:

(a)   provide accurate, complete and concise information for effective decision-making

(b)   analyse and/or evaluate the results of work or research

(c)   inform others of a problem, situation or development

(d)   provide an accurate record of a sequence of events or the stages of an investigation

(e)   indicate the likely effects of a proposed course of action

(f)   influence or persuade others of the advisability of a course of action.

The first purpose listed is common to *all* reports and must be kept firmly in mind by the writer if his or her report is to be effective.

In order to achieve any of these purposes, as a writer of a report one must be very clear about a number of points before even considering writing. It is necessary to ask and secure firm answers to the following questions.

(a)   *What is the objective?*
      Is it for information only or to persuade someone to take a course of action?

(b) *Why is it required?*

     (i) How is the report going to be used?

     (ii) Is it to be used by a superior only or for other people to refer to in discussion meetings?

     (iii) Is it for circulation to a number of departments, organisations or to be published for the general public?

(c) *Who will read it?*

     (i) How many people will be reading it?

     (ii) Will their interests and objectives in reading it be the same or different?

     (iii) What is their likely level of familiarity with the subject, content and terminology?

The answers to these questions should decide:

(a) what material needs to be included

(b) what research methods are needed to secure the facts

(c) in what order it is best arranged to meet the interest of the reader(s) and promote their understanding

(d) what methods are best used to convey information quickly, easily and effectively

(e) what language should be chosen for the reader(s) to ensure their comprehension and a favourable response.

It is useful to go through this checklist of questions before beginning and keep the answers visible to ensure one remains "on track".

A further question affecting the structure and content is: *What type of report is required?*

TYPES OF REPORT

There are two main categories of report; their characteristics and the problems associated with them are given below. First there are routine reports which:

(a) are produced frequently or regularly

(b) give specific information

(c) are either presented on a pre-designed form or on a memo form.

Examples of routine reports are: accident reports, performance appraisal reports, progress reports, up-date reports and work completion reports. The problems with these reports often stem from the design of the forms which may encourage inadequate or inaccurate information. In memo form reports, the main problems are likely to occur in structuring the information to achieve a logical sequence.

The second category of reports is special reports which:

(a) are produced in response to a specific situation

(b) usually conform to a basic structure but the sequence or presentation will vary according to the material, circumstances and situation.

Examples of special reports are: project reports, sales reports, financial reports, test results reports, investigatory/feasibility studies, meeting or conference reports and market surveys. The main problems with special reports are poor structuring of information, poor layout of information, incomplete information, verbosity, use of jargon and inappropriate style.

We will now look at each category in greater detail.

Routine Reports

Routine reports on forms   The first reports which anyone may be required to prepare will probably be of this type. Some of these may have occurred in answer to Activity 1 (an accident report form at work, for the police or for an insurance company). On these forms, it is often a legal requirement that specific information is presented briefly and accurately.

These reports should be relatively easy to prepare because the form itself indicates what information should be provided. However well the form is designed to obtain the information needed, the usefulness of what it contains will depend on the effort, ability and systematic approach of the person compiling the report. The report writer must give accurate and complete information directly relevant to the form's purpose, intended use and readership.

One type of routine report form one may be required to complete soon after joining an organisation is the employee's part of the appraisal report. Many companies now incorporate the appraisee's assessment as part of the performance review. An example of such a form is given on pages 181–3.

Routine reports on memorandum forms   These are usually prepared for a superior or for colleagues who are familiar with the situation/type of information/work/project/subject matter but who need up-dating on any new facts or data which require their attention. An example is shown on page 184.

Common faults to avoid when producing these types of report are:

APPRAISAL
EMPLOYEE PREPARATION FORM

This form is optional and may help you to:

    A. identify your current job strengths and needs

    B. consider your career interests

    C. express your development needs.

This is a guide to help you prepare for a useful discussion during your interview. You do not need to complete it unless you want to or adhere to it during the interview, or show it to your manager. After the interview you may keep this form or ask for it to be kept with your Employee Development Plan.

A.   YOUR CURRENT JOB STRENGTHS AND NEEDS

1. Which aspects of your present job give you greatest satisfaction?

2. Are there additional skills developed elsewhere which give you satisfaction, but which are not used in your job?

3. In which job objectives have you done well? Why?

4. Which job objectives have you found the most difficult? Why?

5. Under what conditions do you work most effectively (deadlines, type of manager, working alone or with others, etc)?

6. What are your key job skills and areas of strength?

7. What skills or knowledge do you feel you lack?

B. YOUR CAREER INTERESTS

1. What is your main career interest?

2. What are some alternative career interests?

3. What work areas or activities do you think would lead to these?

4. In what work areas do you believe your next job could possibly be in the next two to three years?

C. YOUR DEVELOPMENT NEEDS

Look over what you have said about yourself. Now, consider what actions and commitments may be necessary on your part.

1. What are your main development needs?

2. Has the lack of any skill or knowledge limited your progress in your job or career? If so, how can you overcome this limitation?

3. What actions could be planned to meet these development needs?

4. What additional education, training or experience do you need?

5. Are there any other considerations you need to take into account to achieve these plans? (Mobility, personal aspects, etc.)

6. Is there any more information you need to make a realistic plan — from your manager or anyone else?

Any other comments

(a) producing overlong, verbose reports which are consequently "skimmed" and not read

(b) producing poorly constructed reports which are difficult to follow

(c) producing reports which are too brief and only give bare facts

(d) assuming that such reports do not need to be itemised and/or provided with subheadings.

Effective brief routine reports, apart from fulfilling the initial checklist of questions on purpose and readership, should be arranged logically as indicated below. The report should include:

(a) appropriate headings with correctly recorded reference date, to, from, subject, reference number (if appropriate)

(b) an introductory sentence setting the report in context — subject, purpose, reference to request for report if necessary

Example of a brief information report on a memo form

Worthingtons
plc

MEMORANDUM

FROM: Mrs K E Bates
        Training Officer

TO: Mr L S Harvey
        Administration Services Manager

DATE: 11 May 19–

SUBJECT: Training courses in report writing

In answer to your request of 5 May 19–, I have enquired about short courses in the local area which might be suitable for your staff.

1. Courses available

    1.1 Oakhampton College of Further Education provide a 2 day course on an on-going basis. The dates for the next two are Tuesday/Wednesday 8/9 June and Thursday/Friday 20/21 July. Cost is £60 per delegate.

    1.2 The Training Society will run a 2 day course in-house on a date to be arranged by us for £70 per delegate.

2. Additional information

    2.1 Many staff are on holiday in June/July.

    2.2 Public transport to and from the college is frequent.

    2.3 The committee room could be made available for training and we have some training resources such as overhead projectors, flips charts.

My own conclusion is that the Training Society may be a more convenient option, but the final decision will rest on which of your staff need this course and when they can attend. I would be glad if you could ring me by the end of the week to discuss the final arrangements.

KEB

(c) itemised facts, with any reasons and commentary briefly stated. These should be numbered and, if necessary, given an underlined topic sub-heading

(d) a concluding sentence, either emphasising any important or priority point and/or stating any action or the next stage now required.

Special Reports

Special reports are those which respond to the needs of a specific situation which may be "one-off". For this reason, no form exists as a guide, although there are some main subdivisions into which such reports are normally ordered. For this kind of report, we will provide more detailed guidance on preparation, planning layout and style.

Although such reports are prepared for a variety of reasons and may fulfil different objectives, for the purposes of planning and structure they fall into two distinct groups:

(a) the information report

(b) the investigation report.

The *information report* is produced to inform others of a situation, event, procedure, policy or set of data. It is really a brief subheaded summary of the material which needs to be communicated.

This type of report may be used to provide information on a number of subjects, for example:

(a) a report for the training manager on arrangements for the training of counter staff in customer care within a chain of fast food restaurants

(b) a report for the recreation officer on the usage of specific facilities within a leisure centre

(c) a report for the head of a laboratory on an outline of research which has been conducted

(d) a report for a manager on population/market trends which may affect demand for a product or service.

The *investigation report* records the investigation of a problem or presents a proposal for change. It usually requires some recommendations which advise on future actions for the consideration of those who requested the report. One might be asked to produce such a report for a number of reasons, for example:

(a) making proposals on how work within a section could be re-organised to be more profitable or efficient

(b) proposing changes to the layout of an office, area within a leisure facility, section of a country park, kitchens or restaurant, workshop

(c) investigating a particular problem, eg an outbreak of petty pilfering or low morale within a work section or a series of complaints from customers or clients.

The layout and structure of both information and investigation reports are very similar, although there are minor differences which will be discussed later. The presentation and planning stages follow the same principles.

Preparation of special reports

ACTIVITY 2

The organisation for which you work is to consider introducing flexi-time working. Assuming that you have been asked to help with this report, what information would you need and what methods would you use to collect it?

Our suggestions appear at the end of the chapter.

The answers given to this activity include two types of information gathering from two sources. These sources are:

(a) *primary sources* — direct observation, interviews, discussions, experiments, etc — where the researcher is directly involved and where the material has never previously been collected

(b) *secondary sources* — other reports, articles, published results, reference books, files, periodicals, etc — where the researcher can refer to information collected previously.

Whenever there is a report to prepare, it is worth jotting down a list of all the available sources and brainstorming all the methods by which one could gather the required information. Inevitably, it will then be necessary to eliminate some of these; there may be sources which are:

(a) unavailable or

(b) impracticable in terms of the time constraints of the report, cost or accessibility of the information.

Finally, one should arrive at a list of those sources and methods which can and should be used. Remember, always check secondary sources first. Desk research amongst published material may save time and effort in covering the same ground by primary methods.

Planning special reports   The planning stage involves three processes:

(a)   Selecting the material in order to meet the writer's objectives, those of the reader(s) and the level of his or her knowledge, understanding and interest. The selection must be based on what the reader needs, ie what is relevant. It is not a matter of presenting the reader with every detail and allowing him or her to pick out what is relevant.

(b)   Grouping related facts and ideas together.

(c)   Arranging these sections of information into an ordered sequence which is logical and understandable to the reader.

Here again, a quick checklist of questions can help to achieve effective results. Try asking yourself the following questions at the planning stage:

(a)   *Now that I have gathered all the information, is there some which is irrelevant to the purpose of the report and to the readers' objectives?*

If the answer is yes, ruthlessly reject such material; this is a difficult task, particularly as we all become committed to our own knowledge.

(b)   *Of the remaining facts and ideas, which relate to one another and can thus be grouped together?*
Sometimes it is helpful to draw a "mind map" to show relationships — we introduced this concept in Chapter 3. An example of a mind map representing some facts relating to the introduction of flexi-time working is given on page 188. Lines and arrows are used to show relationships between points.

(c)   *What subheadings are most helpful to summarise the groups of related facts and to act as a clear guide to the reader?*
Remember that a reader may wish to refer to only one subsection — if the report is to be discussed at a meeting for example.

ACTIVITY 3

Can you think of some useful subheadings under which the points linked in the mind map on flexi-time could be helpfully grouped?

Our suggestions appear at the end of the chapter.

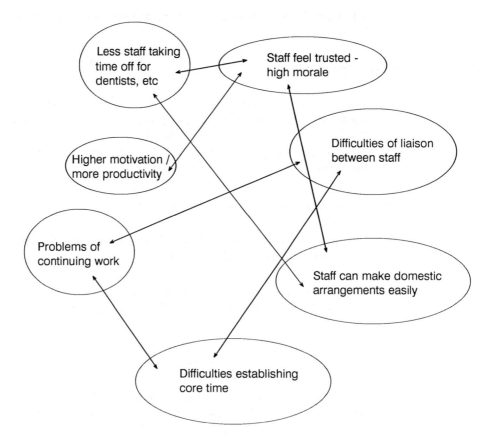

Mind map to prepare for a report on flexi-time

(d) *What sequence of information will be most logical for the reader?*
It is a common mistake for the writers of reports to present the information in a sequence more understandable to them than to the reader. It is vital to respond to the readers' needs rather than one's own.

(e) *Have I checked that I have included everything that the reader needs to know?*
Reports form the basis of decisions; ensure that all the facts and ideas needed to make them are present.

Structure and layout The structure and layout of information reports and investigation reports are similar but there are one or two minor differences. There are also some extra sections which can be added to both kinds of report if they are lengthy. These additions may be appropriate in a project, for example.

(a) *Title*
It is important to aim for clarity and precision in the title to a report rather than brevity. The title is intended to *focus the attention* of the reader. Often the title

of a report will appear on a title page, together with the name(s) of the report writer(s), the name(s) of the person(s) for whom it is intended and the date.

(b) *Contents page*
This is useful in a longer report or project so that page references are given to the main sections and subheadings of the report. Long reports would include page references for illustrations and/or appendices here too.

(c) *Introductory section*
This may differ slightly according to the house style preferred by the organisation or the nature of the report. It usually includes:

  (i)   the purpose, subject and scope of the report;
  (ii) any background information needed by the reader to understand the context of the report.

The alternative layouts are given below for information and investigation reports.

Layout of introductory section for information and investigation reports

Information report	**Investigation report**
Purpose and subject: a statement of these, together with the name/positions of the person(s) compiling and requesting the report and the date for submission.	*Terms of reference*: giving purpose, scope and any limitations imposed by time/cost constraints or availability of the information. This sometimes also gives name/positions of person(s) compiling and requesting the report and the date for submission
Background to the occasion, event, situation or set of data to be presented with any necessary definitions.	*Background* to the problem, situation to be investigated or to the change proposed; reasons why the investigation is taking place.
Sources of information listing any source documents used and any other ways in which the report writer obtained information, eg dates/locations of visits, etc.	*Methods of investigation* listing all the methods used for the investigation, both primary and secondary.

(d) *Main body of the report*
This may be headed "Analysis of information" or sometimes, in the case of an investigation report "Findings". It may not have any main heading at all but

189

simply proceed with the subheadings which the writer has decided give the best shape and sequence to the material.

As this section will be the longest and most complex, setting out the facts and ideas in detail, it is essential that there are clear and appropriate subheadings to guide the reader and that these should appear in a logical order. It is also important that all headings, subheadings and points should be numbered and that the numbering should be clear and consistent.

(e) *Conclusion*

A conclusion summarises the important or priority points for attention briefly and may evaluate the material previously discussed. It is important that no new material appears here.

An information report will finish with this section, so the conclusion is important to remind the reader of the major facts or ideas which should now be considered.

(f) *Recommendations*

These only appear at the end of an investigation report. They should emerge clearly from the findings and conclusions and give specific actions which should now be carried out to effect the change or solve the problem investigated. They are advisory for the person(s) who requested the report and therefore should state such actions clearly.

(g) *Appendix*

This usually contains any graphs, tables of figures, diagrams, illustrations, maps, etc which relate to the subject matter of the report as a whole and which would interrupt the sequence of the main report by distracting the reader's attention. These items appear at the end of the report and must be referred to in the text, eg see Appendix A.

ACTIVITY 4

Can you think of any instance where the kind of material which we have stated usually appears in an appendix would be better included in the main body of the report itself? Give some thought to this before reading on.

You may have thought of a report where a particular diagram is used as an essential part of the text to explain a process or layout and where one or two paragraphs refer closely to it. In this case, it may be better for the reader if it appears opposite the relevant explanation rather than at the end. The main deciding factor is the ease with which the reader can understand the information.

(h) *Bibliography and list of acknowledgements*
These usually appear at the end of reports, especially those which are lengthy and/or have been the subject of extensive research. The bibliography lists the published sources, with all relevant details such as publisher, date of publication, etc. The acknowledgements should list all the people who have been consulted.

(i) *Synopsis or summary*
This usually appears at the beginning of a long report or project in order to summarise briefly

  (i)   the outline of the report
  (ii) the methods used
  (iii) the main conclusions and recommendations.

It exists to guide the readers and, again, is very useful where there are a number of readers with differing levels of interest and needs. Synopses are therefore frequently found attached to reports for committees or members of boards.

(j) *Numbering*
One last requirement in the layout and structure of reports is for clear numbering. There are several systems which might be used; probably the most common is the decimal system, as shown below.

  1. Main subheading
      1.1 Subheading
      1.2 Subheading
      1.3 Subheading
           1.3.1 First subdivision under subheading
           1.3.2 Second subdivision under subheading

In contrast, there are systems which alternate different types of numbers and letters. For example:

  A. Main subheading
      1. Subheading
      2. Subheading
      3. Subheading
          (a) First subdivision under subheading
          (b) Second subdivision under subheading

With the decimal system, if there are a number of subdivisions under a subheading, the conglomeration of digits becomes rather confusing. Equally, with the alternating system, it could become difficult to follow. Therefore it is useful to keep the subdivisions down to a minimum. Occasionally the two systems are integrated, if it helps clarity, eg

1. Main subheading
    1.1
    1.2
    1.3
        (a)
        (b)

Every organisation has a preferred numbering system. Whatever system is used, the important principle of numbering is that it is consistent and easy to follow.

Finally, all reports should be signed and dated.

As we have already given an example of an information report on a memo form (see page 184), we will end this section on special reports by giving an example of an investigation report (see pages 193 and 194) which builds on the work completed in Activity 3.

When you have finally prepared your draft report, remember to revise — go back to your original checklist and make absolutely sure that:

(a) everything is included which is needed

(b) the language is understandable to the reader

(c) the sequence and numbering are logical.

Even then the report may not be finished. It is possible that the writer of the report may be required to be present at a meeting which discusses the written report and that he or she may have to give a brief oral presentation of its subject matter. So, before the end of this chapter on report writing, it is worth giving some space to the techniques of presenting a report.

ORAL PRESENTATION OF REPORTS

The most common mistake made by report writers required to present their reports orally is simply to read the report.

ACTIVITY 6

(a) Why do you think this is a mistake?
(b) What should be some of the differences between a written report and its oral presentation?

Think about these questions before reading on.

Example of investigation report (short)

The feasibility of introducing flexi-time to the clerical and administrative staff at Worthingtons plc

1. TERMS OF REFERENCE

   The Personnel Manager requested the Administrative Manager to investigate the possibilities of introducing flexi-time to the staff within the Administration Department. A report was to be forwarded not later than 10 May 19. ., so that it could be discussed at the quarterly Heads of Departments' Meeting.

2. METHODS OF INVESTIGATION

   The following methods were used.

   2.1 A range of published material on flexi-time was read including published articles concerning similar organisations and equivalent members of staff.

   2.2 A cross-section of staff within the Administration Department was interviewed to find out their views.

   2.3 The Information Services Manager at Lows Ltd and the Management Services Manager at Marchants plc were visited to see their flexi-time system in operation.

3. ANALYSIS OF INFORMATION

   3.1 Advantages for management

   The following advantages were noted:

   — Less time was taken off by staff for essential appointments.

   — There was greater motivation amongst the staff leading to higher productivity.

   These advantages were found in both companies already operating flexi-time.

   3.2 Disadvantages for management

   There was an initial difficulty in establishing a suitable core time and some early problems in controlling work flow. These were usually overcome within the first few weeks of the system being introduced.

   3.3 Advantages for staff

   All the staff interviewed mentioned that:

    — they would be able to organise domestic arrangements more freely which would lead to less stress;

    — they would have freedom to control when they arrived and departed and this would help with transport and punctuality;

    — they would enjoy the sense of trust and responsibility.

3.4 Disadvantages for staff

Some staff expressed concern that liaison both within the department and with other departments might be more difficult. They stipulated that a clear and adequate core time must be established.

4. CONCLUSIONS

4.1 The advantages for both staff and management appear to outweigh the disadvantages; motivation and productivity would both be increased.

4.2 There is a need to establish sufficient core time and to develop clear procedures for control and liaison.

5. RECOMMENDATIONS

The following recommendations are made:

5.1 Flexi-time should be introduced within the Administration Department and given a trial period of three months.

5.2 Consultation should now take place between the Personnel Manager and the Administration Department about the most appropriate core time and control/liaison procedures.

5.3 The system introduced should be subject to careful briefing and close monitoring during the three month period.

5.4 The final decision concerning whether to retain the system and, if so whether to make any modifications, should be made at the end of the three month trial period.

Signed:
Dated:

Merely to read a report to a group of people who already have a copy in front of them is a waste of time and boring. Oral presenting is an opportunity to summarise and emphasise those aspects which are most important to all concerned. Simply reading a report also encourages all the worst personal presentation faults: ie head down, voice muffled and a lack of eye contact.

The differences between a written report and its oral presentation are that:

(a) the language will be different

(b) other presentation methods can be used to help understanding — overhead projector with viewfoils, slides, extracts from videos, board displays, models, etc.

Preparing an Oral Report

A review of Chapter 2 on Effective Self-Presentation will help here, but here is some of that information summarised in a checklist.

WHO?: the audience

▶ Who will be listening to me?

▶ How many are there?

▶ What are their objectives, knowledge, background, interests?

WHAT?: the objectives

▶ What is the response I want from them?

▶ How might I achieve this?

▶ What is the best approach and language?

HOW LONG?: the schedule

▶ How long is there before the presentation for preparation?

▶ How long will each stage of the planning take (preparation of visual aids, rehears-ing, etc)?

▶ How long is the presentation itself to be?

WHERE?: the location

▶ Where is the presentation to take place?

▶ What is the size of the room?

▶ What are the seating arrangements?

▶ What facilities does the room have?

▶ What equipment and materials can be used there?

▶ What are the acoustics like?

▶ What will be the speaker's position in relation to the audience?

WHICH?: the methods and language

In the light of all the above:

▶ Which methods of presentation should be chosen?

▶ Which words are best to achieve understanding and show enthusiasm?

HOW MUCH?: selecting the important points

This will be dependent on the previous answers but remember to:

▶ keep notes to a minimum

▶ highlight points which will need to be referred to in the report.

Above all, *rehearse*. Use a tape or a friendly colleague to check timing and structure. Check the equipment in advance; not only whether it is in working order but also whether it will be really effective.

Delivering an Oral Report

The structure of the presentation should be logical and should therefore include:

(a) an introduction which states what the report is about, why it has been pro- duced, what methods are going to be used to present it and how long the presentation will be. This is a briefing for the audience. It states the *purpose* of the presentation.

(b) A clearly structured discussion of the main points and facts with appropriate illustrations where relevant. For investigation reports, this will often involve identifying:

    (i) the *current position* that exists

        (ii)   the *problems* involved in the current situation

        (iii) the *possible alternatives* for resolving the problems that were investigated.

(c)   A conclusion, giving an outline of the conclusions and recommendations contained within the report. For an investigation report, this part of the presentation involves stating the *proposals*.

Of course, all the points mentioned in Chapter 2 concerning personal delivery should be followed.

CONCLUSION

We hope that this chapter has clarified the importance of reports to accurate recording and informed decision-making. There are many kinds of report but they share these common objectives. In addition, they all need to respond to similar principles.

ANSWERS TO ACTIVITIES IN CHAPTER 12

Activity 2

Information needed	*Research methods*
Types of flexi-time systems	— books and articles on different systems
Staff views	— questionnaire
	— interviews
The degree to which the system has been workable in similar organisations	— published material from other organisations or in periodicals
	— interviews with relevant personnel in similar organisations which have tried the system.

Activity 3

Suggested sub-headings might be:

1. *Advantages for staff*

    — staff feel trusted — higher morale

    — staff can make domestic arrangements more easily.

2. *Advantages for management*

    — more productivity

    — fewer staff taking time off.

3. *Disadvantages for staff*

    — problems of liaison.

4. *Disadvantages for management*

    — difficulty of controlling work

    — difficulty of establishing core time.

SECTION 3: INTERPERSONAL SKILLS WITH EXTERNAL CONTACTS

INTRODUCTION

This section will be devoted to developing your skills as an "ambassador" of your organisation. Many of you will be employed in roles that will bring you into contact with those outside the organisation; for some, the contact will be frequent, for others, it will be occasional. These contacts may be:

(a) customers or clients

(b) members of the public

(c) salespeople or buyers from other organisations

(d) prospective employees

(e) fellow professionals or experts from similar organisations

(f) representatives from external regulatory or advisory bodies

(g) representatives from the press, radio or television

(h) members of central or local government.

Your contact may be by letter, by telephone, in one-to-one discussions or in group meetings. It may be on your own territory, their territory or at a neutral location. You may have to relate to people who are friendly and helpful or aggressive and obstructive.

Whoever you encounter outside your organisation, they will be judging your organisation, in part, from the impression you convey. If you, as the ambassador, handle the encounter well, they are likely to develop confidence in your organisation as being efficient and well-organised. If you show yourself to be ill-informed or ill-prepared with poor personal presentation, they are likely to judge your organisation as ineffective.

In order to develop the right approach you will need to draw on all the skills mentioned in Section 1 and be able to apply them to:

(a) developing an appropriate approach and image

(b) writing effective letters

(c) handling face-to-face encounters assertively

(d) developing good telephone techniques

(e) dealing with problems, complaints and difficult people

(f) handling the media — the press and television

(g) being effective at negotiating.

Section 3 contains chapters on each of these topics.

13 Projecting the Right Image

Whatever your specialism, you will be employed by an organisation that is in business to achieve certain objectives. These may include making a profit, being cost effective, providing a quality service, etc. It cannot achieve these objectives without fulfilling the needs and demands of the people outside the organisation who may:

(a)   use the product or service — customers or clients

(b)   regulate the conditions under which production takes place or control quality standards — eg factory inspectors, environmental health officers, and a range of regulatory boards

(c)   live in the surrounding area of the organisation — local residents

(d)   be affected by the provision or sale of the product or service — eg competitors, members of the public

(e)   provide components or information or ideas for the organisation — eg suppliers, sub-contractors, research institutes, consultants

(f)   act as intermediaries between the organisation and its customers or clients — eg agents, brokers, distributors.

All these groups can influence the success or failure of an organisation and it is necessary for an organisation to maintain the right kind of image with them.

RESPONSIBILITY FOR GOOD PUBLIC RELATIONS

When referring to public relations, it is useful to think of the "public" as all those external groups which may have an interest in the organisation and with which it must maintain a good relationship.

The Role of the Public Relations Specialist

It is tempting to think that public relations is the concern of a specialist individual or function within the organisation, ie the publicity officer or the public relations department; to a certain extent this is true. If a department has this function, its responsibility will be to ensure that the organisation maintains a high and reputable profile in the market place and in the national and local media, etc.

Individual Responsibility for Good Relationships

However, today, organisations have recognised that a good image is not just the responsibility of one specialist section — it is the responsibility of every employee — the scientist, engineer, administrator and caterer. When an outsider has contact with an organisation, anything can condition his or her experiences and reactions. As a member of an organisation one needs to consider one's own external contacts and how important the impressions made by those contacts may be to an employer.

ACTIVITY 1

With whom do you come into contact outside the organisation in your particular role (either as an employee or as a student)? What is the importance of each contact for the *organisation*? Make a list under these two headings:

Outside contact   *Importance to organisation*

Make your list before reading on.

You will find your answers show that people outside the organisation possess power which they can use for or against the organisation. That power may be used negatively if their impressions of you or the organisation are bad, eg by refusing to enter a contract with you, refusing permission to allow a particular process or activity to go ahead, refusing finance for projects, etc. If you are a student, you may be able to think of an occasion when a poor image projected by your college has affected its activities. For example, in one college, the right to hold a "rag" was taken away when student behaviour alienated the local community.

Progressive organisations have recognised the importance of each contact made by an employee and have embarked on courses of internal training which promote the importance of total quality and customer care throughout the company. The emphasis has been placed on care of the customer because this is the outside group that ultimately determines the success of the organisation. However, remember that every contact is in some respects a customer for your organisation.

TOTAL QUALITY AND CUSTOMER CARE

To understand what we mean by this concept, try the exercise on page 205.

ACTIVITY 2

Think back to a time when you required service yourself, ie a service on your car, a visit to a restaurant, a request from a government department.

1. Did the service giver find out fully about requirements? If not, how did this affect your impression of that person and the organisation?
2. What kind of expectation did you have in relation to the quality of the service?

Think about this before reading on.

When we are on the receiving end, we expect the person giving the service to check our requirements fully before attending to our needs. Contacts outside the organisation expect the same consideration. They want to know what is on offer, where they stand in relation to the organisation, so that they can clearly understand whether they should be transacting business with the organisation or not.

Other expectations one might have had in terms of quality in the situation above (Activity 2) are that:

(a) on the initial contact, someone attends to your requirements promptly

(b) the person appears interested and enthusiastic about providing the service

(c) the price is kept within the quotation or estimate given

(d) any agreed timescales are maintained

(e) any person you meet from that company knows about your needs, can deal with enquiries and is polite and helpful

(f) any documentation received from the company is clear and accurate

(g) if further appointments are required, they keep those appointments and are punctual

(h) the service satisfies your needs.

You may have other expectations to add.

In many ways your own contacts are expecting the same. What most people want from their dealings with a business organisation is a good, reliable product or service, provided by staff who seem to care about their needs. Therefore your most important objectives when dealing with people outside the organisation are to give a quality service and customer satisfaction.

The Individual's Role in Providing a Quality Product or Service

Some job roles are directly related to producing a product or delivering a service and therefore have a major impact on their quality. Other functions within an organisation may have a more indirect relationship with the production or delivery of the product or service.

ACTIVITY 3

Which of the following occupations would you say have

(a)   direct responsibility for providing quality to the ultimate customer

(b)   indirect responsibility for providing quality to the ultimate customer?

Tick under the appropriate heading shown below.

Direct responsibility for quality   *Indirect responsibility for quality*

Research worker in R and D
Executive officer in the Civil Service
Computer programmer
Telecommunications engineer
Works manager
Personnel manager
Hotel manager
Work study officer
Area sales manager
Solicitor
Chartered accountant
Cost accountant
Company secretary
Organisation and methods officer
Social worker

Now check your list against ours at the end of the chapter.

The important point to realise after doing this activity is that whether one's job is directly or indirectly related to the quality of the product or service, everyone has the same responsibility for the ultimate quality of the product or service. For example:

(a)   If a programmer produces a poor program or administrators do not process information correctly and promptly, the more direct activities of research, production, sales or delivery cannot take place, ie items are likely to be produced to the wrong specification, or be sent to the wrong customers.

(b)   If personnel do not select the right people to fill posts, then jobs will not be carried out competently.

Everyone has a responsibility for ensuring that the product or service which reaches the customer or client is of a quality that will satisfy their needs.

The Individual's Role in Giving Customer Satisfaction

Again there are some job roles which may be seen as directly concerned with caring for the customer:

(a)   sales assistants in shops

(b)   commercial and industrial salespeople

(c)   counter clerks in building societies, banks, etc

(d)   those in the professional services — doctors, solicitors, etc

(e)   waiters, waitresses, bar staff

(f)   receptionists and telephonists

(g)   sports coaches, entertainers, tour guides, country park wardens.

These are the people who come into contact with people outside the organisation every day. However, customers do see the results of other people's work. For example:

(a)   they receive letters, forms and other business documents

(b)   if they visit premises, they note the attitude of any staff they encounter in car parks, offices or corridors, as well as the standard of maintenance and appearance of the buildings, etc.

This means that those who have "back room" jobs — clerks, administrators, machine operators, cleaners, security staff, as well as those who manage them, also have a responsibility for customer satisfaction.

A PRACTICAL APPROACH TO DEVELOPING THE RIGHT ATTITUDES TO OUTSIDE CONTACTS

In this section we will concentrate on dealing with customers but the same points are also true for other external contacts.

Recognise the Importance of the Customer

This applies to everyone, whatever their specialism or position within an organisation.

(a) Without the customer there is no business and no employment.

(b) It is therefore customers who pay salaries.

(c) If you satisfy customers' needs they will have a good image of you and the organisation you represent and will tell other people. They are also less trouble and make a job easier to do.

(d) If you disappoint customers, bad news travels even faster! They also become irritable and aggressive and make your job more difficult to do.

Recognise Ways of Upsetting Customers

There are many ways of upsetting people and sometimes you may be unaware of your own behaviour. Anyone outside an organisation will be dissatisfied when they are made to feel:

▶ unwelcome

▶ annoyed

▶ in the way

▶ embarrassed

▶ uncomfortable.

ACTIVITY 4

Try to identify behaviour which might make an outsider visiting your organisation feel any of the above.

Set down your own ideas before reading on.

Such behaviour can probably be divided into three categories: appearance, voice and action. We have mentioned a few possible causes in the lists below.

APPEARING ▶ uninterested in clients or their business

▶ bored or apathetic

▶ cross

▶ untidy, dirty or unprofessional

▶ disorganised.

SOUNDING ▶ aggressive or rude

▶ too submissive or uncertain

▶ unco-operative

▶ sarcastic

▶ patronising.

BEHAVING ▶ leaving customers without assistance for too long
BADLY by

▶ turning away from them

▶ turning one's back on them

▶ chatting to other employees about seemingly trivial matters in front of clients.

A Positive Approach

The most important step you can take is to start looking at yourself and your organisation through the customer's eyes. This is why we asked you to carry out Activity 2 on page 205. Try to meet the same high standards that you would expect when you want good service. As you progress up the management ladder, it will be part of your managerial responsibility to ensure that your staff are able to take the same positive approach.

You can make a start by thinking carefully about the way you:

▶ look

▶ listen

▶ speak

▶ behave.

Appearance

(a) All employees should always look clean and tidy as this creates an image of efficiency. Remember that looking efficient is halfway to being efficient!

(b) All employees should dress in a manner which supports the image the organisation wants to convey, not totally according to their own preferences. Always check whether there is a "dress code" in existence.

(c) Make sure body language creates a welcoming, helpful impression. Maintain good eye contact (but do not stare), smile, show open friendly gestures (avoid jabbing or pointing of fingers).

(d) If contact is by written communication, make sure that all documents look neat, follow the company's house style, with correct sentence construction, spelling and appropriate vocabulary. (For more details see Chapter 14.)

Speaking and listening

(a) Speak clearly and audibly so that people do not have to ask for information to be repeated.

(b) Ensure that your tone conveys courtesy, interest and lively concern.

(c) Listen carefully and attentively using "Um", "I see", etc to demonstrate attention without interrupting the speaker.

(d) When giving information, sound confident.

Behaviour

(a) Always give the other person full attention, even in difficult circumstances.

(b) Always acknowledge the presence of a visitor immediately. If it is necessary to complete a conversation with another employee, apologise to the visitor and conclude the conversation as quickly as possible.

(c) Always try to help visitors or outside contacts whether it is your specific responsibility or not. If you cannot answer their queries or provide the information, make sure they find someone who can. Take the initiative in approaching those who look lost, confused or upset and offer assistance.

CONCLUSION

If you follow these simple guidelines whenever you have contact with those outside your organisation, you will find that you can project a positive image of yourself and your employer. You will find the other chapters in this section continue this theme, by helping you to create the right image in specific business situations. The first of these concerns writing effective business letters.

ANSWER TO ACTIVITY IN CHAPTER 13

Activity 3

Direct responsibility for quality	*Indirect responsibility for quality*
Research worker in R and D	Executive officer in the Civil Service
Telecommunications engineer	Computer programmer
Works manager	Personnel manager
Hotel manager	Cost accountant
Area sales manager	Company secretary
Solicitor	Work study officer
Chartered accountant	Organisation and methods officer
Social worker	

14 Business Letters

A certain amount of contact with people outside an organisation must be maintained through correspondence. In fact, it is estimated that a manager may spend up to 25 per cent of his or her time on writing and dictating; a substantial part of this will be letters. You will remember the advantages and disadvantages of the written word as a form of communication from Chapter 1.

Despite the importance of letters as a form of external communication, it is surprising how bad senior managers can be at composing them. Letters are part of the armoury of the "ambassadorial role" of the manager, yet many are content to allow letters to leave their office which are poorly laid out, badly structured, full of officialese, syntax errors and spelling mistakes. Think how you respond if you receive a letter that looks scruffy or needs two or three readings before you understand it. You are probably tempted to put it to one side to read when you have more time and you develop a very poor impression of the writer and the organisation he or she represents.

Our intention in this chapter is to enable you to write better business letters. We will not waste time going over basic concepts, which we hope you have already covered.

THE ESSENTIAL POINTS ABOUT BUSINESS LETTER WRITING

The important point to bear in mind about letter writing is that it is very close to a one-way communication method since one cannot control the time, place or circumstances in which the letter will be read. There is no body language to help understanding. The message depends entirely on layout, structure and style to convey the right information and persuade the reader to respond in a favourable manner. To do this, letters must fulfil the six Cs of good communication.

ACTIVITY 1

This is a recap activity. See if you can remember the six Cs and think about them in relation to letter writing before reading on.

It is essential to ensure that:

(a) the layout of the letter is clear and the overall appearance attracts the reader to the contents

(b) the information contained within each letter is correct, complete and comprehensive

(c) the structure of the letter is concise and clear so that the reader can follow the logical progression of ideas easily

(d) the sentence construction, punctuation, spelling and use of vocabulary is correct, concise and clear

(e) the style and tone of writing is courteous and appropriate for the purpose and the reader.

Much of this is dependent upon good preparation.

PREPARING BUSINESS LETTERS

There is a simple process to be followed in preparing successful business letters. It may be necessary to think through these stages very consciously early in your career. Later on the process will become automatic. The simple preparatory stages can be presented as a checklist.

▶ *Why am I writing this letter*? What is the purpose?

▶ *To whom am I writing*? What do I know about him or her? If it is someone with whom I have already had some contact, what do I know about:

(a) his or her existing knowledge of the topic?

(b) his or her age, attitudes and personality?

(c) his or her level of authority?

▶ *Do I need to refer to any previous correspondence or documents*? Do I have them to hand?

▶ *What is the relevant information to be conveyed*?

Purpose

This requires the writer to identify the type of letter he or she is writing. For each type, it is necessary to consider the desired purpose, whether the letter is in connection with sales, sales promotion, recruitment and selection, buying or finance.

For example, there are letters of:

(a) enquiry   (c) adjustment
(b) information   (d) application

(e) appointment
(f) dismissal
(g) refusal
(h) acknowledgement
(i) complaint

(j) collection
(k) reference
(l) resignation
(m) invitation

as well as those that convey

(a) an order
(b) a sales promotion

(c) a quotation.

ACTIVITY 2

Decide your purpose in writing the following types of letters:

(a) a letter of application
(b) a collection letter
(c) a letter of complaint
(d) a letter of adjustment
(e) a sales promotion letter.

Then compare your answers with ours at the end of this chapter.

The type of letter and its purpose determines the content, structure and style. Some are much easier to compose than others.

ACTIVITY 3

This is an activity which should develop your critical evaluation of how writers achieve their purpose.

(a) Look through some of the letters (including "junk mail") you receive in the next few weeks. Allocate them according to the categories shown on pages 214–215.

(b) Then look at them more closely to see how they achieve their purpose through the sequencing of information and the tone and vocabulary used.

This research activity should prepare you for some of the points that follow.

The Reader

Each letter should be composed for the reader. When you are composing a standard or circular letter, it is necessary to design one to which the majority of readers could not take exception; the writer must decide on the average reader and aim it at this group. When it is correspondence to one individual, plan the content, structure and style for that one person. Gauge that person's existing knowledge of the topic, so that he or she is not provided with too few or too many facts; be careful not to appear too familiar, too austere, too patronising, too curt or too eager through choice of words and phrasing.

Organising the Information

First, it is necessary to collect together the information required to compose the letter. Check that the correct files, documents, leaflets, enclosures, etc are to hand. This should encourage the flow of dictation or writing because it will not be interrupted in order to find the appropriate file, etc.

Planning

Sort the facts into a logical sequence in an outline plan before starting to dictate or write.

DESIGNING A STRUCTURE FOR BUSINESS LETTERS

All business letters follow a basic structure.

General Structure for a Business Letter

This is as follows:

(a) subject heading

(b) introductory paragraph which puts the message into a particular context

(c) main body of one or more paragraphs which provide the detail

(d) closing paragraph which states the action to be taken.

Subject heading This should *always* appear after the salutation in business letters. It should be short, simple and summarise the content of the letter. This serves a number of purposes:

(a) it identifies the content so that the postroom can distribute it to the most relevant person if no name or job title is included in the address

(b) it categorises the contents for identification by the reader

(c) it can help when subject classification is used for filing.

Introductory paragraph   The opening paragraph should put the message in context by any of the following means:

(a)   referring to the event or situation prompting the letter

(b)   acknowledging the receipt, date and subject of any correspondence received

(c)   explaining the purpose of the letter.

This should be done simply and directly, without the use of outdated expressions such as "We are in receipt of", "Thank you for your esteemed enquiry" or unnecessary phrases such as "I am writing to . . .".

Main body   The main body of the letter contains the facts and details. These may be contained in a single paragraph or several paragraphs depending on the amount of information needed to ensure that the letter is complete and comprehensive.

If several paragraphs are involved, each one should deal with a specific aspect of the topic. The information should be presented in a sequence which is easy for the reader to follow.

Concluding paragraph   The final paragraph is the one which the reader will remember most easily. It is therefore in this paragraph that any follow-up action to the letter should be identified. This must be extremely clear, with precise dates, times, locations, etc. Vague phrases such as "as soon as possible" or "at your convenience" may be polite but can be misinterpreted.

Structure for Specific Types of Letters

The actual sequence used for a letter depends on its type. A simple classification for structuring letters is by purpose whether they convey straightforward information or attempt persuasion; whether they are giving good news or bad news. We have given some structural formats for the sequencing of information in certain types of letters in the tables below.

Sequence for straightforward information (eg enquiry, explanation, application)	**Sequence for letters conveying good news** (eg successful application, successful tender)
Aim: To convey information clearly and concisely	*Aim:* To convey good news quickly and clearly and show enthusiasm
Subject heading	*Subject heading*
Opening paragraph As general structure above	*Opening paragraph* Convey good news at once

Middle paragraphs Provide explanatory details	*Middle paragraphs* Provide explanatory details
Closing paragraph State action needed from receiver or to be taken by writer	*Closing paragraph* Convey congratulations and state any follow-up action needed

Sequence for letters attempting persuasion (eg promotional letters, direct marketing)	**Sequence for letters conveying bad news** (eg refusals, closures)
Aim: To persuade the reader into action by creating impact and curiosity	*Aim:* To present bad news clearly but with tact; to avoid offence. Sometimes to elicit action despite difficult circumstances
Subject heading Bold and startling	*Subject heading* Neutral
Opening paragraph Dramatic opening sentence to attract attention, eg question or provocative statement	*Opening paragraph* Set context for bad news but keep relatively neutral at this stage — should prepare the reader
Middle paragraphs Provides detailed facts while maintaining interest through use of vocabulary and sentence construction	*Middle paragraphs* Leads into circumstances or reasons for bad news. Then states the news and its implications plus stating any positive factors arising from the situation
Closing paragraph An appeal for action often using an incentive, eg "bring this coupon for your free gift"	*Closing paragraph* Some statement which attempts to alleviate the unpleasantness; any action which can be taken on their part

Sequence for letter of complaint	**Sequence for letter of adjustment to complaint**
Aim: To state the nature of the complaint clearly and usually to ask for some form of action/recompense	*Aim:* To express regret at the occurrence, give an explanation and offer recompense if complaint is justified. Also to restore the reader's confidence
Subject heading Clear	*Subject heading* Clear

218

Opening paragraph
Context of complaint, brief statement of what, who, when, where

Opening paragraph
Acknowledgement of letter; expression of regret; indication that nature of the complaint has been understood

Middle paragraphs
Provide detail about precise nature of complaint and implications for writer (eg lost time, delay, lost business, etc)

Middle paragraphs
Statement of results of investigation into the complaint and what kind of adjustment is to be offered. Sometimes it is useful to pose alternatives. If no justification for the complaint, the results of investigation must be fully explained in a tactful manner which shows understanding of the writer's concern

Closing paragraph
Action sought to remedy the complaint and any time limits within which action should be taken

Closing paragraph
Restate apology and express hope that action taken will allow goodwill to be retained

Examples of a number of letters are shown on pages 220–224.

STYLE

Letter writing style is a highly contentious subject. Most organisations develop a "house style" — a way of writing that they require all their employees to adopt. It is necessary to observe this to maintain a good relationship with an employer. However, house styles do change over the years and, if one considers an organisation's house style is deficient in some way, it is possible to encourage it to consider new styles which are more appropriate.

The basic objective of any letter writing style is to convey information *correctly, concisely, clearly and courteously*. It should always be possible to judge letters against these criteria.

Example of a letter conveying good news

National Leisure Ltd

31-33 Oxford Square, London W.1

Telephone: 071-666 2489   Fax: 071-666 2597

5 September 19. .

Mr A Cook
Country Craft Kitchens Ltd
10 The Links
OCKINGHAM
Beckhampshire OK5 6PL

Dear Mr Cook

Your quotation 1207 for design and installation of kitchen fittings

I am pleased to tell you that National Leisure Ltd have accepted your quotation for the design and installation of kitchen fittings for our new teashop at the Waterloo Country Park in Ockingham.

You will be receiving an official order for this work within the next three days. We will need the installation to be completed by 5 April 19. ., so that the teashop can open for business at the beginning of the Easter holiday.

I would like to meet you early next week to discuss the plans you submitted. I suggest Tuesday 13 September at 11.00 am in the reception area of the Waterloo Country Park. Could you confirm the date and time with me by telephone on the above number, extension 35?

Yours sincerely

P Fox
Development Manager

Example of a letter conveying bad news

Save & Build Building Society
62 High Street,
Deddingham,
Dedhamshire DG6 2XO
Tel: 0963–72843
Fax: 0963–74382

5 September 19. .

Mr S March
The Willows
Cross Street
DEDDINGHAM
Dedhamshire DE1 5SN

Dear Mr March

Mortgage application

The Society has now completed its investigations and survey on Stable Cottage, Minkles Lane, Deddingham and I enclose a copy of the surveyor's report.

The surveyor found a number of faults, the most serious of which are:

— evidence of subsidence in part of the house;
— weak roofing supports;
— signs of wet rot in most timber frames.

Generally, the house is in a very poor state of repair. The Society has therefore decided that it cannot make you a mortgage offer on this property.

However, I must emphasise that the decision applies only to Stable Cottage. Save and Build Building Society would be happy to consider any mortgage application from you on another property.

Please telephone me on the above number if you have any queries concerning the surveyor's report.

Yours sincerely

D Catherall
Mortgage Applications Manager

Enc Surveyor's report

Example of letter making a complaint

Wells & Gough

High Class Butchers

10 The Withies, OCKINGHAM, Beckhampshire OF6 1XP

Telephone: 0666| 57890

---

5 September 19. .

The Manager
Royal Hotel
Western Parade
OCKINGHAM
Beckhampshire OK3 2RG

Dear Sir

Duty telephonist 1 September 19. .

On 1 September 19. . , I telephoned your hotel to tell your Assistant Catering Manager, John Bowman, about problems in securing game birds for the celebration dinner that evening. I found the duty telephonist that day rude and unhelpful.

The facts are as follows. I attempted to make contact three times. The first time she assumed I was asking for a guest and put the phone down before I had time to correct her. When I redialled, she accused me of not knowing what I wanted and wasting her time. She then left me waiting to be put through for five minutes. When I tried later that morning, I was told curtly that Mr Bowman was out and there was no-one else who could take my call. Since the matter had become urgent, I had to visit the hotel personally to resolve it. I found that Mr Bowman had been in the hotel all morning.

This encounter made be feel annoyed, put me to unnecessary trouble and did very little for the reputation of your hotel. Since other clients and suppliers may be receiving similar treatment, I decided to make a formal written complaint.

I hope you will be able to improve your telephonist's behaviour and would appreciate reassurance that corrective action has been taken.

Yours faithfully

M Gough

Example of a letter replying to a complaint (ie adjustment)

The Royal Hotel

WESTERN PARADE, OCKINGHAM,
BECKHAMPSHIRE OK3 2RG
Tel: 0666 89076   Fax:0666 89076

7 September 19.

Mr M Gough
Wells & Gough
10 The Withies
OCKINGHAM
Beckhampshire OF6 1XP

Dear Mr Gough

Thank you for your letter dated 5 September 19. . telling me about the behaviour of our duty telephonist. I apologise for the inconvenience caused by this incident.

I have investigated the matter and have found that we hired a relief telephonist from a local agency for 1 September because of sickness amongst our own staff. We were at fault in not checking her telephone manner before allowing her to deal with calls.

I am glad that you have made this complaint as it highlights a problem in our hotel service when relief staff have to take over duties at short notice. We will be vetting agency staff more carefully as well as ensuring that any relief staff are provided with simple written guidelines on appropriate procedures and behaviour.

I am very sorry you were treated with discourtesy. Our hotel appreciates the excellent service your firm has given us over the past few years and we would like to continue our business contact.

Yours sincerely

J Croft
Manager

Example of a promotional letter

(NB This would be produced by a mailmerge so space has been left for the personalised details, eg name of contact, name of organisation, etc.)

Stinton Training

19 Russley Green Wokingham Berks
WK6 5PP
Telephone: 0739 71794

---

5 November 19. .

Dear (space for personalised name)

Can you meet the challenge of the 1990s?

The 1990s will be a period of rapid change in which only organisations with a well-trained workforce will survive. Does (space for inserting company name) want to meet this challenge? If so, WE can help you.

Our organisation has over fifteen years' experience in training staff from top British companies. The courses we offer can be tailor-made to the special needs of (space for inserting company name) and can take place on (space for company name) premises or at suitable hotel complexes — the choice is yours!

Our trainers are experienced in a wide range of management skills including: total quality and customer care, team building, negotiation, managing change. Perhaps your staff need a "crash" course in foreign languages to handle delicate overseas contracts. We can make them proficient in French, German or Spanish in three weeks; Japanese and Russian take a little longer.

If you have a training need, STINTON TRAINING can help YOU. Don't be left behind! Send for our FREE BROCHURE today, or contact Sue on the above number. The rest is up to us!

Yours sincerely

B Kempworthy
Director

Correct

This means that any letter must say exactly what the writer means. This involves choosing precise vocabulary and correct sentence construction.

Use of the correct vocabulary It is very easy to confuse some words. For example, a common mistake is the confusion of the word "morals" with "morale". Consider how the use of the wrong word in the following sentence completely changes its meaning: "When three engineers were made redundant in the factory, it led to very low morals".

We are not always aware of the precise meaning of some words and therefore use one which is incorrect. We have selected a number of words which commonly create problems for letter writers in the activity below.

ACTIVITY 4

The following pairs of words are often confused. Give an accurate description of each word. Then check your answers with ours at the end of the chapter.

The first set are words which sound the same but have different meanings or usages.

complement	council	dependent
compliment	counsel	dependant
discreet	practice	principal
discrete	practise	principle
sight	stationary	weather
site	stationery	wether
		whether

The next group are ones which people tend to use interchangeably but in fact have different meanings.

affect	alternately	continually	imply
effect	alternatively	continuously	infer

Check your answers against ours at the end of the chapter.

Use the correct spelling, punctuation and sentence construction A dictionary is an essential part of letter writing equipment or use the spell check on your word processing package (but beware — some of these will give you the American spelling!). Always check words about which you have *any* doubts. A letter which has several spelling errors looks careless. Think about the impression on your reader — if you cannot get the spelling right, are the facts correct?

ACTIVITY 5

Check your own spelling ability on the following frequently misspelt words.

Word	Definition
ac — dation	housing or lodging
arg — ent	a quarrel
ben — f — ed	gained an advantage from
co — tee	a formal meeting
d — f — te	precise, firm
emba — sed	confused, self-concious
envir — ment	habitat, background
fu — fi —	carry out an undertaking
ind — p — nt	self-reliant, self-sufficient
knowledg —	knowing a lot
lia — on	a connection with or an illicit affair
mis — el — ous	mixed, an assortment
nec — sary	needed
oc — as — on	an incident or a celebration
oc — red	happened
prof — sion	an occupation requiring advanced qualifications
questio — ire	a form containing a number of questions
rec — ve	accept
sep — r — te	to come between

You can check the correct spelling at the end of the chapter.

ACTIVITY 6

Test your own knowledge of sentence construction and punctuation by stating whether the following are examples of correct usage in business letters.

(a) Thanking you for your attention.
(b) I wish to order the following items: envelopes, headed notepaper, pencils and pens.
(c) You are owed several months' salary.
(d) Each of the three companies have an interest in this development.

You can find the answers at the end of the chapter.

Also, remember the basic principle of writing in short, simple sentences so that sentence construction and punctuation are likely to be correct.

Concise

All the relevant information concerning the topic should be included, but it should be presented in as brief a form as possible. Observing the following principles will help:

(a) Keep sentences relatively short; each one should express a single thought. It is likely that the reader will have to read long sentences which contain several ideas more than once to understand them. However, do not go to the opposite extreme and make every sentence short since this will lead to a disjointed letter.

(b) Each paragraph should deal with a specific aspect of the subject of the letter. Therefore, create a new paragraph for a new aspect of the matter.

(c) Write in a direct manner. Do not include redundant phrases which do not say anything. Such phrases are often used because they "sound impressive" or "make the letter sound more polite" but consider whether they are necessary or merely provide "padding". The basic test is, "Can this phrase be deleted without altering the meaning of the sentence?" If the answer is "Yes", delete it.

Clear

There are a number of points that will help to keep the message clear. The purpose in writing a business letter is for the reader to understand the contents as quickly and easily as possible and then to respond positively. The choice of vocabulary must therefore help this process. So, the basic rules are:

(a) Use precise vocabulary and avoid vague words or phrases, eg nice, things, some, several, a lot.

(b) Avoid using jargon which the reader may not understand.

(c) Use simple two syllable words in preference to longer, more obscure words.

(d) Use simple, direct phrases in preference to stilted "officialese".

If in doubt refer back to the basic principles in Chapter 3.

While these three criteria of being correct, concise and clear are important for all business letters, the exact style of the letter and the tone used will be governed by the purpose of the letter and the readership. Some letters will need to be written:

(a) *objectively* — presentation of facts with very little scope for individual sentiments, eg requesting or giving information, explaining, complaining.

(b) *subjectively* — with the emphasis on an emotive argument to surround a few basic facts, eg letters that persuade, sell or attempt to secure help or advice.

ACTIVITY 7

Look at the examples of the letter giving bad news on page 221 (factual) and the sales promotion letter on page 224 (emotive). Try to identify how the use of sentence construction and vocabulary achieves the different objectives. Look at these examples carefully before reading on.

▶ *Factual letters are*: concise; they use short sentences to make statements, they use concrete nouns, they use precise terms, and limit the use of adjectives and adverbs.

▶ *Emotive letters are*: often longer and use greater variety in length of sentences; the sentences often pose questions or make exclamations; more abstract nouns are used initially to create images; emotive words, particularly adjectives and adverbs are used.

Another important aspect about good style is to make letters interesting to read. One common fault made by inexperienced letter writers is to repeat the same words constantly. Vocabulary should be varied. Again, help is at hand in a "thesaurus" which gives the synonyms for many thousands of English words. Today, many word processing packages include a thesaurus so that it is possible to check the meaning of a word as well as find a suitable synonym.

APPEARANCE OF BUSINESS LETTERS

We do not intend to go into details on the format of letters, styles of address, salutations, complimentary closes, etc because it is likely that readers are familiar with the rules and conventions. Note, however, that most organisations today prefer the fully blocked letter format with open punctuation, in which all information starts at the left hand margin and no punctuation marks are used except in the body of the letter. All the examples in this book use this format. The reasons for this are practical. It enables a typist or word processor to make fewer key strokes and therefore correspondence can be produced more quickly and with less likelihood of mistakes.

It is also important that, to create the right impression, the quality of the printed type and the paper is good.

Remember that responsibility for an effective business letter belongs to the writer, not to a typist or word processor operator. He or she will need to play a part but ultimately the writer must check that your letters meet the highest standards. If someone else produces your letters you will need to work as a team. Agree the layout in advance rather than pass adverse comments after the job is finished.

CHECKLIST FOR EFFECTIVE BUSINESS LETTERS

It may be useful to go through the following checklist when drafting or checking any letter.

(a) Does the overall appearance of the letter create a good impression of the writer and the organisation?

(b) Have the conventions of letter layout been followed?

(c) Is the purpose of the letter clear?

(d) Does the letter convey correct information in sufficient detail to achieve its purpose?

(e) Has the information been presented in the most logical sequence to achieve its purpose?

(f) Has paragraphing been used properly?

(g) Are the style and tone appropriate for the purpose and the reader?

(h) Is the language simple, direct and appropriate for the reader?

(i) Are the sentence construction, punctuation and spelling correct?

(j) Is the meaning of each sentence absolutely clear so that there can be no possible misunderstanding?

(k) Is the overall message, however unpleasant, presented in a courteous manner?

Obviously, the answer to all these questions should be "yes".

Avoid:

(a) officialese

(b) redundant phrases

(c) jargon

(d) vague or ambiguous words

(e) over-familiarity

(f) sarcasm

    (g)   rudeness.

Finally, check the clarity of business letters occasionally by using the fog factor formula (see Chapter 3).

DICTATING CORRESPONDENCE

You may write your own letters in longhand to be copied by a typist or you may produce a rough draft on your own microcomputer to be edited into final copy by a word processor operator. Alternatively, if your correspondence load is heavy, you may be required to give shorthand or audio dictation. We have therefore included some guidelines in this chapter on giving dictation.

Preparation

▶ *Pre-plan correspondence before a dictation session*
Identify the main points for each letter and know the sequence for presenting the information. This may be in the form of rough notes, not a full rough draft.

▶ *Consider the typist.*
Anticipate the problems he or she may encounter with the corrrespondence.

▶ *Organise a dictation session at an appropriate time.*
This should be when your mind is fresh and your can concentrate.

Initial Instructions

▶ *Greet the typist.*
If giving audio-dictation, greet the typist at the beginning of a batch of dictated correspondence.

▶ *Identify the nature of the work on the tape.*
He or she then knows what to expect, ie two short letters or a long session of several letters plus a report.

▶ *Give full instructions at the beginning of each piece of correspondence.*

    (a)   The type of document
    (b)   Its approximate length
    (c)   How many copies are required
    (d)   The quality or type of paper to be used (if there is a choice)
    (e)   Any other special instructions, eg files or documents from which he or she may need to extract information, special layout instructions, etc.

The typist then knows what to expect and can be prepared.

Sequence

▶ *Dictate information in the order in which the typist produces the letter.*
This needs some forethought, ie your reference; our reference; date; addressee; address; salutation; subject heading; main body of the letter; complimentary close; enclosures/copies.

General Guidelines

▶ *Be aware of the effect of background noise or interference.*
Try to dictate in as quiet a place as possible; close windows and doors.

▶ *Speak clearly and audibly.*
Remember that little things like chewing, smoking or sucking the end of a pencil, swinging around in the chair or walking up and down can all impede clear diction.

▶ *Use natural phrasing.*
Pause at commas and at the ends of sentences.

▶ *Avoid dropping your voice at the ends of words or sentences.*

▶ *Dictate punctuation as you go along.*
If you have confidence in the typist, dictate only unusual punctuation. If in doubt, dictate each comma, full stop and capital letter.

▶ *Dictate paragraphing.*
Use the words "new paragraph".

▶ *Spell out words over which the typist is likely to experience difficulty.*
This applies particularly to proper names and numbers. Use the phonetic alphabet shown on page 232 if necessary. Numbers can be distinguished by, for example, fifteen = one five, fifty = five o.

▶ *If it is necessary to give instructions in the middle of dictation, or make a correction, precede the instruction with the word "typist" or his or her name.*
This will attract his or her attention and cause him or her to stop typing; otherwise he or she will be typing the instruction in the middle of the letter!

▶ *Indicate when the end of each piece of correspondence has been reached.*

▶ *Indicate when the end of the batch of dictation has been reached.*
Do not just lapse into silence. Also, remember to thank the typist.

▶ *Check through the tape quickly to ensure that it has recorded properly.*

Phonetic Alphabet
(used internationally by British Telecom)

A	Alpha	J	Juliet	S	Sierra
B	Bravo	K	Kilo	T	Tango
C	Charlie	L	Lima	U	Uniform
D	Delta	M	Mike	V	Victor
E	Echo	N	November	W	Whisky
F	Foxtrot	O	Oscar	X	X-ray
G	Golf	P	Papa	Y	Yankee
H	Hotel	Q	Quebec	Z	Zulu
I	India	R	Romeo		

MODERN TECHNOLOGY AND CORRESPONDENCE

Today, conventional mail may not enable written messages to be conveyed with sufficient speed. One should therefore be familiar with new methods of transmitting letters or alternatives for conventional letters.

Fast Transmission of Letters

FAX This stands for facsimile transfer and is a means by which handwritten notes, letters, reports, maps, diagrams and photographs can be transmitted in a few seconds or minutes by the telecommunications network. For example an A4 letter can be transmitted in about 15 to 20 seconds. This method enables an exact copy (facsimile) to be conveyed by electronic signals along a telephone line between two compatible FAX transceivers. Despite its speed, FAX will not replace conventional hard copy letters immediately as it is expensive to send a letter by this means and it lacks quality.

FAX is extremely useful for sending documents between organisations where speed may be the most important criterion (eg for contracts).

Electronic mail Today it is possible for electronic letters to be produced through an inbuilt program on a word processor or desk top computer using the "house style" layout for the organisation and then transmitted using one of the E-mail (electronic mail) systems, eg Telecom Gold. E-mail will also enable the same standard letter to be sent to numerous recipients simultaneously.

Alternatives to Conventional Letters

Telex   Although an exact copy of a letter can be transmitted quickly by FAX, many organisations still use the telex system for some messages that might otherwise be sent by letter. Telexes can now be sent from many networked computer terminals without the use of a dedicated teleprinter.

A telex message can be prepared, edited and checked on the microcomputer and VDU and then kept on electronic file until a suitable transmission time. The layout of a telex message is shown below. Since transmission on the telex network is charged by time, an abbreviated note form is likely to be used. The ability to be correct, clear and concise is important.

Annotated telex message

```
87-08-12   16:22                            Date and time
007
AB179 16.22*
311890 MGPUBS G                             Code of sender
KEY+7170842+
ERNEX AA170842                              Code of receiver
311890 MGPUBS G                             Transaction number
3462  87-08-12   16:23                      Date and time repeated


ATTN CHRIS PLAYER

RE: PARADIGM DISTRIBUTION IN AUSTRALIA

I RECEIVED MESSAGE THAT YOU AGREE TO
REPRESENT PARADIGM BUT AM AWAITING
CONFIRMATION BY POST. I WOULD LIKE TO       Message
INCLUDE ASTAM. PLEASE ADVISE.

REGARDS
ADAM MARSHALL
PARADIGM PUBLISHING

*
ERNEX AA170842                              Code of sender repeated
311890 MGPUBS G                             Code of receiver repeated
```

Telemessage   This is an electronic letter service, available in this country, which can be used when information in letter format needs to be transmitted very quickly. It replaces the old internal telegram system. Telemessages can be sent by telephone, telex machine or computer and once the message has been received by British Telecom it will be transmitted electronically to a computer terminal for printing at a post office near its destination. It is then delivered in the first class post on the next working day.

CONCLUSION

Obviously, your letters and dictation of letters will deal with a specialist area and we are only able to give you some general guidelines. However, whatever your specialism, you want to achieve a clear understanding on the part of the readers and to leave them with an impression that you are efficient, professional and caring.

ANSWERS TO ACTIVITIES IN CHAPTER 14

Activity 2

(a) The purpose of a letter of application is to promote yourself in writing so that you are shortlisted for interview.

(b) The purpose of a collection letter is to bring a debt to the attention of the debtor, request prompt payment and inform the recipient of likely action if the debt is not repaid.

(c) The purpose of a letter of complaint is to present the full circumstances of the complaint and to state clearly what form of action you want taken.

(d) The purpose of a letter of adjustment is to apologise to a complainant for any inconvenience suffered and, if the complaint is justified, to state what form of recompense is to be offered.

(e) The purpose of a sales promotion letter is to persuade a potential customer or client to use the product or service.

Activity 4

complement (noun or verb)	= something which completes
compliment (noun or verb)	= an expression of thanks or praise
council (noun)	= a body of people which discusses, makes decisions
counsel (noun or verb)	= advice, someone who gives advice or to give advice
dependent (adjective)	= depending on, relying on, contingent upon
dependant (noun)	= a person who depends on another
discreet (adjective)	= prudent, cautious
discrete (adjective)	= separate, distinct
practice (noun)	= a method, habit, action
practise (verb)	= to carry out the action
principal (adjective and noun)	= main, most important, the head, the leader
principle (noun)	= a rule, a standard, a belief, a code
sight (noun and verb)	= seeing, a scene, a spectacle or to see
site (noun and verb)	= a place, a plot or to locate, to place

stationary (adjective)	= at a standstill
stationery (noun)	= writing materials
weather (noun and verb)	= atmospheric conditions or to wear away, to discolour
wether (noun)	= a castrated ram
whether (conjunction)	= expressing doubt or a choice between alternatives
affect (verb)	= to influence, to pretend, to move
effect (noun and verb)	= a result, an impression, to bring about, to accomplish
alternately (adverb)	= every other one
alternatively (adverb)	= one of two, ie a choice
continually (adverb)	= happening frequently
continuously (adverb)	= uninterrupted, happening without a break
imply (verb)	= to hint, to suggest that
infer (verb)	= to deduce from, to conclude

Activity 5

accommodation	liaison
argument	miscellaneous
benefited	necessary
committee	occasion
definite	occurred
embarrassed	profession
environment	questionnaire
fulfil	receive
independent	separate
knowledgeable	

Activity 6

1. This is incorrect usage. It is an example of a hanging participle and leaves the sentence incomplete. This is a common fault in business letters. To correct this fault, you would need to change it to:

   "Thank you for your letter".

2. This is correct usage of the colon and commas. Remember that a colon is used to introduce a list and that commas are used to separate items in a list.

3. This is correct use of the apostrophe. Since the salary relates to more than one month the apostrophe comes after the "s".

4. There is incorrect agreement of subject and verb in this sentence. To correct this you would need to change it to:

   "Each (singular) of the three companies has (singular) an interest in this development".

15 Face-to-Face Encounters

In this chapter, we will be looking at some techniques which will enable you to handle face-to-face encounters with confidence and courtesy. Meeting people outside your organisation is one of the more interesting aspects of any job but is also a challenge. You may be meeting them on a one-to-one basis in a meeting or interview, at a joint meeting or conference, or even by closed circuit television.

Whatever the situation, this type of encounter means that communication is oral and visual. You can speak, listen and use body language. When these forms of communication are in harmony and used effectively they will have a strong positive influence on the other person. When one of them is defective or out of harmony, you are likely to promote doubt, confusion and antagonism. In all encounters, you should have a number of objectives:

(a) to deal with the matter in hand efficiently, however difficult

(b) to leave the other person with a positive impression of yourself and your organisation

(c) to say the right thing in the right way at the right time

(d) to feel satisfied with the outcome of the situation.

ASSERTIVENESS

Many people confuse assertiveness with aggressiveness. For this reason some organisations may prefer to call assertion self-confidence.

ACTIVITY 1

Which of the following phrases (one or more) do you think best describes assertiveness?

(a) Manipulating people to do what you want.
(b) Making sure that other people have to listen to your point of view.
(c) Holding back instead of speaking up.

(d) Being honest with yourself and others.

(e) Behaving in a rational adult way.

Think about this before reading on.

In fact, the last two phrases are both important aspects of assertiveness. It is having self respect as well as respect for other people which then enables one to act rationally and logically instead of emotionally. This can be difficult in the face of people who are behaving in a difficult, antagonistic way. However, there are some simple steps which are easy to learn but take some practice to use.

To give a full definition, assertiveness is:

▶ being honest with yourself and with others

▶ being able to say what you want, need or feel but not at the expense of other people's feelings

▶ understanding the other person's point of view

▶ being positive

▶ behaving in a rational, logical manner.

Recognising Influences on Our Own Behaviour

Although we all can exhibit submissive, aggressive and assertive behaviour, our own behaviour is likely to veer towards aggressiveness or submissiveness in the face of difficulty. This happens for a number of reasons:

(a) *Fight/flight syndrome*
When we get into a difficult situation, the adrenalin starts pumping. This is the body's way of providing energy to do one of two things — fight or run away as fast as possible (ie aggression or submission).

(b) *Culture/gender conditioning*
To some extent our tendency towards aggression or submission may be the result of cultural influences or gender conditioning. For example, despite greater equality in opportunities and work boys are still encouraged to be strong, tough, not to show weakness, to win, not to back down, etc, while girls are encouraged not to hurt others, to be sensitive, subtle, gentle, not to argue or get angry.

We must recognise that this may influence not only our own behaviour but also the way *other people may attempt to treat us*.

Assertive and Non-Assertive Behaviour

Before anyone can become more assertive, he or she needs to recognise the characteristics of the other extremes.

Aggression Being aggressive is an outcome of only wanting to achieve one's own goals and regarding encounters as contests in which one must beat the other person. Aggression involves:

(a) putting one's own ideas and feelings forward but ignoring the right of others to do so

(b) attempting to ridicule others and their ideas

(c) insisting that one is never wrong

(d) using sarcasm to belittle others

(e) being patronising.

An aggressive person:

(a) makes much use of the word "I"

(b) sounds loud and strident

(c) uses rapid speech or deliberate slow sarcasm

(d) uses very direct eye contact (staring)

(e) has a firm set to the jaw or a jutting chin

(f) attempts to encroach on other people's space by leaning forwards or leaning over

(g) points or jabs a finger while talking or thumps the table.

Submission Submissiveness means constantly trying to avoid hurting or upsetting other people or letting other people have their way in order to gain their approval or avoid their displeasure. Submission involves:

(a) giving in to other people

(b) not volunteering one's own ideas or feelings

(c) always agreeing, even when one knows it is wrong

(d) always being apologetic about one's ideas or behaviour.

A submissive person:

(a) precedes sentences with apologies

(b) is hesitant and may stutter

(c) speaks very quietly

(d) allows sentences to trail off into silence

(e) maintains very little eye contact

(f) makes nervous, jerky movements — may be clumsy

(g) hunches his or her shoulders

(h) has a worried expression

(j) crosses his or her arms frequently for protection.

ACTIVITY 2

(a) Identify two situations, one in which you have behaved aggressively and one in which you behaved submissively.

(b) In each case, identify in what ways your approach was aggressive or submissive. What did you say? What non-verbal signals were there?

(c) How did you feel after the encounter was over?

(d) What was the eventual outcome of the encounter?

Try to recall this as precisely as possible before reading on.

This activity should help you to analyse your own behaviour. It will also cause you to question how we feel after such encounters. For example, you may feel very good after being aggressive if it made the other person submissive. You felt you had won. But how did they feel? Submission tends to make us feel resentful about our own behaviour and about the person who made us feel so awful. This can lead to a "revenge psychology", and can be damaging for future relationships. It is better to work towards being assertive.

The Basic Steps in Becoming Assertive

In face-to-face encounters, however difficult, try the following basic steps:

(a) Listen attentively and show to the other person you understand his or her position; this is more positive than thinking how to defend your own position or attack his or hers.

(b)   State your thoughts or feelings calmly and with control.

(c)   Say what you think should happen.

This can be done effectively by practising assertive language and non-verbal signals.

Assertive language   Vocabulary should indicate recognition of everyone's right to an opinion, eg "I believe . . . what do you think?" "I would like to do . . . How do you respond to this suggestion?" Use language which shows that you have been listening and that you have understood what others said (even if you do not agree with them). Good linking words between their ideas and yours are "however", "alternatively", "nevertheless" — they are softer and sound more reasonable than "but".

As well as showing concern for both points of view they are also concerned about performing tasks effectively. Assertive people speak calmly with a steady, medium pitched voice and with natural phrasing and pace.

ACTIVITY 3

Look at the following situation and note the differences between the aggressive, submissive and assertive replies. Then state the effect you think each would have on the customer.

Situation
You work in a wholesaler's and are talking on the telephone to a retail manageress who wants you to bring forward the delivery date on her order. It is extremely important to her. You know that your own supplier will not have made a delivery to you by the date that the retailer wants delivery.

Replies

(a)   "Well . . . er. It's rather difficult you see. I'm sorry but our supplier . . . Oh well, if it's that important to you, perhaps I can have a word with them. . . ."

(b)   "By when? You must be joking! That's impossible! Be reasonable, my good woman. Do you think we can work miracles here?"

(c)   "I can understand that it is important for you to have a delivery by the 10th; however, our own supplier will not have made a delivery to us by then. We could deliver two thirds of the order from our existing stocks and let you have the balance by the 20th. Would that help you out?"

Check your answers against ours at the end of the chapter.

Assertive body language   Assertive people:

(a)   maintain good eye contact

(b)   stand or sit in an upright but relaxed posture

(c)   use gestures, facial expressions and tone which reflect the message they are putting across.

Some Problem Face-to-Face Situations Requiring Assertiveness

Meeting people for the first time   It is very easy to give the wrong impression at this early stage. If someone looks away, hangs back, lets others make the first move or mumbles a greeting, people will assume straight away that he or she is submissive and may try to exploit that. On the other hand, if someone stares hard at others, strides right up to them (very close), grasps their hand and their arm and then starts talking about himself or herself, he or she will appear too dominant and forthright.

So, at the first encounter:

(a)   establish eye contact and smile

(b)   move towards the other person and extend your hand straight out in a greeting

(c)   introduce yourself

(d)   ask an open question to start the conversation

(e)   maintain the conversation through a sequence of questions, answers, comments and opinions, being careful to include all the parties involved and without blocking any contributions through inattention, rudeness or aggressive body language.

Making a request   Asking someone to do something for you can be another embarrassing situation. Many people are frightened of rejection. Therefore, it is necessary to look and sound confident. If making a request:

(a)   be clear in your message

(b)   be direct in your language

(c)   maintain strong eye contact

(d)   smile

(e)   use a pleasant tone.

If you use all these techniques, it will be much harder for the other person to refuse the request.

Saying "no" and refusing requests   We have just mentioned that it can be difficult to say no. Perhaps there have been times when you know you should have refused a request, you wanted to say no but could not actually do so. Perhaps you did not want the other person to get cross or you did not want to hurt him or her by a refusal; perhaps you thought it would make you appear rude or churlish.

Unfortunately, whenever we agree to something, when our basic motivation is to refuse, we tend to comply with the request grudgingly and harbour resentment. We probably do not carry out the task very well as a result. Remember, if there is a reason to say no to the request you have a right to make that response without feeling guilty. Although people do not like negative responses, most would probably prefer to receive an honest no at the start, rather than a grudging compliance, possibly only to be let down later.

In saying no, try to show that an understanding of the other person's position in making the request and give the reason for refusal. Try saying something along the following lines:

"I can see why it is important for you to have the information by Thursday. However, our organisation could not guarantee that it would be correct or accurate within this timescale; therefore, I cannot comply with your request. I can have it on your desk by 9.00 am Monday morning."

Expressing one's feelings and standing up for oneself   Remember that while other people have a right to their ideas, opinion and feelings, you also have a right to yours. If someone is using rudeness, sarcasm, joking at your expense, or persisting in asking you to do something you consider wrong or unreasonable, then calmly and evenly let that person know how you feel when he or she does this. For example, "I don't think your sarcasm is helping us resolve this problem. It makes me feel annoyed and uncooperative. Could we try working together rather than against one another? I think we may solve it if we do."

Being persistent and coping with refusals   There are many times when it is necessary to be persistent. One may be selling a product, persuading someone to use a service, overcoming someone's objections, applying for jobs or trying to see the right person. In many of these situations, people will not listen properly and will be anxious to get away.

The basic technique, as most salespeople will say, is to repeat the message firmly but politely until the other person really listens.

This does not mean raising one's voice and shouting the same phrase to drown out the other person's objections or insisting on one's rights. It does mean:

(a) deciding on the key phrase to convey

(b) bringing this phrase into the conversation in many different ways

(c) showing understanding of the other person's objections (eg too busy, previous experiences, lack of funds, etc).

Showing appreciation   Showing appreciation is often hard for us to do. When other people meet our expectations or demands we just accept it without a word. Too often, one will hear the phrase, "We only hear from him when we've done something wrong; never a word of thanks or praise".

Do you like your efforts to go unrecognised (a good assignment, a task completed well)? Probably not. Being able to give a compliment and say "thank you" is a sign of a caring, confident person.

Accepting compliments   We like appreciation for our efforts, but some people find it difficult to respond. Hearing the words can make people embarrassed, turn red, avoid eye contact or even become terse and abrupt or walk away. If someone has gone to the trouble of giving a compliment, always acknowledge it with a smile and an appreciative comment.

Making an apology   There will be times when you make mistakes and need to apologise or when you need to show concern that you have caused negative emotions in others. We often avoid making apologies. Too often, we hope time will allow the other person to forget the incident. This may cause us to avoid seeing or speaking to that person for some time. This can hurt our own relationship with them and that of the employing organisation. It is far better to confront the situation and make the apology. Do this simply, directly and with sincerity:

(a) "I'm sorry . . . . . . happened. I am taking positive steps to ensure it does not occur again."

(b) "I'm sorry you feel this way about the matter. I didn't intend to upset you."

Being positive   This involves a way of thinking as well as a way of behaving. It is looking for opportunities rather than threats, dwelling on strengths rather than weaknesses, looking for something "good" in the blackest situation. In meeting people, it can be easy to become negative and pessimistic, anticipating the worst possible outcome, imagining all the mistakes one can make.

One way to develop a positive attitude is to give yourself a mental "talking to", particularly before a difficult or unwelcome encounter. Remind yourself of your abilities and knowledge, list the opportunities presented by the situation, counter all your negative thoughts with positive ones.

Example: "I know it's going to be a difficult meeting with . . . today and I do find him awkward to deal with. However, I've done my research, my figures are right and I know the justification for each point. If he becomes aggressive, I will remain calm and will not allow him to goad me."

If encounters do go wrong, do not dwell on the failure; but do not ignore it either. Try to evaluate what went wrong and why so that you can adopt alternative tactics in any new encounter. Learn from your mistakes; do not try to explain them away.

DECIDING APPROPRIATE LOCATIONS FOR MEETINGS

Just as there can be a right time to conduct business, so there can be a right place.

Concept of Territory

We all have our own territory — *our* home, *our* office, *our* lecture room — the places that we regard as "ours" in which we feel more comfortable and in which we feel we have control.

When we visit another person's territory we become more conscious of ourselves, more wary and less at ease.

When we meet on neutral territory such as a pub, a restaurant, a hotel or a conference, the place may be strange to us but there is no psychological association for either person and therefore both parties can feel relatively relaxed.

It is necessary to be aware of our territorial consciousness when arranging face-to-face encounters. One should think very carefully about the purpose of the meeting and the best location to achieve that purpose.

Locations to Suit Particular Purposes

Look at some examples below.

Situations when it is necessary to demonstrate authority   If it is important to demonstrate authority to another person or to try to impress him or her, have the meeting in your own organisation or office. You will then be surrounded by all your authority symbols. The other person will be more uneasy and it is easier to control the encounter.

Situations when it is necessary to ask a favour   If you want to ask someone for a favour, then arrange to meet on that person's territory where he or she will feel at home and more relaxed. This might put him or her in a better mood to comply with your wishes.

Situations when it is necessary to reach a negotiated compromise   During negotiations both parties are likely to be aware of their authority and the importance of not making unsuitable concessions. If an acceptable compromise is to be reached, it is preferable to take both parties away from their normal surroundings onto neutral territory.

Situations when it is necessary to create ideas or solve complex problems When creating joint ideas or solving joint problems, it is often preferable to meet on neutral territory. This is because everyone needs to be able to concentrate exclusively on the matter in hand and if the meeting is in either party's office, normal office routine may intrude (telephone calls, queries from other staff, etc).

THE BASIC STAGES IN ANY FACE-TO-FACE ENCOUNTER

Whatever the reason for a face-to-face encounter, it is necessary to pass through some specific stages. These can be remembered through the mnemonic WASP.

W Welcome

A Acquire information

S Supply information

P Part

Welcome

If the meeting is on your territory, you should initiate the welcome. Ensure that you greet your contact in the assertive manner outlined above. If it is the first time you have met, explain clearly who you are, who you represent, your authority to conduct business and your purpose in holding the meeting.

If the meeting is on his or her territory, allow the other person to control the welcome but still retain your assertive behaviour. Provide the relevant information about yourself and your organisation.

Acquire Information

There are a number of points to bear in mind when asking questions:

(a) *Use the right kind of questions*:

    (i) closed questions requiring yes or no answers to confirm facts
    (ii) open questions to secure details, probe reasons, etc.

(b) *Listen to other people's answers attentively*, so that you do not miss points and do not have to ask them to repeat information. Show that you are listening through body language and paralinguistics.

(c)   *Make notes of the most important points* so that you have a record of the meeting.

(d)   *Make maximum use of body language* to reinforce the questions; look quizzical when someone says something which you do not fully understand; nod your head in agreement, look thoughtful when you are giving an idea due consideration.

Supply Information

The points to remember here are:

(a)   Have *all* the facts and figures necessary for the meeting close at hand.

(b)   Have appropriate material, ie flip chart, paper, board available for jotting down ideas — it is easier to consider a point when both parties can see it.

(c)   Do not try to convey too much complex information orally — you will probably find yourself drawing pictures in the air with your hands! Have some supportive literature such as a written fact sheet available.

(d)   Supply information in a form which the visitor will understand quickly and easily — think whether diagrams, sketches, charts or graphs will help.

Parting

Once the business is concluded, one person needs to draw the meeting to a close. Normally this will be the person on whose territory the meeting is taking place. On neutral territory, it could be either person. Before parting, it is necessary to be absolutely sure that both parties have the same interpretation of the outcome. Therefore a good method of parting is to:

(a)   Summarise the business transacted and ask whether the other person agrees with this view.

(b)   Check any further action to be taken arising from the meeting, to ensure there is agreement on:

    (i)   what the action is
    (ii)   who is taking it
    (iii)   any deadlines by which it must be completed and
    (iv)   details on how or where.

(c)   Thank the other person for his or her time and say goodbye.

CONCLUSION

We have provided some basic techniques for handling any face-to-face encounter effectively. Obviously, not all contacts will be co-operative and pleasant. One may have to deal with unpleasant, aggressive or rude people or people who are complaining about the service they have received. The basic points remain the same but we will give some further guidance on handling complaints and difficult people in Chapter 17.

ANSWER TO ACTIVITY IN CHAPTER 15

Activity 3

(a) *Submissive response*

You are giving way to the pressure of the situation and not wanting to say no. Consequently, the customer thinks you are going to comply with her request. If you cannot persuade your supplier to speed up its own deliveries, you will ultimately disappoint the customer and run the risk of losing her business in future. Also she will not trust you.

(b) *Aggressive response*

You are likely to be creating resentment in the customer by stating that her request is totally unreasonable. You do not appreciate her viewpoint. You are not dealing with the problem or suggesting any solutions to it. She will have a very poor opinion of you and your company and is likely to take her business elsewhere if at all possible.

(c) *Assertive response*

You have shown that you appreciate her position and have clearly stated your own. You are also prepared to offer a compromise that may assist. Whatever the outcome, she should be left with the impression of someone who tried to be helpful.

16 Telephone Behaviour

Today, if we want to contact someone a few hundred yards or several thousand miles away, we probably reach for the telephone. We use this method of communication because it:

(a) is convenient — we only have to reach for it

(b) saves time — we avoid having to spend time travelling to see the person

(c) should be cheaper — we can accomplish our business quickly and it saves travelling expenses.

However, the more the telephone is used the more the opportunity exists for poor telephone technique and behaviour. Since for many external relationships, the telephone may be the main contact, the way calls are received and made can affect the way an organisation is seen by others. Even unskilled telephone users often have good intentions in being helpful and efficient, so why do so many problems arise?

COMMON PROBLEMS IN TELEPHONE COMMUNICATION

Everyone has complained about other people's telephone behaviour at some time, so let us use this as a starting point for identifying the common problems.

ACTIVITY 1

What problems have you experienced when making telephone calls to other organisations? Try listing these.

Then check your experiences with ours at the end of the chapter.

Problems can be grouped under several headings:

(a) *Poor reception of the call* — both at the switchboard and by the extension.

(b) *Poor attitude* — people being unhelpful or obstructive.

(c) *Bad listeners* — are those people who insist on talking or who do not demonstrate in any way that they are listening to the other person's part of the conversation.

(d) *Bad organisation* — those people who are not prepared for taking telephone calls (unable to find a pencil, paper, files, etc).

(e) *Ineffective* — dealing with people who cannot get around to actually *doing* something to help.

Now you have identified your own frustrations with other people's telephone behaviour, take another look through the list to see if any of them could apply to you!

OTHER PITFALLS IN USING THE TELEPHONE

These may be our common complaints about telephone users. However, there are some inbuilt pitfalls in using the telephone as a means of communication which need to be faced and overcome.

These are:

(a) *Difficulty in establishing rapport with the other person.*
When dealing with someone on the telephone it is not possible to use body language to get "on the same wavelength". You are totally reliant on the voice.

(b) *Inability to determine the other person's situation.*
Over the telephone, one cannot determine the conditions in which the receiver is taking the call. It may come at an inconvenient time when he or she is pre-occupied with a work problem. You may call when someone else is in the office and the receiver does not want to speak in front of him or her.

(c) *Misinterpretation.*
When you are dependent on words and tone alone, it is quite easy to make wrong assumptions or jump to conclusions.

(d) *Barriers to concentration.*
It is difficult to command the attention of the other person on the end of a phone. Either party to the call may be subject to all kinds of distractions from noise inside or outside their office, interruptions by staff or other telephones, or trying to complete other work while making the call.

These pitfalls need to be anticipated and steps taken to overcome them. So far this has been a rather negative analysis, so let us look at the positive aspects of telephone contact.

ADVANTAGES OF THE TELEPHONE

It is necessary to recognise that there are also some advantages to be gained from using the telephone, particularly if one has an effective telephone technique.

(a) *It establishes contact.*
    Since it is a quick and easy method of making contact, most business is done over the telephone. Remember that many people, whether at work or home, are unable to ignore a ringing telephone!

(b) *There are some benefits to a lack of visual contact.*
    The inability of the caller to see the other party can have some benefits. It is easier to assert authority on the telephone when no-one can see your confusion, blushes or appearance. You can sound self-assured, confident or determined in situations where otherwise you might be more submissive.

(c) *Easier control.*
    With effective telephone technique, it is easier to control a discussion over the telephone than when in a meeting.

DEVELOPING EFFECTIVE TELEPHONE TECHNIQUES

There are five important stages to effective telephone behaviour when making calls. These are:

(a) preparing for the call

(b) giving the verbal handshake

(c) receiving information

(d) giving information

(e) parting.

We will examine what is involved in each of these stages.

Preparing for the Call

Too often, we remember that we must call someone, grab the telephone, establish contact and *then* start thinking about what we want to say. We are committing a number of sins here:

(a) we have not organised our thoughts or the necessary factual information

    (b)   we have not considered whether this is the most economic time for us to call or the most convenient time for the other party to receive the call.

When receiving calls, we may swear to ourselves because the call has interrupted our own priorities in work; perhaps we allow it to ring for ages in the hope that the caller will ring off or someone else may answer it. Finally we answer the phone with a distracted or curt "Hello". *We are not always prepared to receive calls.*

Receiving calls   It is necessary to consider some preparation for receiving calls. One may think there is nothing one can do to prepare in advance but there are a number of things that can help in the reception of calls.

    (a)   *Know the organisation well.*
          This includes people, products and services, departments, etc. This helps in answering queries, transferring calls quickly, etc.

    (b)   *Keep a message pad and pen handy, plus the internal telephone list.*
          This will assist in making notes, taking messages for others and transferring calls.

    (c)   *Know how to transfer calls using the organisation's telephone system.*

Making calls   The essential ingredients of good preparation are:

    (a)   identify the purpose of the call — so that you do not become sidetracked

    (b)   make notes of the main points to be covered in achieving that purpose

    (c)   organise names, telephone numbers, factual information or data or relevant files close to the telephone for reference. Make sure there is a message pad and pen close at hand to make notes during the call

    (d)   if you do not have a contact name and extension number, determine in advance the type of person in the organisation most likely to be able to help

    (e)   decide the priority of a call. If it is non-urgent, delay making the call until the cheaper time rates (ie after 1.00 pm on weekdays)

    (f)   balance the above against what time is most likely to be convenient to the receiver (and therefore help you to achieve your purpose). For example, consider the time differences when making calls abroad; allow people time to open their post in the morning; do not make important or lengthy calls last thing on Friday afternoon.

Now you are prepared, you are ready to make the call.

Giving the Verbal Handshake

When meeting someone face-to-face for the first time, you are likely to walk towards him or her, smile, extend a hand in greeting and then introduce yourself. To establish rapport with the person at the other end of a telephone, it is necessary to achieve the same effect. However, only words and tone are available to do this.

ACTIVITY 2

Try to identify what is wrong in the following telephone dialogue.

Receiver: (answers on the 10th ring, sounding impatient) "Yes. What is it?"

Caller:　"Er. . . . I hope you can help me. I want to enquire about some . . . er . . . software for the Astra computer. You see my son . . ."

Receiver: "If you want computer games, you need the Games Section. You'll have to ring them."

Caller:　"But wait, you see my son is . . ." (click)
". . . in hospital and wanted to check that the bulk order of business software for his company . . ."

Misunderstanding occurred here because both parties ignored the verbal handshake. Neither knew to whom they were speaking and there was no attempt to be helpful on the part of the receiver.

Verbal handshake when receiving calls　When receiving calls you should:

(a) answer promptly (puts caller in a good mood)

(b) give a greeting (according to the time of day)

(c) announce the name of the department and your own name clearly and slowly (The caller then knows that he or she is through to the right department and to whom he or she is speaking. It also gives time to "switch on" to starting the conversation proper.)

(d) ask how you can help the caller

(e) sound lively and alert throughout this greeting

(f) smile while speaking — it *does* comes through in the tone of your voice.

So a typical greeting might be:

Receiver: "Good morning; Business Software Department, Philip Jones speaking. How can I help you?"

▶ If, for any reason, it is not possible to take the call at a particular moment, explain briefly why it is inconvenient and arrange a time to ring the caller back. This is preferable to carrying on with the call and sounding impatient with the caller.

Verbal handshake when making a call It is really the responsibility of the receiver of a call to initiate the verbal handshake. In reply you should:

(a) state your name, organisation and department or job title

(b) announce the purpose of the call. However, if any uncertainty or pre-occupation is detected in the other party's verbal handshake, you should politely enquire whether it is convenient for him or her to receive a call at that time.

Also, when in contact with an unskilled telephone handler who merely says "Yes" or "Hello", take the initiative with an announcement along the lines of: "Good morning. This is Carol Parsons of Taylor and Smith. I am ringing on behalf of my son, Peter, the Managing Director. To whom am I speaking?" Again, sound cheerful and alert.

Receiving Information

The same rules apply here whether one is a caller or a receiver. It is necessary to apply the skills of listening. British Telecom has a useful mnemonic it uses in its own training programme about listening on the telephone:

L Limit your own conversation to essentials

I Impatience is audible

S Shut out distractions

T Two ears — one mouth (We have two ears because we need to listen perhaps more than we need to speak.)

E Examine information and ideas

N Notes.

this is very sound advice. We would like to add a few more points.

(a) Remember paralinguistics (see Chapter 2). It is often difficult for people to sustain a one-sided explanation for very long. They need re-assurance that you are still listening.

(b) "Read back" key points at appropriate breaks in the explanation so that they know you have the information noted down correctly.

(c) Help the other person to explain his or her needs by asking the right kind of questions, ie

  (i) If confirmation is required from him or her that the information received and noted down is correct, ask a closed question which merely requires a yes or no answer.

  (ii) If more detail is required, ask open questions — these start with "who", "where", "when", "how", "why", etc.

(d) Once committed to a call, *concentrate* on it. Do not try to do two things at once, especially maintaining a conversation in the office as well as the one on the telephone.

ACTIVITY 3

Having read the above points, try to identify the mistake being made by the caller before reading on.

Caller: "That's arranged then. You'll come in and sort out our accounts?"

Receiver: "Yes."

Caller: "Will you be able to come on the 22nd?"

Receiver: "No."

Caller: "The 23rd then?"

Receiver: "No."

Caller: "Friday the 24th then?"

Receiver: "No."

Caller: (exasperated) "When will you be able to come?"

Receiver: "Any time the following week."

Caller: "Will Mr Jones be coming with you?"

Receiver: "Yes."

Caller: "Will there be anyone else?"

Receiver: "Yes."

Caller: "Who's that?"

Receiver: "John Partridge, our assistant accountant."

When you see this conversation on paper, it is easy to see how the caller was wasting time by asking closed instead of open questions to secure the information he or she needed. However, it is very easy to fall into this trap when speaking on the telephone.

Giving Information

Some key points here are:

(a) keep the other person fully informed at all times about what is happening. For example, do not disappear in the middle of a call to get information from a file without telling the other person. Do not leave him or her with a "Hang on a moment". The caller cannot see you; he or she only hears the silence on the other end of the phone — will you be gone for five seconds or five minutes?

(b) make a positive effort to be helpful. Volunteer information before being asked for it.

(c) make notes throughout the call of any information which has been supplied and concerning what action is to be taken.

(d) explain any action that will be taken as a result of a call. This should include: what action will be taken, by whom and when.

(e) if there are options available in the kind of action which can be taken identify them clearly and ask the other person for a preference.

Parting

ACTIVITY 4

Identify the faults in this ending to a telephone conversation before reading on.

Receiver: "Is that all then?"

Caller: "I think so. Is there anything else you need to tell me about the equipment?"

Receiver: "I can't think of anything."

Caller: 'Well if you do think of anything you've got my telephone number, haven't you?'

Receiver: "Yes, of course."

Caller: "Well then . . ."

Receiver: "Yes, well . . ."

(Silence at both ends)

Many people find it difficult to bring a telephone conversation to an end. The conversation wanders on aimlessly after the purpose has been achieved because neither party actually wishes to initiate the parting. Once business has been transacted, the best way of finishing is for the receiver to summarise the action to be taken, thank the caller and then to say firmly "Goodbye".

GENERAL POINTS IN TELEPHONE TECHNIQUES

Unless you know the other person quite well, do not offend him or her by use of inappropriate words or tone of voice. It is therefore wise to avoid:

(a) using technical jargon which may not be understood but the other party is too polite or embarrassed to request an explanation

(b) being over familiar by using words such as "love", "darling" or "guv"

(c) using negative or unhelpful words such as "can't", "won't", "don't know", "no"

(d) allowing a negative emotional tone to creep into one's voice.

Remember, the other party will be forming a picture of the caller from the words said and that picture should be a positive one. Again, British Telecom has a useful mnemonic indicating what to think about when speaking on the telephone.

P Pitch — a low pitch comes across a telephone more effectively

I Inflection — allow the rise and fall of your voice to indicate questions and statements

C Courtesy — *always* be polite; try using the other person's name during the conversation

T Tone — keep it positive

U Understandability — use words that can be understood by the other person

R Rate — talk a little more slowly than normal on the telephone

E Enunciation — pronounce words clearly and audibly.

If you follow some of these simple techniques, your telephone behaviour should be more effective in future. However, we have left the tricky problem of dealing with telephone complaints or awkward callers for discussion in Chapter 17.

USING MOBILE TELEPHONES

One difficulty that may arise these days in adopting effective telephone behaviour is the increasing use of mobile telephones. These may be the fitted mobiles in cars which give the user a "hands free" facility or the portable type that can be carried around with the user.

ACTIVITY 5

(a) Would you find a mobile telephone useful. If so, why?
(b) What problems might you experience in using one (once you had learned how to make and receive calls)?

Try to answer these questions before reading on.

Certainly, mobile phones enable more successful connections to take place since people can be contacted whether they are in the office or on the move. Mobile phones also give the caller greater freedom in determining the time and place to make a call.

However, there are problems attached to their use as well.

(a) The chance of being caught at an inconvenient time is greater. The caller does not know whether the receiver is cruising on a straight dual carriageway, getting frustrated in a congested city centre or having dinner in an intimate restaurant.

(b) Engaging in a lengthy conversation while driving along a busy road is dangerous: it also breaks the "avoid doing two things at the same time" communication rule.

(c) A receiver is more likely to come across on the telephone as impatient, preoccupied or curt if trying to hold a telephone conversation while making tricky road manoeuvres.

(d) It is not possible to make notes whilst driving (although it is possible to key in telephone numbers for making return calls).

This is not intended as a condemnation of mobile telephones, but offers a word of caution about their use. It is probably better to offer to ring a person back at a convenient moment rather than to continue a conversation on the move.

USING A TELEPHONE ANSWERING MACHINE

ACTIVITY 6

If you call someone and get a recorded message, do you

(a) Swear under your breath but leave a short message?
(b) Put the phone down quickly?
(c) Chatter away to the machine?

Be honest about your answers before reading on.

Many people dislike contact with answering machines and may give answer (b) above. However, they have become a fact of business life and therefore one should learn to use them effectively (which eliminates (b) and (c)). Answer (a) is fine provided the person listening to the recording does not hear the muttering preceding the message. But it does indicate a poor attitude.

It is therefore important to be able to record an announcement for a machine and also to leave an appropriate message.

Recording an Announcement

The essential information on a recorded message is:

(a) an identification of the organisation by name

(b) a courteous explanation that no member of staff is available at the time to deal with calls

(c) either a message giving appropriate information to the caller or (if the equipment has a recording facility) an invitation to the caller to leave his or her name, telephone number and a message, and an indication of when to speak (ie "after the tone") plus an assurance that the matter will be dealt with as quickly as possible

(d) a "thank you" for calling.

It is necessary to speak clearly and sufficiently slowly for the caller to understand and respond to the message and to sound sufficiently friendly and interested so that the caller does not ring off.

It is a good idea to write out the words of the recording first so that it can be read in a confident voice.

Responding to Recorded Messages

Listen to the recordings immediately and respond quickly.

Leaving a Message

The best way of dealing with fear of answering machines is always to anticipate that a machine may answer the call. If one is prepared properly for an ordinary call, all the information necessary for leaving a message should be to hand; it is only necessary to concentrate on giving the information in a logical order. The type of information requested is as follows:

(a) name, organisation and telephone number

(b) an identification of who the message is for

(c) a very brief statement of what the call is about

(d) a day or time and extension number for the return call.

The message should be as short as possible — some machines have a time limit for recording (often three minutes).

BEING AWARE OF TELEPHONE FACILITIES

It is only possible to use the telephone in the most effective manner if one is aware of all the facilities a telephone system has to offer. Most organisations today have sophisticated electronic private automatic branch exchanges (PABX) and it is necessary to be familiar with the facilities these offer.

A list of possible facilities is given below.

(a)	abbreviated dialling	— frequently used numbers can be dialled using a one or two digit code
(b)	alarm call	— allows any extension user to arrange for a call to be made to a nominated extension at a given time, eg for meetings
(c)	amplification of call	— enables several people in a room to hear the caller
(d)	automatic recall	— automatically redials a busy number

(e)	break in	— allows a caller to break into a conversation in an emergency
(f)	call barring	— restricts connection availability on certain extensions
(g)	call forwarding	— ability to divert calls to other extensions
(h)	call hold	— keeps a line open to a caller while the extension user is located
(i)	call waiting	— ability to let an extension user know there is another incoming call
(j)	conference call	— ability to link several extension users together over the phone system and with an outside caller
(k)	direct inward dialling	— ability to enable an incoming call to be routed directly to a selected extension by adding the extension number to the ordinary number
(l)	direct outward dialling	— ability to have direct access to the external telephone network
(m)	dictation access	— access to a central dictation facility
(n)	do not disturb	— allows the user to bar any incoming calls until further notice
(o)	follow me	— allows calls to be routed to further extensions as the extension user moves around the building
(p)	group hunting	— ability to seek out any one of a named group of extension users to take a call by trying each one in turn
(q)	night service	— allows an extension user to receive and make calls after the operator has gone home.

ACTIVITY 6

Find out which of the above facilities are available on the telephone system within your own company or college and, if possible, how you use them.

CONCLUSION

Always remember that the reaction you get from other people on the telephone is partly conditioned by your own behaviour. They will have formed a picture of you from your words and tone and will react accordingly. Always be clear about the picture *you* want them to have.

ANSWER TO ACTIVITY IN CHAPTER 16

Activity 1

Some of our complaints about telephone calls included:

(a)   the telephone being allowed to ring for a long time before anyone answers it (especially when the caller *knows* there is someone there!)

(b)   unintelligible greetings or just "Hello"

(c)   being left stranded on the end of a dead line

(d)   being transferred around an organisation

(e)   being told there is no one in

(f)   not knowing to whom you are talking or whether he or she has the authority to help you

(g)   having to deal with someone who does not sound as though they want to help you (their boredom, impatience, pre-occupation or antagonism is obvious)

(h)   having to deal with people who keep on interrupting you or who anticipate (wrongly) what you want

(i)   people who do not demonstrate they are listening

(j)   having to deal with people who do not have pencil or paper to hand and who go away from the phone for minutes at a time to check information or who do not write messages down

(k)   people who are unable to find files

(l)   having to deal with people who make trivial conversation rather than taking action

(m)   people who insist on controlling the conversation with questions which do not allow you to express your needs.

This is a formidable list — we expect your own was similar.

17 Handling Awkward Customers and Complaints

So far we have examined the techniques of relating to people outside the organisation in writing, during face-to-face meetings and on the telephone. These encounters are easy when the other person is also applying the correct techniques or does not present any problems.

However, we all have our own dread of encountering certain types of people, particularly when they are "being difficult" or complaining about our organisation's products or services. Too often we react emotionally to these people and become overly aggressive or too submissive.

In this chapter, we will try to identify some of the problem characters one may come across in the course of one's work. However, remember that these are stereotypes; in fact each person is an individual and must be treated as such. It is in these situations that assertiveness techniques will be useful. However, it is also important to be able to see the situation from the complainant's point of view.

PROBLEM TYPES

ACTIVITY 1

What types of people do you most dread meeting or having to speak to on the telephone? Why do these types create difficulties for you? Think about these questions carefully before reading on.

Obviously, we do not know your answers to these questions.

However, in the rest of this section we will identify some "difficult" types and the emotional reactions they are likely to arouse.

The Rude Aggressive Person

Readers should remember the description of this type from Chapter 15. When dealing with such people they are likely to arouse strong emotions and put one on the defensive, particularly if they are using anger and rudeness to make a complaint.

The temptation is to react emotionally by:

(a)   becoming equally angry and aggressive

(b)   saying and doing things that might be regretted later because they provide a "release" at the time.

or

(c)   being intimidated by this approach

(d)   sounding hesitant, overly submissive and flustered.

Both these reactions prevent one from dealing effectively with the situation causing the difficulty.

There are probably two types of aggressive people:

(a)   those who adopt this pattern of behaviour when they become angry and exasperated over a particular incident or problem

(b)   those who are habitually rude in all encounters and situations.

The Submissive, Withdrawn Type

It is also possible to recognise this type of person from the description in Chapter 15. One may not immediately think of these people as a problem because it is easy to manipulate their thoughts and behaviour.

It is all too easy to react to them by becoming dominant and virtually intimidating them into agreeing with your own proposals. However, you always need to ask yourself whether they might be withholding useful ideas, opinions, etc or whether they are agreeing too easily to a second-rate solution.

The Talkative Type

Readers may recognise this type of difficult encounter. This person:

(a)   insists on doing all the talking

(b)   frequently goes off the point of the encounter

(c)   never pauses for breath to allow an interruption

(d)   may talk over you (by increasing volume or speed) when you do try to interrupt.

Such people may be more pleasant in manner than the angry aggressive type, but they can create just as many problems because they are taking up valuable time which could be spent more productively.

The probable (emotional) reaction to this type of person is to do *anything* to stop the flood of words. This may include:

(a)   becoming increasingly curt and rude

(b)   showing boredom by stretching and yawning

(c)   finding an excuse to get rid of them

(d)   passing them on to someone (anyone) else.

The Persistent Questioner

This type can be recognised by a tendency to:

(a)   never accept what someone says

(b)   keep repeating or returning to the same questions

(c)   look very doubtful at anything others may say

(d)   gloat when they trip others up in a contradiction

(e)   reject others' authority for dealing with their situation or problem

(f)   sound and look scornful.

This type of person is likely to make others feel:

(a)   resentful

(b)   humiliated

(c)   angry (there is a temptation then to stop being courteous)

(d)   they want to adopt a "take it or leave it" attitude

because they will not accept that others have the correct information or the authority to deal with them and that undermines self-esteem.

The Superior Type

These people are determined to show that they know more than others by:

(a) using a range of facial expressions, including challenging eye contact, quizzical looks, arched eyebrows

(b) emitting heavy sighs whenever others put forward ideas or opinions

(c) standing when others are sitting or using "the-leaning-back-in-chair-hands-behind-head" posture

(d) using complex vocabulary when simple direct words would be more appropriate

(e) belittling others' ideas, opinions and actions or totally ignoring them

(f) questioning whether others have the authority to deal with them.

Obviously their purpose is to make others feel inferior and act submissively so that they can manipulate the situation to their advantage. Too often such people achieve their purpose. Dealing with this type of person is a little like banging your head against a brick wall. They do not respond to anything you say or do. They are likely to make you feel:

(a) exasperated

(b) annoyed

(c) doubtful of your own knowledge and ability.

These are all emotional reactions which allow them to retain the upper hand. Alternatively, you may be tempted to show them that your knowledge is superior by proving them wrong. Once this kind of person has lost face, he or she will never want to deal with the organisation again.

These types will be encountered in all kinds of situations. Some of them may work in the same organisation as colleagues or superiors. They will certainly be found amongst customers, clients, suppliers and advisors. When your are representing an organisation to someone else it is essential that you handle awkward people effectively so that business can be transacted successfully. The key to this is to be *assertive* and to *understand* their point of view.

UNDERSTANDING THE COMPLAINANT

Start by considering why people may behave as they do. Let us take anger as an example.

Angry People

ACTIVITY 2

Think back to any time when you have become angry when making a complaint and vented that anger on a bank employee, a shop assistant, etc. Why did you get angry?

Try to examine the reasons carefully before reading on.

We would expect numerous different answers here depending on the person answering the question. For example, here are just six reasons why people may show anger.

(a) They consider themselves justifiably cross about poor workmanship or service (ie the product or service did not meet expectations).

(b) The other person was not *doing* anything to resolve the problem.

(c) They do not like complaining and have to work themselves up into anger to be able to do it at all.

(d) They reacted badly to something the other person said which made them "see red".

(e) They find that getting annoyed gets action faster than being polite.

(f) They enjoy the power of making other people become submissive when they get angry.

If you turn this the other way round, it is possible to appreciate that anyone who becomes angry when complaining could have any of the above motives; it is wrong, however, to assume that it is anything as deliberate as the last two.

Talkative People

Talkative people may be talking a lot because:

(a) they are naturally extrovert

(b) it is a nervous reaction to a problem situation

(c)   they are lonely and want someone to talk to.

The Persistent Questioner

Persistent questioners may be annoying but it is possible that they:

(a)   need frequent reassurance that information is correct

(b)   may be faced with an even more difficult person waiting for them who wants detailed answers

(c)   may think that you look rather young to know much about the topic or problem being discussed.

It is only when doubting is mixed with gloating and scorn that you are up against someone who enjoys putting other people through an interrogation.

Superior People

There may be a variety of motives behind this type of behaviour.

(a)   They are proud of the knowledge they possess; it may have been acquired recently and they want to "air" it.

(b)   They crave admiration and flattery which they hope they may secure if they can prove themselves to be knowledgeable.

(c)   They believe in reinforcing differences in authority or status.

(d)   They think their approach is the only way to get good service.

Always be generous is ascribing motives to other people's behaviour, initially.

HANDLING COMPLAINTS

The basic rules for handling complaints and difficult people are the same whether they are on the telephone or face-to-face. When people complain, they want an answer to their problem, understanding of the inconvenience that has been caused or recompense for their loss. All the talk, bluster and anger is reinforcement to achieve this end.

Therefore the solution is relatively simple — *get on with action*. This involves the following methods.

(a)   Stay calm and in control of your emotions — be assertive.

(b)   Find out what is wrong.

(c)   Show sympathy with the situation — apologise for any inconvenience.

(d)   Show that action is being taken to get the problem sorted out.

(e)   Keep the person informed of the action being taken.

Let us look at each of these points in more detail.

Stay Calm

This is probably the hardest stage. Many people who create problems for us are often difficult to handle because they have let their emotions, whether anger, suspicion, fear, etc, get the better of them. If you become reduced to the same state, the end result is likely to be disaster. If there is a genuine reason for their behaviour, it is easier to remain calm. However, with those who are rude, or are intent on belittling you, the situation is easier to handle if you can depersonalise their behaviour. Remember, they are probably like that to everyone.

Find Out What is Wrong

No complaint can be dealt with until:

(a)   the complainer calms down

(b)   the full facts are known.

Too often we rush into trying to get the facts of the complaint while the complainant is still in an emotional state.

(a)   *Initially, let them do the talking.*
It is better to let an angry person give vent to his or her feelings, a talkative person explain and a questioner raise queries without interruption at first. Lengthy explanations, justifications, or righteous indignation will only fuel emotions at this stage.

(b)   *Use sympathetic paralinguistics.*
Demonstrate attentiveness; write notes of any relevant information (names, dates, times, etc). This information will be needed and it shows that the problem is being taken seriously.

(c)   *Show empathy with complainants.*
This can be by a direct apology for the inconvenience they have been caused in having to complain and/or a phrase which shows understanding for their problem or point of view. Sound sincere in this!

When dealing with a complaint about the organisation, do not accept responsibility for the situation at this point — it could amount to legal acceptance of negligence on the part of the organisation!

(d) *Start asking a combination of open and closed questions to get the full facts.*
Different customers respond to different kinds of questioning.

Talkative person The techniques for questioning a talkative person are:

(a) break into the monologue by picking up on a key word which enables you to respond pleasantly by asking a simple question and allows his or her conversation to take off on a more positive line. Persist in this technique — it probably will not work the first time.

(b) use the person's name near the beginning of a question. This attracts attention and can be followed up with a closed question. It also shows courtesy.

(c) use closed questions as much as possible since you are likely to get a simple yes or no in answer before he or she carries on the description.

ACTIVITY 3

Consider how you could break into this monologue to find out the necessary factual details. The customer is complaining about losing a jacket in your country park. You have discovered her name is Mrs Fitch.

"Well, I'm sure I had the jacket when I was down by the lake. You see George, that's my youngest son — the little terror, was pulling at my arm — my bad arm that is. I hurt it last week playing badminton — I fell you see. I carried on and won though. Well, you see he was pulling my arm that had the jacket over it and I remember it slipping down my arm and I had to transfer it to my good arm — the left one. He wanted to go in a canoe on the lake. He went on one last year on holiday and enjoyed it so much. I gave him the money — it was in the jacket pocket. You do charge a lot for canoes, don't you? He went off and I sat down by the boathouse to watch. I sat on the jacket because the grass was wet. After that we went on one of the nature trails. It was then that the weather turned and it started raining. We got so wet — I'm sure I've caught a cold as a result."

Our suggestions appear at the end of the chapter.

Angry person This is more tricky since you must judge whether an open or closed question suits the situation better. The guiding principle is to use a combination of questions which get the exact information and allow you to get on with taking action as quickly as possible. We have shown below how you might handle an encounter with an angry Mrs Fitch, rather than just a talkative one.

Mrs Fitch	"What kind of business do you run here? I turn round for two minutes and someone runs off with my belongings."
You	"Have you lost something in our park?" (Ignore attack and get on with establishing the nature of the complaint.)
Mrs Fitch	"Lost! More likely stolen. Its my green jacket, new this week.. You can't trust anyone these days. What are you going to do about it, young man? I need it urgently."
You	"I can understand your concern about losing it so I'll try to trace it as soon as possible. Can you tell me the places you visited that day?" (Calming by showing a willingness to get on with some kind of action.)
Mrs Fitch	"You expect me to remember all my movements."
You	"Did you visit the lake?" (Ignore rudeness and ask closed question to seek confirmation of possible location.)
Mrs Fitch	"Yes, I was sitting by the boathouse. You should provide seats you know. I had to sit on my jacket."
You	"You had it at that point then. Did you go along the red or blue nature trail?" (Follow up with forced choice questions to find out movements.)
Mrs Fitch	"We went along some trail or other. How should I know what colour it was?"
You	"Did it start near the lake and finish just outside the car park?" (A closed question to narrow choice of location.)
Mrs Fitch	"Yes."
You	"That's the blue trail. I'll call the warden for that area." (Statement on action to be taken.)

Submissive A submissive complainant who finds it difficult to explain would need help through more probing open questions. Think of a hesitant Mrs Fitch in this situation.

Mrs Fitch	"I'm terribly sorry to take up your time but I seem to have lost a . . . jacket."

You	"What kind of jacket did you lose, Mrs Fitch?"
Mrs Fitch	"It was a lady's jacket, short length and dark green. Oh dear, I'm so silly, I don't know where it can be!"
You	"Can you tell me what parts of the country park you visited that day, Mrs Fitch? Perhaps it's been handed in at one of these locations."
Mrs Fitch	"Let me see. I went to the lake with my son, sat down by the boathouse and then went for a walk along the blue trail. It started raining halfway through and it was then I noticed I didn't have my jacket. Do you think someone may have found it?"
You	"I'll just check with the warden for that area."

Note that in this case, the open questioning provides a more supportive, encouraging approach.

Take Action

Initially it is necessary to decide whether one has the authority to resolve the problem oneself. In some cases the solution may lie with someone else in the organisation.

If one can deal with the matter oneself, explain the action which will be taken clearly and then get on with it. If there are two or more options available explain these to the customer clearly and let him or her make the choice, eg "I can do [X] or [Y]. Which would you prefer?" This way he or she is allowed to retain some control over decision-making in the situation. Providing a forced choice is also a good way of prompting a decision.

If follow-up action is involved, give the other person an indication of the timescale involved. ("I'll get back to you soon/as soon as possible" may mean within the next three hours to the other person but within the next three days to you.)

If it is not possible to take action oneself, explain clearly to whom the matter has been referred (ie name, job title, extension number, etc).

RESPONSE FROM A DIFFICULT CUSTOMER OR COMPLAINANT

One of the satisfactions in many jobs is to be able to handle a situation well and send a customer away satisfied, particularly one who has expressed appreciation. One may not always get a "thank you" from difficult customers but this should not discourage one from dealing with them effectively. If one has taken action which resolves their problem:

(a) angry or rude customers will recognise that their situation was handled effectively and there is a good chance they will remain a customer

(b) talkative customers will tell someone else (at length) about how helpful the organisation was

(c) persistent questioners and superior types are likely to enhance the organisation's reputation amongst their contacts.

CONCLUSION

Awkward, complaining people create difficulties, it is true but one can learn to deal with them and bring such encounters to a successful conclusion. In the last two chapters, we will provide some assistance in two encounter situations which may be difficult to control — handling the media and negotiating.

ANSWER TO ACTIVITY IN CHAPTER 17

Activity 3

Some possible interventions in Mrs Fitch's monologue would be:

(a) When she is talking about her arm try, "That must have been painful Mrs Fitch. It was your jacket, was it?".

(b) When she mentions sitting on the jacket try, "Was it a waterproof jacket then?".

(c) When she is talking about the nature trails try, "Mrs Fitch, would that be the red or blue trail?".

18 Handling the Media

This chapter may seem to be more suited to a book on public relations; in a large organisation, it will be the PR department's responsibility to ensure that the activities of the company get coverage in the press and on television and radio. In smaller companies, there may not be anyone to take on this role and you may become involved in having to prepare press releases or give a radio or local television interview. These are specialist communication skills of which you should be aware.

With the proliferation of local television and radio stations, it is becoming more likely that local residents, sportspeople and club members, as well as employees even of small businesses, may become involved with the media.

If a company or local authority or service is newsworthy for some important event, or possibly some business scandal, the media will attempt to gain access to "a good human touch" story by putting pressure on employees to talk.

For these reasons, we have considered it relevant to include a short chapter on handling the media.

CONFIDENTIALITY

Although a business wants good publicity in the media, there are likely to be many aspects of its activities that it does not want to divulge. From the media's point of view the cameraman wants a dramatic picture, the reporter wants a newsworthy story and the interviewer wants a new slant on a topic. In trying to achieve their objectives, they may well put pressure on employees to divulge as much inside information as possible. Employees must be extremely careful what they say. They should always check back with a higher authority before saying anything to the media and get clearance for all facts and figures. They should never be tricked into talking "spontaneously" about other employees, financial information, products, markets, etc.

It is good policy never to see any visitors without an appointment — that way you can do your own research on them before a meeting.

ISSUING PRESS RELEASES

One communication method which is used by companies to inform the public of important events is to issue a press release. In this section, we will deal with the kind of press release that is written by a member of the organisation and then sent to a number of papers in the hope that the item is sufficiently newsworthy to be included in the local or national press.

To write a good press release it is necessary to be able to put yourself in the place of the newspaper reader — then write what the reader would want to know. The article that will appear in a paper is different from other forms of business communication. While facts and figures are still important, it is the way the information is presented that is important.

ACTIVITY 1

Turn to the business pages of a quality newspaper. Read an article about a particular organisation. Try the same exercise in a popular tabloid. Then attempt to identify how journalism compares and contrasts with the forms of written business communication you have encountered so far in this book. When you have answered this activity, read on.

Some of the points you may note are as follows:

(a) The length of the sentences and the complexity of the language will vary with the type of paper. However, short, simple sentences and direct, straightforward vocabulary have the greatest impact.

(b) The heading for the passage is not a straighforward objective summary of the contents — it must act as a stimulus. This is often achieved through some degree of ambiguity or vagueness so that the reader is persuaded to read on for clarification.

(c) The first sentence is extremely important. It must attract the reader to stop and look at the rest of the passage.

(d) Although facts and figures are provided, they are worked into a vivid description, often full of human interest and direct quotes from people working within or associated with the organisation.

(e) Much greater use than normal is made of adjectives and adverbs to add emphasis and create interest.

Depending on the agreement with the paper, the press release may be printed in its original form as provided by the organisation's representative or may be edited by the paper's own staff to suit the style of the paper and the space available. However, even if the paper's own journalist uses his or her expertise to adapt the information in a press release, the original must be sufficiently well written to attract attention in the first place.

Here are a few guidelines about preparing and presenting a press release.

Content

▶ Passages in the press are short, therefore confine the facts to one or two sides of A4. If it is necessary to provide considerable detail running to several pages, provide a half page summary as well.

▶ Provide a headline that attracts attention, eg
    not: Mayor opens new bowling green
    but: Mayor is bowled over.

If no headline is provided, the paper's journalist will devise his or her own.

▶ Ensure that the first sentence attracts attention. After all, papers are getting many press releases from organisations and they will choose those which catch their eye.

▶ Provide complete information. Ensure that the questions "what", "who", "when", "where" and "how" are answered in the release. These are the hard facts that readers want to know.

▶ Provide the human touch. This is best achieved by using some direct quotes such as: " 'This has been the best year ever' said Managing Director, Geoff Horton".

Layout

▶ Type the press release on the organisation's headed paper; this provides essential information about the organisation.

▶ Give a contact name and extension number at the top of the page so that the recipients can raise any queries with the right person.

▶ Mark the sheet "Press Release" so that it can be recognised quickly and easily.

▶ Identify at the top whether the item is for "immediate release" or "release on or after . . . ." (insert date).

▶ Use double line spacing and wide margins on either side of the paper so that there is room for editorial comments.

▶ If the release is more than one page, write "more" at the bottom of each page and number the pages. Write "end" at the bottom of the passage. These words help the editor to recognise whether there are pages missing.

▶ Date the press release — for reference purposes.

Style

▶ Write in short sentences. Use simple, direct vocabulary.

▶ Use adjectives and adverbs freely but be careful not to distort the facts.

ACTIVITY 2

1. Select an event that has happened at your college or company recently. Write a press release of not more than one side of A4 that could be sent to a local paper. Try to find an interest slant for the story which provides the human touch.

2. Check back to ensure that you have followed the principles given.

3. Ask someone not associated with your organisation to read your press release and comment on its appeal.

No answers are given for this, since clearly responses will be individual.

PRESS CONFERENCES

Some organisations prefer to bring the press to them rather than send out a press release. Often this will be for more dramatic occasions such as a company merger, the launch of a new product, or even for more unpleasant events such as a fire, a site closure, etc. This allows reporters and cameramen all to be in the same place and receive exactly the same information.

On these occasions, top management may be available to answer questions or (as seen in political press conferences) a pre-prepared press release will be read out to the press. Once the press release has been read and questions have been asked and answered, reporters will phone through their stories to their papers. They are usually given a written copy of the press release for reference. It is therefore important that the facts are clearly presented and an appropriate image of the organisation is created.

You are unlikely to be directly involved in the press question/answer session until you are part of senior management but you could be involved in the practical arrangements for a press conference. Since it is a very important communication exercise, you will need to view all the practical arrangements from a communication/relationship perspective. The venue must be suitable for the occasion; it must be quiet, have appropriate acoustics and provide access to telephones for reporters to phone through their stories.

HANDLING A FACE-TO-FACE INTERVIEW

With the proliferation of local radio and television stations, it is becoming more likely that local business people will be asked to give interviews. Such interviews may be on location at a business fair or exhibition, at one's own work premises or may be recorded at a studio.

We have covered self-presentation at an interview in Chapter 6 and face-to-face encounters in Chapter 15; readers will realise that many of these points are relevant here. There are, however, additional problems involved in any kind of radio or television interview. The first problem is that of the stress involved.

Facing Stress

You are likely to find a radio or television interview a nerve-wracking experience. A mass audience will hear the answers. Every hesitation and misplaced word will be noted. At the same time, you want to hold the attention of that mass audience so that they do not switch to another channel.

If the interview is at a studio, you will have to face this strange environment. The loneliness of the radio studio may be disconcerting — just interviewer, interviewee and the microphone, and then the faces behind the glass in the control room. In a television studio, it is necessary to dress in colours that transmit effectively, make-up will be applied and there are a mass of lights and cameras to adjust to.

Radio may be the ultimate test of oral communication skills. Only the voice is available; it must be used to inform, instruct, persuade and convince. The audience has to be caught up in the speaker's enthusiasm for the subject and be impressed by his or her breadth and depth of knowledge.

Television is probably more testing of non-verbal skills. Although people listen to what is being said, they are drawn to how people look and how they behave on screen. We remember more of what we see than what we hear. Therefore, it is necessary to look appropriate for the interview and use body language to maximum advantage.

It is necessary to be sure that one can handle stress and do justice to the topic of the interview. Therefore think carefully before agreeing to an interview.

Handling the Programme Organisers

Apart from the stress involved, there are other reasons for giving careful thought to whether an interview is in your interests or not. The interview must allow you to present yourself and your organisation in the best possible light. You do not want to become a party to an interview programme where the aim is to belittle the interviewees in order to develop the image of the presenter. It is therefore wise to ask questions about:

(a)   which programme? (Is it reputable?)

(b)   when and where? (Is it convenient for you and does it give you time to prepare?)

(c)   who will be conducting the interview? (Is he or she the kind of person who will enable you to present yourself well or is he or she likely to provoke you?)

(d)   how long will the interview last? (Can you spare the time; is it long enough to do justice to the topic?)

(e)   will you be allowed to check the questions and organise your answers before the programme? (You do not want to be asked embarrassing questions or to have to refuse to answer a question.)

(f)   will the programme be live or recorded? (Recorded may be better because of the points made above.)

(g)   why have you been chosen? (Is it your expertise, your personality, your access to information or are you a good "target" for attack or ridicule?)

(h)   who else is on the programme? (For example, will it be a programme where fellow guests are compatible or where conflict is being deliberately encouraged?)

Checking Questions and Preparing Answers

It is always wise to ask the programme organiser for an outline of the questions to be asked within the interview. If you are representing your organisation, your management are likely to want a list of the exact questions so that they can delete or respond to any which relate to information they do not want divulged.

Once you have the outline structure of the questions, prepare your answers to suit the time available. Ensure you include the relevant information — the points you want to make. Do not try to make more than three or four basic points within an interview — any more will be lost on the audience. Also think carefully about how you can convey these points to best advantage. Pure facts can sound boring. Can you liven up the presentation by anecdotes or analogies which bring the facts to life?

Preparing Yourself

You need to prepare physically and mentally for any interview. Think about how to sit. You want to be comfortable but also to show enthusiasm, interest and alertness. Consider the body language you may need to use to reinforce what you are saying.

Effective Interview Behaviour

ACTIVITY 3

Watch a television interview on a politically or organisationally sensitive topic with an experienced interviewer and an inexperienced interviewee.

Try to list

(a)   the faults made by the interviewee
(b)   the ways in which the interviewer manipulated the interviewee.

You can check some of the common faults at the end of the chapter.

Now we have noted some of the aspects of poor media interviews in the above activity, let us finish by making some positive points about behaviour.

DO

▶ present your "good" side to the camera

▶ lean slightly forward and look alert

▶ speak clearly and distinctly

▶ remember assertiveness techniques

▶ use facial expressions and limited gestures to reinforce your words

▶ be and sound enthusiastic and sincere

▶ know your facts

▶ make sure you put your key points across — it does not matter what the questions are. You can learn this technique from interviews with politicians

▶ anticipate the way questions are leading and steer the conversation back from contentious, difficult areas

▶ use techniques such as blowing your nose, cleaning glasses, starting your sentence with something like "I'm glad you asked me that" if you want to stall for time when thinking up your answer to a tricky question.

ACTIVITY 4

Watch an interview between an experienced interviewer and an experienced politician on television. Identify the key points the politician wants to make and the key areas the interviewer wants to question. What techniques does each side use to achieve their purpose?

Note down any useful phrases that are used by the interviewee for evading or twisting awkward questions for his or her own use.

CONCLUSION

Writing a successful press release or handling a radio or television interview well can be a rewarding experience. However, never underestimate the need for the media to get "a good story" even at your expense. The criterion for success in using the media is to be able to put across to the public the information *you* want them to have. If you can do this, then the media is working for your organisation.

ANSWER TO ACTIVITY IN CHAPTER 18

Activity 3

Some common faults amongst inexperienced interviewees are:

(a) They become defensive, aggressive or rude and this detracts from their information and can bore the audience.

(b) They use technical jargon which the audience does not understand.

(c) They stray off the point so it is difficult to follow their argument.

(d) They use noisy or distracting gestures which create microphone noise or look too flamboyant.

(e) They are unnerved by silence and feel an obligation to keep the conversation flowing, even if they have already made their point.

(f) They are too vague — their answers are full of non-committal phrases — "sort of", "things", "and so on" — so that you do not feel that they are conveying reliable information.

You probably detected many other faults.

Below are some of the ways in which interviewers manipulate interviewees. We have added some actions which can be taken by the interviewee if this happens.

(a) He or she dominates the interviewee and the conversation. Interviewees should remain assertive and insist on making their points.

(b) He or she interrupts before interviewees have made their point. Interviewees should come back to the point they were attempting to make before continuing.

(c) He or she deliberately misquotes facts. Interviewees should insist on correcting them.

(d) He or she misinterprets interviewees' statements by summarising them and giving a new emphasis. Action for interviewees is the same as above.

(e) He or she attempts to sidetrack interviewees into minor issues. Interviewees should bring the conversation back to the main issues.

(f) He or she inserts unrehearsed questions in an attempt to embarrass or trip up interviewees. If questions have been previously vetted, interviewees should refuse to answer these undisclosed ones.

(g) He or she attempts to provoke interviewees into showing a range of emotions (eg fear, distress, anger or resentment) in order to "liven up" the interview or to distract viewers from the facts. Interviewees should remain calm and in control.

(h) He or she attempts to slip in a derogatory last statement at the close of the interview. Interviewees should insist on having the last word.

19 Negotiating

Readers' initial impressions on reading this heading may be — my job will not involve this. However, we need the skills involved in these activities many times in our working lives. Negotiating techniques are not confined to the publicised wrangles between management and unions; they are used in agreeing contracts, in arranging facilities for exhibitions and conferences and even in trying to secure a personal increase in pay or some time off!

Negotiating is also about reaching agreement. In many situations where one is trying to persuade someone to buy ideas or services, there are bound to be differences on all kinds of issues. Negotiation is based on conflict, ie perceived differences between two parties. It does not have to be a power struggle or an unpleasant encounter in which insults are hurled across the table. It may be necessary to negotiate over:

   (a)   differences in how to solve a problem

   (b)   differences in methods or procedures to use to achieve an objective

   (c)   different needs regarding cost or price

   (d)   different ideas concerning time-scales or deadlines.

Most children are experienced negotiators — particularly over staying up to watch their favourite programmes on television!

As we grow up, we often lose sight of some of the basic techniques we used then.

IMPORTANCE OF WIN-WIN SOLUTIONS

Perhaps one of the important aspects about negotiation that children learn is that if one wants something from someone else it is probably necessary to concede something that he or she might want, eg "I'll swap my comic for your sweets". The outcome of negotiation should enable both sides to get most of what they wanted. It must be a win-win result.

Too often, adults turn negotiation into a power struggle which must be won and therefore nothing must be conceded to the other side. The outcome from this approach is win-lose. Try the following exercise to appreciate why a win-lose outcome is undesirable.

ACTIVITY 1

(a) If you win an argument, how do you feel?

(b) If you lose an argument, a serious game, or a negotiation, how do you feel?

Jot down your own feelings before reading on.

Most people would admit that winning makes them feel good but would also admit to one or more of the following sentiments when losing. "Losing makes me feel:

(a) annoyed with myself

(b) inadequate

(c) humiliated

(d) cross

(e) resentful

(f) out for revenge."

Basically, whether we place the blame for losing on ourselves or the other party, we do not like having to give way. If this happens in a business negotiation it is going to sour future relationships between the two parties involved and possibly between the two organisations they represent.

In order to achieve a win-win outcome it is necessary to follow some basic stages to secure the objective.

THE STAGES FOR A NEGOTIATION

There are five basic stages to any negotiation. These are:

(a) prepare

(b) discuss

(c) propose

(d) bargain

(e) settle.

Before we move through the stages there is one important concept that must be appreciated in successful negotiation. This is to view every aspect from the opponent's position. It is no good going into a negotiation with only your own version of the situation considered. You will become blinkered, lose opportunities for settlement and probably antagonise the other party by short-sighted behaviour.

Prepare

This is the most important stage. One cannot reach a good agreement without preparation. All preparations need to be noted down on a *negotiation planning sheet*. There are several aspects which it is necessary to prepare.

ACTIVITY 2

If you were about to negotiate with your boss for a pay rise, what preparation might you make before asking for a meeting?

Compare your list with ours at the end of the chapter.

In any type of negotiation, preparation can be a complex activity because one needs to consider:

The issues involved People have to negotiate because they are in conflict over one or more issues. It is therefore important that before they meet they have a full appreciation of all the issues involved. Very often, what appears to be a single issue has a number of sub-issues. Each one is likely to be seen differently by the two parties.

As an example, imagine you want to book accommodation and conference facilities at a local hotel for two days of training for computer sales staff. You have to agree a price for these facilities. Consider the issues involved for you and the hotel manager.

You	The hotel manager
To pay the least possible for the facilities needed	To make the maximum profit from the booking
To delay payment for as long as possible	To secure payment as soon as possible
To secure discount for bulk booking	To limit discounts
To have exclusive use of facilities	To achieve economies of scale in use of staff, food, etc
	To secure future bookings

As the buyer in this situation, you have got to recognise that the seller may be talking about the same topics but the issues involved are different. Also try to prioritise the issues.

Setting negotiation objectives It is necessary to work out in advance, the agreement you would like to have, ie the optimum package you could hope for. This is the optimum settlement.

It is also necessary to work out the minimum you could possibly accept to enter any kind of business contract. This is the fall-back position. Recognise that unless the other person is totally in accord with you on all issues, you are unlikely to achieve the optimum settlement, but in setting high expectations it gives some flexibility to manoeuvre.

Now, anticipate what will be the other person's optimum and fall-back positions. Try to think like him or her and see the negotiation from his or her point of view.

Researching the total situation Accurate knowledge is important in successful negotiation; therefore research is essential. This includes:

(a) Information about the topic to be negotiated — full, accurate facts.

(b) Information about the other person and organisation. Find out as much as possible about his or her position and authority within the organisation, the nature of the organisation's business, its financial standing, how badly it needs to negotiate and whether there are other organisations to which it might turn.

(c) Information about your own organisation. Make sure you know how important an agreement is to them; what advantages you have over competing organisations; what authority you have to settle; the nature of previous relationships with the other organisation.

(d) Information about the economic and social environment. It can affect people's bargaining strengths whether you are negotiating in a time of economic expansion or recession and/or whether your current reputation in the industry or local community is high or low.

Preparing a strategy This involves thinking about how to achieve objectives. Essentially this means:

(a) Identify points on which concessions can be made. If agreement is to be reached between the two optimum settlements, concessions will have to be made. Without preparation there is a danger of giving way on the wrong points under pressure.

(b) Consider the concessions you may want to secure from the other party in exchange.

Preparing tactics   At this stage, it is worth reminding yourself of the skills you will need to employ during the negotiation. These would include:

(a)   assertiveness throughout

(b)   good oral communication skills

(c)   listening skills

(d)   positive body language.

In addition, you should remind yourself of the appropriate stages through which the negotiation should progress.

Discuss

The first stage when you actually meet the other party is to discuss the issues. You will need to articulate your case clearly and listen attentively to the demands made by the other side. You will need to identify the underlying logic behind these demands and ask yourself whether the assumptions you made at the preparation stage are correct.

You will need to ask probing questions to secure maximum information, but to recognise that the other party may be reluctant to divulge too much information. If the other party asks you probing questions, answer them clearly but do not volunteer additional information, unless it is in your interests to do so.

Try not to respond emotionally to his or her demands or to put your own case too aggressively. At this stage, you are really "sizing up" the opposition, finding out his or her objectives, testing out the strength of his or her commitment to various issues. It is unlikely that the other party will agree to your terms so early even if you put your case clearly with logical justification. Once you know where you both stand on all the issues involved, there needs to be some movement towards concessions before agreement can be reached. However, this is a step which both sides are often reluctant to take. This is because making a movement towards the other side may be viewed as "giving way" and you will find yourself conceding too much.

Propose

You will recognise when you have moved into the proposal stage because statements will contain an element of compromise ("I might be prepared to do . . ." "If you were to . . .") However, it is quite difficult for an inexperienced negotiator to detect when the other party is prepared to consider proposals. In fact, most people give out verbal or body language "signals".

ACTIVITY 3

If you were negotiating with someone, what signals might you look for which would indicate that the other side was willing to consider proposals?

Write down your own ideas before reading on.

These signals may be phrases such as:

(a) "I couldn't consider that *at the present time*" (ie "I might consider it in the future").

(b) "*As things stand*, I would find it difficult to agree that price" (ie "I don't like what I've heard so far, but I might be willing to adjust the price if you put other incentives to me".

Listen for qualitative words which creep into statements indicating that the other party is prepared to be more adaptable. These might be words such as perhaps, might, relatively, quite, possibly.

Also, people use body language to signal a willingness to move their position. This can be:

(a) an evaluative gesture, eg stroking the chin (shows careful thought)

(b) an expectant look and a pause in speech (shows they are expecting you to add something else)

(c) leaning forward and looking keen (they are ready to respond to something you have said).

However, do not wait indefinitely for the other party to make the move. It may be necessary to signal one's own willingness to move instead. This can be done by any of the means mentioned above or by actually putting a proposal in words (eg "What if I were to . . . would you then be prepared to . . ."). By making these tentative proposals, you will find out the areas where you are relatively close in your thinking and those on which you must still work hard to bring you closer together.

Do not make firm promises at this stage. Remember that often you are negotiating a package deal. You want to be able to trade off one item against another. If you have already agreed a compromise on a particular point, you cannot use it for later "trade-offs".

Bargain

As you move closer together you will find that your tentative "What if you were to . . . then I might be prepared to . . ." firms up to definite concessions and counter concessions. However, do remember two basic principles if you want a good agreement with which both sides are happy.

(a)   Concede something which is valuable to the other party but is cheap for you to give away.

(b)   Always trade-off one concession for another, ie always get something in return.

You should appreciate now why preparation is so important, ie you have already estimated what the other side might value and what is cheap for you.

For example: you are negotiating a service contract and from your research you have established that:

(a)   getting the job done within very tight time constraints is one of the most important criteria for the other party

(b)   your organisation is going through a relatively slack period so you could divert additional staff to working on this contract.

You could concede a tight time schedule (cheap for you) in return for a high price (valuable to you).

Settle

An inexperienced negotiator is often so glad to have reached this stage that he or she forgets to check what has been agreed. It is always important to make this final check. It is very easy for two parties to leave a negotiation with different interpretations of the agreement which has been reached. Always confirm a negotiated agreement in writing.

SOME SKILLS TO HELP NEGOTIATION

It is simple to identify the stages; it is more difficult to actually follow them. Some practical techniques which can help are as follows:

(a)   *Be a good listener*
       This enables you not to antagonise the other party by misunderstanding crucial points.

    (i)   Always ensure replies to the other party follow on from his or her statements or questions.
    (ii) Avoid parallel conversations.
    (iii) Check your understanding of the point you have reached every so often with a statement such as: "Let me get this clear. If we are prepared to . . . , you would . . . Is that right?".

(b) *Communicate well*

    (i)   Speak clearly and confidently.

    (ii) Make sure you do not allow doubt, annoyance or impatience to sound in your voice.

    (iii) Try not to use emotive language which could provoke a "slanging match". Emotive exchanges end up in what are known as defence-attack spirals with arguments going round and round.

    (iv) Control the speed of your speech; use pauses strategically to show emphasis and to allow the other person to appreciate fully the point you are making.

    (v) Ask many open questions.

(c) *Use positive, helpful body language*
The table on pages 295–6 should identify some body language which you should use and some you should avoid. It is quite alarming how we can react to these body language messages subconciously!

(d) *Use breaks*
If you feel that your negotiation is not progressing well or you are in danger of a stalemate situation, try a break. Suggest going into another room for a cup of coffee or taking a break for lunch. Often such breaks can restore physical and mental energy.

It might even be appropriate to suggest a change of environment for the negotiation, eg moving onto neutral territory.

Good and bad body language in negotiations

Positive body language	*Unhelpful body language*
Open palms — which show honesty, integrity	Clenched fists or pointing, jabbing fingers show aggression. Hiding palms indicates a desire to conceal
Good eye contact shows confidence and willingness to meet the other party	Fixed eye contact — staring — shows aggression. Avoidance of eye contact shows submission and lack of confidence
Sitting in an upright but relaxed position leaning slightly towards them shows interest, alertness and desire to agree	Leaning back in chair, particularly with hands behind head issues a challenge. Sitting on the edge of the chair shows nervousness

Nodding agreement on points and smiling offers encouragement to proceed	Shaking head and frowning can act as a disincentive for other person to proceed or make concessions
Sitting with unfolded arms and legs — indicates a "no barrier" attitude	Sitting with tightly folded arms and/or legs indicates a desire to set up barriers
	Drumming fingers on desk indicates impatience
	Adjusting clothes or hair indicates nervousness
Using a conversational seating arrangement or a round table help to reinforce equality and willingness to negotiate	Using a bigger chair or settling behind a large desk indicates a desire to dominate

TACTICS FOR HANDLING HARD NEGOTIATORS

You will probably encounter at least one person who regards himself or herself as a "hard" negotiator. Such people believe in the win-lose approach and they are determined you will lose! They will use anything to press home an advantage. Here are a few tactics they may try. They may:

(a) be insulting or personally abusive in the hope that you will lose your temper and lose control of your strategy and tactics

(b) accuse you of incompetence or wasting their time in the hope that it will undermine your confidence and you will lose control

(c) use threats of withdrawal or of referring the matter to arbitration in the hope that you will be rushed into making unwise concessions.

In the face of all these your tactics should be to:

(a) recognise the tactics for what they are

(b) stay calm and in control of your emotions and behaviour. Remember to be assertive

(c) state how their behaviour makes you feel and ask them to behave more rationally

(d) if they persist, withdraw from the negotiation until they are prepared to behave more reasonably.

CONCLUSION

Your negotiating techniques will improve with practice. You will not be totally successful at first. However, you will find that if you work through these stages you will have a firm foundation on which to base your facts and your behaviour and, in time, both aspects will come more naturally to you.

ANSWER TO ACTIVITY IN CHAPTER 19

Activity 2

In preparing to negotiate with your boss for a pay rise it would be a good idea to determine:

(a) the amount you would like to receive

(b) the minimum amount you would accept to remain in the job

(c) any benefits you might consider in place of a cash increase.

You should also consider:

(a) How favourable was your last appraisal report/interview? (What evidence can you extract to support your case? What might he or she bring up that could be damaging to your case?)

(b) What is the financial position of the organisation? (Is it in a position to pay you what you are seeking?)

(c) What concessions might you be prepared to make to secure the pay increase? (Would you be prepared to assume more responsibilities, work longer hours, be more flexible?)

(d) What do you know about your boss? (When and where would be the best time and place for this negotiation?)

You have probably thought of other preparations you would make, particularly if you have a specific boss in mind. The important point is to research the situation thoroughly and have as much information to hand as possible.

20 Training Videos on Communication and Interpersonal Skills

By the time you have reached this chapter, you will have covered a wide range of skills you will need as a manager of staff. One way of reinforcing learning in these vital skills is to watch other people:

(a) making mistakes

(b) demonstrating skilled behaviour.

Training videos play a useful role in giving you this kind of secondhand experience.

ACCESS TO TRAINING VIDEOS

There are a number of sources of videos:

(a) Those at college can ask a tutor, librarian or visual aids section whether they have any of the videos listed available for viewing.

(b) Those at work can talk to the training section which may have one or more of the videos listed and may be able to provide access for viewing.

(c) Most video film production firms hold viewing sessions in centres throughout the country or take their videos "on tour" round hotels in major towns. It is worth getting in touch with the companies to find out whether there is a centre or hotel near you where you might view the videos. Some will charge a small fee for this (up to £10).

(d) Most regions of the country hold business exhibitions from time to time or there are central locations at which a prominent training video company will present non-stop viewing of their most popular training videos.

(e) Some independent suppliers of a range of equipment include preview facilities free as part of their promotional activity.

VIDEOS AVAILABLE

These are listed by section. (NB Some chapters may not be covered by relevant videos.)

Section 1   Basic Principles

Chapter 1   Communication principles

Gower

Communication or what's that noise (28 minutes) — covers reading, writing, speaking and listening.

Rank
Training

A question of may (23 minutes) — deals with barriers to communication.

Chapter 2   Effective oral communication

Speaking
Gower

Verbal communication: the power of words (30 minutes) — covers the principles and pitfalls of communicating.

Gower

Applause (26 minutes) — takes viewers through seven basic steps for gaining self-confidence in presentation skills.

Melrose

Bravo! What a presentation! (19 minutes) — how to give an effective presentation.

Rank
Training

Effective speaking (24 minutes) — some simple rules for successful public speaking.

Video Arts

Making your case (25 minutes) — how to plan and deliver a formal presentation.

Body language
Gower

Body language (60 minutes in 3 × 20 minutes sections) — a very detailed and amusing analysis of body language and its importance.

Gower

Communication: it's not just what you say (21 minutes) — how to use and interpret body language.

Gower

Communication: the non-verbal agenda (30 minutes) — the use of words and body language.

Listening
Gower

Listening makes a difference (7 minutes) — on the importance of active listening skills.

Gower   *The power of listening* (26 minutes) — identifies barriers to effective listening.

Melrose   *Listen!* (20 minutes) — the importance of effective listening skills in various jobs.

Rank Training   *Listening* (18 minutes) — demonstrates how not listening can be costly.

Chapter 4   Visual communication

Video Arts   *Can we please have that the right way round?* (22 minutes) — deals with slide projection used in presentations.

Section 2   Internal Communications

Chapter 6   Self-presentation at an interview

BBC Enterprises   *The interview game: body language* (25 minutes) — a guide to body language in the interview situation.

Industrial Society   *You can't just walk in* (22 minutes) — designed to help young people at job interviews.

Melrose   *What the window cleaner saw* (23 minutes) — the use of body language, particularly in an interview.

Southampton University   *Write, giving full details* (23 minutes) — a guide to the completion of application forms.

Chapter 7   Developing teams

Gower   *Group productivity* (21 minutes) — examines three phases of group development in terms of task and group issues.

Gower   *Team building* (18 minutes) — looks at the various elements which can prevent teams from succeeding and how to build a successful team.

Gower   *Team building: a blueprint for success* (18 minutes) — illustrates a number of important points about team building.

Rank Training   *Teamwork: the play* (29 minutes) — shows how it is possible to work together to achieve objectives.

Chapter 8

Leadership

Guild Training	*Leading to the top* (21 minutes) — Chris Bonnington compares leadership techniques on Everest to those in the workplace.
Guild Training	*Leadership* (23 minutes) — John Adair looks at the three major areas of concern to a leader — the task, the individual and the group.
Industrial Society	*Leadership matters* (25 minutes) — explains what action-centred leadership is and why it is important.
Melrose	*Teams and Leaders* (23 minutes) — how to work within groups/team building.
Rank Training	*Me and We* (17 minutes) — how a manager can build a better team by defining objectives and sharing decision making.
Video Arts	*Where there's a will* (29 minutes) — some practical assistance in effective leadership and motivating a team.
Video Arts	*From No to Yes* (27 minutes) — deals with developing a constructive route to agreement in meetings and groupwork.

Motivation

Gower	*Beyond Theory Y: the contingency approach to management* (14 minutes) — explores styles of leadership.
Gower	*The inside track* (15 minutes) — looks at negative and positive aspects of motivation.
Gower	*Managing motivation* (11 minutes) — how to help employees achieve a higher level of productivity.
Gower	*Maslow's hierarchy of needs* (15 minutes) — examines Maslow's theory and its application to motivation at work.
Gower	*Motivation: the classical concepts* (21 minutes) — examines five classical motivation theories.
Gower	*Theory X and Theory Y: two sets of assumptions about management* (10 minutes) — contrasts the two theories and suggests that assumptions one makes about people determines the style one will choose to manage them.
Guild Training	*The art of motivation* (30 minutes) — examines theories of McGregor and Herzberg.

Melrose   *Motivating the team* (30 minutes) — aimed at first line managers and presents some ideas on motivation in an easily assimilated form.

Rank Training   *The will to work* (25 minutes) — provides easy-to-follow guidelines for supervisors on motivation.

Rank Training   *More than money* (27 minutes) — stresses how motivation varies from person to person and how to identify action to enable people to be more effective.

Chapter 9   Meetings

Guild Training   *Formal meetings* (20 minutes) — how to control and direct formal meetings.

Guild Training   *Take the chair* (25 minutes) — looks at the role of the chairperson and how to draw out the best contributions from members.

Rank Training   *Meeting the meeting challenge* (35 minutes) — leading a meeting to accomplish objectives.

Video Arts   *Talking to the team* (28 minutes) — how to run a team meeting.

Video Arts   *Meetings Bloody Meetings* (30 minutes) — deals with the organisation and control of meetings.

Video Arts   *More Bloody Meetings* (27 minutes) — deals with the people side of meetings.

Chapter 10   Instruction

Industrial Society   *Team briefing* (23 minutes) — shows effective communication through use of team briefing.

Melrose   *Brief encounters* (33 minutes) — a guide to team briefing.

Rank Training   *More than words* (13 minutes) — deals with how to instruct more effectively.

Rank Training   *Welcome aboard* (20 minutes) — how to plan and execute an induction programme.

Video Arts   *You'll soon get the hang of it* (29 minutes) — helps with the techniques of one-to-one training.

Chapter 12

Written reports

Melrose	*The writing programme* (20 minutes) — a guide to clear, direct writing particularly for reports.
Rank Training	*Oh what a lovely report* (26 minutes) — guidelines on how to prepare and produce effective reports.

Oral reporting

Guild Training	*The floor is yours now* (24 minutes) — how to give an effective presentation — geared towards oral reporting.
Rank Training	*The anatomy of a presentation* (33 minutes) — making a presentation to senior management.

Visual aids

Guild Training	*Don't just tell them* (20 minutes) — deals with various types of visual aids.
Melrose	*Talking with pictures* (27 minutes) — a guide to the use of visual aids.

Section 3   External Communications

Chapter 13   Projecting the right image

Melrose	*Quality the only way* (30 minutes) — how everyone is involved in giving a quality service to customers or clients.
Melrose	*Making customer service happen* (27 minutes) — emphasises the importance of all managers being concerned with customer satisfaction.
Video Arts	*The customer is always right* (21 minutes) — how to achieve 100 per cent quality.
Video Arts	*An inside job* (27 minutes) — deals with meeting the needs of internal customers.
Video Arts	*If looks could kill* (28 minutes) — shows the power of behaviour which influences our face-to-face encounters.

Chapter 14   Business lettters

Rank Training	*When letters work* (24 minutes) — explains how letters can influence people and can be part of customer care.

Video Arts   *The Business Letter Business* (26 minutes) — shows how to structure an effective business letter.

Chapter 15 Face-to-face encounters

Assertiveness

Gower   *When I say no I feel guilty* (30 minutes) — a series of four case studies dealing with assertiveness.

Guild
Training   *Asssert yourself* (180 minutes in four parts) — deals with recognising the problems, some techniques, how to say 'no'; advantages of being assertive.

BBC
Enterprises   *Working with assertiveness* (40 minutes) — a basic training in some assertiveness techniques.

Melrose   *Say what you want* (24 minutes) — presents six basic points on being assertive.

Chapter 16 Telephone behaviour

Gower   *Making the most of incoming calls* (27 minutes) — how to receive calls effectively.

Gower   *Telephone skills: courtesy on the line* (14 minutes) — basic steps to using the telephone aimed at those not manning switchboards.

Melrose   *Telephone courtesy pays off* (18 minutes) — handling incoming calls effectively.

Melrose   *Telephone perfection* (23 minutes) — looks at the importance of telephone training for all employees.

Video Arts   *Telephone behaviour* (29 minutes) — a humorous guide to more professional telephone behaviour by covering skills involved in three basic stages.

Chapter 17 Handling difficult encounters

Gower   *Dealing with difficult customers* (13 minutes) — guide to dealing with angry customers.

Gower   *Working with difficult people* (25 minutes) — how to come to terms with awkward and aggressive people.

Melrose   *In the customers' shoes* (28 minutes) — shows how a young woman comes to realise the importance of handling customers correctly together with subsequent analysis of the main training points.

Rank Training	*Handling customer complaints* (25 minutes) — demonstrates three basic steps in dealing with angry customers.

Video Arts	*Awkward customers* (24 minutes) and *More awkward customers* (31 minutes) — show a range of awkward customers and how to handle them.

Video Arts	*Prescription for complaints* (21 minutes) — an objective view of handling customer complaints and turning problems into business opportunities.

Chapter 19 Negotiation

Melrose	*Agreed* (30 minutes) — deals with conflict resolution through empathy and co-operation rather than confrontation and aggression.

Rank Training	*The Art of Negotiation* (29 minutes) — shows the basic stages of a negotiation and the skills involved.

If you would like to obtain the full colour brochures of training videos from the main companies mentioned above the addresses are:

Gower Training Resources
Gower House
Croft Road
Aldershot
Hants GU11 3HR
0252 331551

Guild Training
6 Royce Road
Peterborough
PE1 5YB
0733 315315

Industrial Society
Quadrant Court
49 Calthorpe Road
Edgbaston
Birmingham B15 1TH
021–454 6769

Melrose Film Productions Ltd
16 Brommells Road
London SW4 0BL
071–627 8404

Rank Training
Cullum House,
North Orbital Road
Denham
Uxbridge UB9 5HL
0895 834142

Video Arts Ltd
Dumbarton House
68 Oxford Street
London W1N 9LA
071–637 7288

BBC Enterprises videos are available for hire through Guild Training at its address in Peterborough. The Industrial Society produces a range of inexpensive booklets on many of the topics contained in this book and their catalogue can be obtained from the above address. Likewise, Video Arts produces a range of inexpensive *Briefcase*

Booklets to accompany its videos which contain the basic training points. A brochure outlining these booklets can be obtained from the above address.

Index